ZumaOOH!

859 Walker Avenue
Oakland, CA 94610-2003
USA

Educating the Reflective Practitioner

Toward a New Design for Teaching and Learning in the Professions

Donald A. Schön

Educating the
Reflective Practitioner

JOSSEY-BASS
A Wiley Imprint
www.josseybass.com

Published by Jossey-Bass
A Wiley Imprint
989 Market Street, San Francisco, CA 94103-1741   www.josseybass.com

Jossey-Bass books and products are available through most bookstores. To contact Jossey-Bass directly call our Customer Care Department within the U.S. at 800-956-7739, outside the U.S. at 317-572-3986 or fax 317-572-4002.

Jossey-Bass also publishes its books in a variety of electronic formats. Some content that appears in print may not be available in electronic books.

Library of Congress Cataloging-in-Publication Data

Schön, Donald A.
    Educating the reflective practitioner.

    (Jossey-Bass higher education series)
    Bibliography: p. 345
    Includes index.
    1. Professional education.   2. College teaching.
3. Experiential learning.   4. Educational innovations.
I. Title. II. Series.
LC1059.S45   1986   378'.013   86-45626
ISBN   1-55542-220-9   (alk. paper)

COVER DESIGN BY VICTOR ICHIOKA

In the story of Dani and Michal in Chapter Six, "Dani" refers to Daniel Gat of the Department of Architecture at Technion, in Haifa, Israel. "Michal" is Michal Sofer, now a practicing architect, who was a student of Professor Gat's at the time of this story. Professor Gat presented this case study in 1983 during an academic workshop at the Technion at which I was a guest participant. I am very grateful both to him and to Ms. Sofer.

Printed in the United States of America
FIRST EDITION
PB Printing   20 19 18 17 16 15 14 13

The Jossey-Bass
Higher Education Series

Contents

Preface

In the early nineteen-seventies, when William Porter, then dean of the School of Architecture and Planning at M.I.T., asked me to join a study of architectural education under his direction, I did not anticipate the kind of intellectual journey I was in for. It is a journey that has occupied me for well over a decade, drawn me into debates over the present situation and future prospects of professional education, and caused me to rethink and reconnect ideas that date back to my Ph.D. thesis on John Dewey's theory of inquiry.

In the early stages of the journey, I planned a book on professional knowledge and education. Later, it became clear to me that it would be necessary to split the book in two. In the first part, published in 1983 as *The Reflective Practitioner,* I argued for a new epistemology of practice, one that would stand the question of professional knowledge on its head by taking as its point of departure the competence and artistry already embedded in skillful practice—especially, the reflection-in-action (the "thinking what they are doing while they are doing it") that practitioners sometimes bring to situations of uncertainty, uniqueness, and conflict. In contrast, I claimed, the professional schools of contemporary research universities give privileged status to systematic, preferably scientific, knowledge. Technical rationality, the schools' prevailing epistemology of practice, treats professional competence as the application of privileged knowledge to instrumental problems of practice. The schools' normative curriculum and separation of research from practice leave no room for reflection-in-action, and thereby create—for educators, practitioners, and students—a dilemma of rigor or relevance. The argument of *The Reflective Practitioner* implies a question: What kind of professional education would be appropriate to an epistemology of practice based on reflection-in-action? I left the question unanswered there, to be answered here. In this volume, I propose that university-based professional schools should learn from such deviant traditions of education for practice as studios of art and design, conservatories of music and dance, athletics coaching, and apprenticeship in the crafts, all of which emphasize coaching and learning by doing. Professional education should be redesigned to combine the teaching of applied science with coaching in the artistry of reflection-in-action.

Beginning with a study of architectural education, I take architectural designing and the design studio as prototypes of reflection-in-action and education for artistry in other fields of practice. The generalized educational setting, derived from the design studio, is a *reflective practicum*. Here, students mainly learn by doing, with the help of coaching. Their practicum is "reflective" in two senses: it is intended to help students become proficient in a kind of reflection-in-action; and, when it works well, it involves a dialogue of coach and student that takes the form of reciprocal reflection-in-action.

In Part Two I describe the dynamics of a design studio, with its paradox and predicament of learning to design, rituals of instruction, and styles of coaching artistry. Then, in Part Three, I explore variations on a reflective practicum in three other contexts—master classes in musical performance, psychoanalytic supervision, and a seminar (taught for several years by Chris Argyris and me) in counseling and consulting skills. These explorations highlight similarities in the processes by which students learn—or fail to learn—the artistry of a designlike practice. They also point out how learning and coaching vary with the medium and content of practice. I describe the threefold structure of the coaching task and illustrate models of coaching ("Follow me!" "joint experimentation," and "hall of mirrors") that place different demands on the competence of coach and student and lend themselves to different learning contexts.

Finally, in Part Four, I turn to some of the implications of these ideas for redesigning professional education. I argue from an analysis of the current predicament of the professional schools that redesign is necessary—indeed, long overdue. And I conclude with the story of a modest experiment in curriculum reform that suggests what may be involved in implementing the idea of a reflective practicum.

I have found it necessary here to cover some of the ground already covered in *The Reflective Practitioner;* my argument about education for reflective practice depends on the epistemology of practice articulated in the earlier book. So the first two chapters set out, in revised form, the view of professional knowledge presented there. The model of designing described in Chapter Three appeared in its entirety in *The Reflective Practitioner.* But the discussion of the design studio as a reflective practicum in Part Two, the examples and experiments described in Part Three, and the treatment of implications for professional education in Part Four, are all substantially new.

I would like to say what I have *not* tried to do in this book. I have not considered how the teaching of applied science might best be combined with a reflective practicum. (I have an idea about it—that applied science should be taught as a mode of inquiry like and unlike the reflection-in-action of a skillful practitioner—but I have only touched on it here.) I say little here about wisdom in response to the ethical dilemmas of practice in bureaucratic institutions where professionals spend increasing amounts of time. Nevertheless, in Part Four, I am concerned with institutional forces that restrict discretionary freedoms essential to the exercise of wisdom and artistry alike. And I believe that education for reflective practice, though not a sufficient condition for wise or moral practice, is certainly a necessary one. For how are practitioners to learn wisdom except by reflection on practice dilemmas that call for it?

My emphasis is on the positive side of education for practice. I mainly ask, What goes on in a reflective practicum when it is working well? I have mostly chosen examples of

coaching and learning where a coach's skills and understandings
seem to me worth emulating. I am aware, however, that this is not
always the case. There is a negative side to teaching (Israel
Scheffler calls it a "dark side"). So I also present some "horrible
examples" of coaching. And I also ask, What are the generic
difficulties inherent in a reflective practicum? How may these be
overcome? What can go wrong? How might things be done better?
I consider how students can steer a course between overskepticism,
which prevents their learning anything, and overlearning, which
causes them to become true believers. And I consider how coaches
may become more sharply aware of the potentially destructive
effects of the "help" they offer.

   This book is intended especially for individuals in schools
or practice settings—practitioners, teachers, students, and educational administrators—who are concerned with education for
reflective practice. But it is also intended for all those who share a
lively interest in the elusive phenomena of practice competence
and artistry and the equally elusive processes by which these are
sometimes acquired.

   Like *The Reflective Practitioner,* this book is a primer. My
hope is that some readers, especially in the faculties of the
professional schools, will use it to extend and develop the inquiry
I have begun.

Acknowledgments

   It is literally true that I am indebted to more people than I
can name. Among the persons who have been most helpful to my
efforts to work through the argument of this book are Chris
Argyris, Jeanne Bamberger, and Martin Rein. Israel Scheffler and
Vernon Howard and their colleagues in the Philosophy of Education Seminars at Harvard University gave me valuable opportunities on several occasions to present and discuss earlier
versions of this work. At M.I.T., the Design Research Group—
including professors Louis Bucciarelli, Aaron Fleisher, John

Habraken, William Porter, and Patrick Purcell—have greatly helped my efforts to make some sense of designing.

Turning now to specific chapters, Roger Simmonds furnished me with the protocol of the design review in Chapter Three; I am indebted to discussions with him, Florian Von Buttlar, Imre Halasz, Julian Beinart, and, most of all, William Porter, for their help in discovering what the protocol was about. Jeanne Bamberger suggested the example of a master class considered at length in Chapter Eight and gave me the benefit of her many fruitful ideas and equally fruitful criticisms.

David Sachs, a good friend for many years and a notable psychoanalyst, has instructed me in the ways of psychoanalytic practice and supervision. His articles, coauthored with Stanley Shapiro, figure prominently in Chapter Nine. Chris Argyris was my collaborator in the seminars described in Chapter Ten and joined me in writing that chapter—the most recent of our many collaborations.

E. H. Ahrends of Rockefeller University invited me to attend a series of meetings, under his sponsorship, from which I first got the idea of the "professional squeeze play" described in Chapter Eleven. And I am grateful to several colleagues in the M.I.T. Department of Urban Studies and Planning—Donna Ducharme, Bennett Harrison, Langley Keyes, Tunney Lee, Amy Schechtman, Mark Schuster, and Lawrence Susskind—for partnership in the experiment described in Chapter Twelve and helpful criticisms of my attempts to decribe it.

I have also greatly profited from many opportunities to give talks and workshops on the themes of this book, at professional schools and other institutions, in this country and abroad. Some of the material in Part Two was first presented in 1978 at the University of British Columbia as the Cecil Green Lectures for that year. In 1984, the Royal Institute of British Architects provided me with a grant to support my studies of architectural education and a forum from which to present their results. An earlier version of the chapter on psychoanalytic supervision was presented in 1985, under the auspices of the Chicago Institute for Psychoanalysis, as the first Littner Memorial Lecture. Other parts of this book were first presented, in 1985, as the Queens Lectures at Queens University in Kingston, Ontario; the Harvard University Graduate School of Business Colloquium on Case Teaching in the spring of 1985; and the Leatherbee Research Lecture, at the same institution, in spring 1986.

Finally, my warm and heartfelt thanks to Marion E. Gross, who has had the unrewarding job of initiating me into the mysteries of word processing and who prepared this manuscript with conscientiousness well beyond the call of duty.

Cambridge, Massachusetts   Donald A. Schön
November 1986

The Author

Donald A. Schön is Ford Professor of Urban Studies and Education at the Massachusetts Institute of Technology. Schön holds a B.A. degree (1951) in philosophy from Yale University, and M.A. (1952) and Ph.D. (1955) degrees in philosophy from Harvard University. He also attended the Sorbonne and received a Certificate from the Conservatoire Nationale, Paris, France.

In his work as a researcher and consultant, Schön has focused on organizational learning and professional effectiveness. For seven years previous to his appointment to the faculty at M.I.T., Schön served as president of the Organization for Social and Technical Innovation (OSTI), a nonprofit organization which he helped to found. He has served in numerous other administrative and consultative roles with governmental agencies and private industry.

In 1984, Schön was Queens Quest Lecturer at Queens University and was also made an honorary fellow of the Royal Institute of British Architects. In 1970, he was invited to deliver the Reith Lectures, which were broadcast by the British Broadcasting Corporation. Schön's publications include *The Reflective Practitioner* (1983), *Organizational Learning: A Theory of Action Perspective* (1978, with Chris Argyris), and *Theory in Practice: Increasing Professional Effectiveness* (1974, with Chris Argyris). Schön is active in a number of professional organizations and is a member of the American Academy of Arts and Sciences Commission on the Year 2000 and the National Research Council Commission on Sociotechnical Systems.

Educating the
Reflective Practitioner

*Toward a New Design
for Teaching and Learning
in the Professions*

 *Part One*

Understanding the Need for Artistry in Professional Education

The two chapters of Part One are intended to set the stage for subsequent discussion of the design studio in architecture and variations on the idea of a reflective practicum in other fields of practice.

Chapter One describes the dilemma of rigor or relevance that calls for a new epistemology of practice and a rethinking of education for reflective practice. It presents, in brief, the argument of the book as a whole.

Chapter Two presents the ideas central to my understanding of reflective practice: knowing-in-action, reflection-in-action, and reflection on reflection-in-action. It explores the relations of these ideas to practice artistry and describes the general properties of a reflective practicum.

❦ Chapter One ❦

Preparing Professionals for the Demands of Practice

The Crisis of Confidence in Professional Knowledge

In the varied topography of professional practice, there is a high, hard ground overlooking a swamp. On the high ground, manageable problems lend themselves to solution through the application of research-based theory and technique. In the swampy lowland, messy, confusing problems defy technical solution. The irony of this situation is that the problems of the high ground tend to be relatively unimportant to individuals or society at large, however great their technical interest may be, while in the swamp lie the problems of greatest human concern. The practitioner must choose. Shall he remain on the high ground where he can solve relatively unimportant problems according to prevailing standards of rigor, or shall he descend to the swamp of important problems and nonrigorous inquiry?

This dilemma has two sources: first, the prevailing idea of rigorous professional knowledge, based on technical rationality, and second, awareness of indeterminate, swampy zones of practice that lie beyond its canons.

Technical rationality is an epistemology of practice derived from positivist philosophy, built into the very foundations of the modern research university (Shils, 1978). Technical rationality holds that practitioners are instrumental problem solvers who select technical means best suited to particular purposes. Rigorous professional practitioners solve well-formed instrumental problems by applying theory and technique derived from systematic, preferably scientific knowledge. Medicine, law, and business— Nathan Glazer's "major professions"(Glazer, 1974)—figure in this view as exemplars of professional practice.

But, as we have come to see with increasing clarity over the last twenty or so years, the problems of real-world practice do not present themselves to practitioners as well-formed structures. Indeed, they tend not to present themselves as problems at all but as messy, indeterminate situations. Civil engineers, for example, know how to build roads suited to the conditions of particular sites and specifications. They draw on their knowledge of soil conditions, materials, and construction technologies to define grades, surfaces, and dimensions. When they must decide *what* road to build, however, or whether to build it at all, their problem is not solvable by the application of technical knowledge, not even by the sophisticated techniques of decision theory. They face a complex and ill-defined mélange of topographical, financial, economic, environmental, and political factors. If they are to get a well-formed problem matched to their familiar theories and techniques, they must *construct* it from the materials of a situation that is, to use John Dewey's (1938) term, "problematic." And the problem of problem setting is not well formed.

When a practitioner sets a problem, he chooses and names the things he will notice. In his road-building situation, the civil engineer may see drainage, soil stability, and ease of maintenance; he may not see the differential effects of the road on the economies of the towns that lie along its route. Through complementary acts of naming and framing, the practitioner selects things for attention and organizes them, guided by an appreciation of the situation that gives it coherence and sets a direction for action. So problem setting is an ontological process—in Nelson Goodman's (1978) memorable word, a form of worldmaking.

Depending on our disciplinary backgrounds, organizational roles, past histories, interests, and political/economic perspectives, we frame problematic situations in different ways. A nutritionist, for example, may convert a vague worry about malnourishment among children in developing countries into the problem of selecting an optimal diet. But agronomists may frame the problem in terms of food production; epidemiologists may frame it in terms of diseases that increase the demand for nutrients or prevent their absorption; demographers tend to see it in terms of a rate of population growth that has outstripped agricultural activity; engineers, in terms of inadequate food storage and distribution; economists, in terms of insufficient purchasing power or the inequitable distribution of land or wealth. In the field of malnourishment, professional identities and political/economic perspectives determine how people see a problematic situation, and debates about malnourishment revolve around the construction of a problem to be solved. Debates involve conflicting frames, not easily resolvable—if resolvable at all—by appeal to data. Those who hold conflicting frames pay attention to different facts and make different sense of the facts they notice. It is not by technical problem solving that we convert problematic situations to well-formed problems; rather, it is through naming and framing that technical problem solving becomes possible.

Often, a problematic situation presents itself as a unique case. A physician recognizes a constellation of symptoms that she cannot associate with a known disease. A mechanical engineer encounters a structure for which he cannot, with the tools at his disposal, make a determinate analysis. A teacher of arithmetic, listening to a child's question, becomes aware of a kind of confusion and, at the same time, a kind of intuitive understanding, for which she has no readily available response. Because the unique case falls outside the categories of existing theory and technique, the practitioner cannot treat it as an instrumental problem to be solved by applying one of the rules in her store of professional knowledge. The case is not "in the book." If she is to deal with it competently, she must do so by a kind of improvisation, inventing and testing in the situation strategies of her own devising.

Some problematic situations are situations of conflict among values. Medical technologies such as kidney dialysis or tomography have created demands that stretch the nation's willingness to invest in medical services. How should physicians respond to the conflicting requirements of efficiency, equity, and quality of care? Engineering technologies, powerful and elegant when judged from a narrowly technical perspective, turn out to have unintended and unpredicted side effects that degrade the environment, generate unacceptable risk, or create excessive demands on scarce resources. How, in their actual designing, should engineers take such factors into account? When agronomists recommend efficient methods of soil cultivation that favor the use of large landholdings, they may undermine the viability of the small family farm on which peasant economies depend. How should their practice reflect their recognition of the risk? In such cases, competent practitioners must not only solve technical problems by selecting the means appropriate to clear and self-consistent ends; they must also reconcile, integrate, or choose among conflicting appreciations of a situation so as to construct a coherent problem worth solving.

Often, situations are problematic in several ways at once. A hydrologist, employed to advise officials of a water supply system about capital investment and pricing, may find the hydrological system unique. He may also experience uncertainty because he has no satisfactory model of the system. In addition, he may discover that his client is unwilling to listen to his attempts to describe the situation's uniqueness and uncertainty, insisting on an expert answer that specifies one right way. He will be caught, then, in a thicket of conflicting requirements: a wish to keep his job, a feeling of professional pride in his ability to give usable advice, and a keen sense of his obligation to keep his claims to certainty within the bounds of his actual understanding.

These indeterminate zones of practice—uncertainty, uniqueness, and value conflict—escape the canons of technical rationality. When a problematic situation is uncertain, technical problem solving depends on the prior construction of a well-formed problem—which is not itself a technical task. When a practitioner recognizes a situation as unique, she cannot handle it solely by applying theories or techniques derived from her store of professional knowledge. And in situations of value conflict, there are no clear and self-consistent ends to guide the technical selection of means.

It is just these indeterminate zones of practice, however, that practitioners and critical observers of the professions have come to see with increasing clarity over the past two decades as central to professional practice. And the growing awareness of them has figured prominently in recent controversies about the performance of the professions and their proper place in our society.

When professionals fail to recognize or respond to value conflicts, when they violate their own ethical standards, fall short of self-created expectations for expert performance, or seem blind to public problems they have helped to create, they are increasingly subject to expressions of disapproval and dissatisfaction. Radical critics like Ivan Illich (1970) take them to task for misappropriating and monopolizing knowledge, blithely disregarding social injustices, and mystifying their expertise. Professionals themselves argue that it is impossible to meet heightened societal expectations for their performance in an environment that combines increasing turbulence with increasing regulation of professional activity. They emphasize their lack of control over the larger systems for which they are unfairly held responsible. At the same time, they call attention to the mismatch between traditional divisions of labor and the shifting complexities of present-day society. They call for reforms in professional norms and structures.

In spite of these different emphases, public, radical, and professional critics voice a common complaint: that the most important areas of professional practice now lie beyond the conventional boundaries of professional competence.

The late Everett Hughes, a pioneering sociologist of the professions, once observed that the professions have struck a bargain with society. In return for access to their extraordinary knowledge in matters of great human importance, society has granted them a mandate for social control in their fields of specialization, a high degree of autonomy in their practice, and a license to determine who shall assume the mantle of professional authority (Hughes, 1959). But in the current climate of criticism, controversy, and dissatisfaction, the bargain is coming unstuck. When the professions' claim to extraordinary knowledge is so much in question, why should we continue to grant them extraordinary rights and privileges?

The Crisis of Confidence in Professional Education

The crisis of confidence in professional knowledge corresponds to a similar crisis in professional education. If professions are blamed for ineffectiveness and impropriety, their schools are blamed for failing to teach the rudiments of effective and ethical practice. Chief Justice Warren Burger criticizes the law schools, for example, because trial lawyers are not good at their jobs. In the present climate of dissatisfaction with public schools, schools of education are taken to task. Business schools become targets of criticism when their M.B.A.'s are seen as having failed to exercise responsible stewardship or rise adequately to the Japanese challenge. Schools of engineering lose credibility because they are seen as producing narrowly trained technicians deficient in capacity for design and wisdom to deal with dilemmas of technological development.

Underlying such criticisms is a version of the rigor-or-relevance dilemma. What aspiring practitioners need most to learn, professional schools seem least able to teach. And the schools' version of the dilemma is rooted, like the practitioners', in an underlying and largely unexamined epistemology of professional practice—a model of professional knowledge institutionally embedded in curriculum and arrangements for research and practice.

The professional schools of the modern research university are premised on technical rationality. Their normative curriculum, first adopted in the early decades of the twentieth century as the professions sought to gain prestige by establishing their schools in universities, still embodies the idea that practical competence becomes professional when its instrumental problem solving is grounded in systematic, preferably scientific knowledge. So the normative professional curriculum presents first the relevant basic science, then the relevant applied science, and finally, a practicum in which students are presumed to learn to apply research-based knowledge to the problems of everyday practice (Schein, 1973). And the prevailing view of the proper relationship between professional schools and schools of science and scholarship still conforms to the bargain enunciated many years ago by Thorstein Veblen (1918/1962): from the "lower" technical schools, their unsolved problems; from the "higher" schools, their useful knowledge.

As professional schools have sought to attain higher levels of academic rigor and status, they have oriented themselves toward an ideal most vividly represented by a particular view of medical education: physicians are thought to be trained as biotechnical problem solvers by immersion, first in medical science and then in supervised clinical practice where they learn to apply research-based techniques to diagnosis, treatment, and prevention. In this view of medical education, and its extension in the normative curriculum of other professional schools, there is a hierarchy of knowledge:

> Basic science
> Applied science
> Technical skills of day-to-day practice

The greater one's proximity to basic science, as a rule, the higher one's academic status. General, theoretical, propositional knowledge enjoys a privileged position. Even in the professions least equipped with a secure foundation of systematic professional knowledge—Nathan Glazer's (1974) "minor professions," such as social work, city planning, and education—yearning for the rigor of science-based knowledge and the power of science-based technique leads the schools to import scholars from neighboring departments of social science. And the relative status of the various professions is largely correlated with the extent to which they are able to present themselves as rigorous practitioners of a science-based professional knowledge and embody in their schools a version of the normative professional curriculum.

But, in the throes of external attack and internal self-doubt, the university-based schools of the professions are becoming increasingly aware of troubles in certain foundational assumptions on which they have traditionally depended for their credibility and legitimacy. They have assumed that academic research yields useful professional knowledge and that the professional knowl-

edge taught in the schools prepares students for the demands of
real-world practice. Both assumptions are coming increasingly
into question.

In recent years there has been a growing perception that
researchers, who are supposed to feed the professional schools with
useful knowledge, have less and less to say that practitioners find
useful. Teachers complain that cognitive psychologists have little
of practical utility to teach them. Business managers and even
some business school professors express a "nagging doubt that
some research is getting too academic and that [we] may be
neglecting to teach managers how to put into effect the strategies
which they develop" (Lynton, 1984, p. 14). Policy makers and
politicians express similar doubts about the utility of political
science. Martin Rein and Sheldon White (1980) have recently
observed that research not only is separate from professional
practice but has been increasingly captured by its own agenda,
divergent from the needs and interests of professional practitioners.
And Joseph Gusfield (1979, pp. 22), addressing himself to
sociology's failure to provide a firm and useful grounding for
public policy, has written a passage that could have a much more
general application: "The bright hope had been that sociology, by
the logic of its theories and the power of its empirical findings,
would provide insights and generalizations enabling governments
to frame policies and professionals to engineer programs that
could solve the exigent problems of the society and helping
intellectuals to direct understanding and criticism. Our record has
not been very good. In area after area—gerontology, crime, mental
health, race relations, poverty—we have become doubtful that the
technology claimed is adequate to the demand. . . . It is not that
conflicting interests lead groups to ignore social science. It is
rather that our belief in the legitimacy of our knowledge is itself in
doubt."

At the same time, professional educators have voiced with
increasing frequency their worries about the gap between the
schools' prevailing conception of professional knowledge and the
actual competencies required of practitioners in the field. An
eminent professor of engineering, commenting on the neglect of
engineering design in schools devoted to engineering science,

observed nearly twenty years ago that, if the art of engineering design were known and constant, it could be taught—but it is not constant (Brooks, 1967). Another dean of an engineering school said, at about the same time, that "we know how to teach people how to build ships but not how to figure out what ships to build" (Alfred Kyle, personal communication, 1974). The dean of a well-known school of management observed a decade ago that "we need most to teach students how to make decisions under conditions of uncertainty, but this is just what we don't know how to teach" (William Pownes, personal communication, 1972). Law professors have been discussing for some time the need to teach "lawyering" and, especially, the competences to resolve disputes by other means than litigation. A major school of medicine is undertaking a pilot program one of whose goals is to help students learn to function competently in clinical situations where there are no right answers or standard procedures. In all these examples, educators express their dissatisfactions with a professional curriculum that cannot prepare students for competence in the indeterminate zones of practice.

Awareness of these two gaps, each contributing to and exacerbating the other, undermines the confidence of professional educators in their ability to fulfill their mandate. Nevertheless, many professional schools—certainly those of medicine, law, and business—continue to attract large numbers of students in search of the traditional rewards of status, security, and affluence. Self-doubt coexists with pressure to provide traditional services to students who seek traditional rewards.

Thoughtful practitioners of professional education have tended to see these problems in very different ways. Some, in the fields of medicine, management, and engineering, have focused attention on difficulties created for professional education by the rapidly changing and proliferating mass of knowledge relevant to professional practice. They see the problem as one of "keeping up with" and "integrating" into the professional curriculum the stream of potentially useful research results. Others, in law or architecture, for example, have focused on aspects of practice for which traditional professional education provides no formal preparation. They recommend such marginal additions to the standard curriculum as courses in professional ethics or professional/client relationships. Still others see the problem as a loosening of earlier standards of professional rigor and probity; they want to tighten up the curriculum in order to restore it to its former level of excellence.

These are patchwork approaches to problems seen as peripheral. But another group of critics, including some students, practitioners, and educators, raises a deeper question. Can the prevailing concepts of professional education ever yield a curriculum adequate to the complex, unstable, uncertain, and conflictual worlds of practice? A recent example of this school of thought is a book by Ernst Lynton (1985) that links the troubles of the professional schools to a multidimensional crisis of the university and calls for a fundamental reexamination of the nature and conduct of university education. Such commentaries trace the gaps between professional school and workplace, research and practice, to a flawed conception of professional competence and its relationship to scientific and scholarly research. In this view, if there is a crisis of confidence in the professions and their schools, it is rooted in the prevailing epistemology of practice.

Turning the Problem Upside Down

It is striking that uneasiness about professional knowledge persists even though some practitioners do very well in the indeterminate zones whose importance we are learning to recognize. Some engineers are good at engineering design. Some lawyers are good at lawyering, competent at the skills of negotiation, mediation, and client relations that lie beyond the conventional boundaries of legal knowledge. Some business managers are manifestly better than others at making sense of confusing situations; and some policy makers are significantly endowed with the ability to work out useful integrations of conflicting views and interests.

Few critics of professional practice would deny these things, but few would take them as a source of insight into the crises of professional knowledge and education. The difficulty is not that critics fail to recognize some professional performances as superior to others—on this point there is surprisingly general agreement—but that they cannot assimilate what they recognize to their dominant model of professional knowledge. So outstanding practitioners are not said to have more professional knowledge than others but more "wisdom," "talent," "intuition," or "artistry."

Unfortunately, such terms as these serve not to open up inquiry but to close it off. They are used as junk categories, attaching names to phenomena that elude conventional strategies of explanation. So the dilemma of rigor or relevance here reasserts itself. On the basis of an underlying and largely unexamined epistemology of practice, we distance ourselves from the kinds of performance we need most to understand.

The question of the relationship between practice competence and professional knowledge needs to be turned upside down. We should start not by asking how to make better use of research-based knowledge but by asking what we can learn from a careful examination of artistry, that is, the competence by which practitioners actually handle indeterminate zones of practice—however that competence may relate to technical rationality.

This is the perspective of the present book, which starts from the following premises:

- Inherent in the practice of the professionals we recognize as unusually competent is a core of artistry.
- Artistry is an exercise of intelligence, a kind of knowing, though different in crucial respects from our standard model of professional knowledge. It is not inherently mysterious; it is rigorous in its own terms; and we can learn a great deal about it—within what limits, we should treat as an open question—by carefully studying the performance of unusually competent performers.
- In the terrain of professional practice, applied science and research-based technique occupy a critically important though limited territory, bounded on several sides by artistry. There are an art of problem framing, an art of implementation, and an art of improvisation—all necessary to mediate the use in practice of applied science and technique.

Not only the question of the relationship between competent practice and professional knowledge but also the question of
professional education needs to be turned upside down. Just as we
should inquire into the manifestations of professional artistry, so
we should also examine the various ways in which people actually
acquire it.

When, in the early decades of this century, the professions
began to appropriate the prestige of the university by placing their
schools within it, "professionalization" meant the replacement of
artistry by systematic, preferably scientific, knowledge. As awareness of the crisis of confidence in professional knowledge has
grown, however, educators have begun once again to see artistry as
an essential component of professional competence, to ask whether
the professional schools can or should do anything about it and, if
so, how education for artistry can be made coherent with the
professional curriculum's core of applied science and technique.

The debates surrounding these questions have taken
different forms in different professions and schools. In an
engineering curriculum organized mainly around engineering
science, for example, how should students learn engineering
design? How should students of such policy sciences as economics,
decision theory, operations research, and statistical analysis learn
the political and administrative skills of policy implementation?

Legal education has traditionally aimed at preparing
students to "think like a lawyer." Law schools pioneered in the use
of Christopher Langdell's case method to help students learn how
to make legal arguments, clarify legal issues by adversarial process,
and choose from among plausible judicial precedents the one most
relevant to a particular question of legal interpretation. For some
years, however, faculty members in some of the most eminent law
schools have argued the need to develop competences that go
beyond thinking like a lawyer—for example, skills in trial work,
client relations, negotiation, advocacy, and legal ethics. In medical
education, new programs have been devised to address the
problems of preparing students not only for the biotechnical
demands of clinical practice but also for family practice, management of the chronically ill, and the psychosocial dimensions of
illness. Critics internal and external to the business schools now

question the adequacy of the hallowed case method to the specific demands of management in particular industries as well as to the more general demands of responsible stewardship and management under conditions of uncertainty. In such fields as these, a professional curriculum organized around preparation for presumably generic competences of problem solving and decision making has begun to seem radically incomplete.

In some fields, the question of professional artistry has come up in the context of continuing education. Educators ask how mature professionals can be helped to renew themselves so as to avoid "burnout," how they can be helped to build their repertoires of skills and understandings on a continuing basis. Teacher education is an interesting example. Public awareness of the problems of schools has tended over the past thirty years to move in and out of focus, crystallizing from time to time around such issues as the quality of teaching and the in-service education of teachers. Teachers, who often resent becoming targets of blame for the perceived failures of public education, tend nevertheless to advocate their own versions of the need for professional development and renewal. Critics inside and outside the schools have argued in recent years that we must foster and reward development of the craft of teaching.

Where the core curriculum of professional education is relatively diffuse, unstable, and insecure, as in Nathan Glazer's "minor professions," the problem of education for artistry tends to take a different form. In social work, city planning, divinity, and educational administration, for example, educators tend to ask more open-endedly what competences ought to be acquired, through what methods, and in what domains of practice and even to wonder aloud whether what needs most to be learned can best be learned in a professional school. Here education for artistry becomes embroiled in the larger question of the legitimacy of professional education.

As we consider the artistry of extraordinary practitioners and explore the ways they actually acquire it, we are led inevitably to certain deviant traditions of education for practice—traditions that stand outside or alongside the normative curricula of the schools.

There are deviant traditions in the professional schools themselves. In medical schools and schools modeled at least in part on medicine, one often finds a dual curriculum. When interns and residents under the guidance of senior clinicians work with real patients on the wards, they learn more than application of medical science taught in the classroom. There is at least an implicit recognition that research-based models of diagnosis and treatment cannot be made to work until the students acquire an art that falls outside the models; and on this view, widely held by practicing physicians, the medical practicum is as much concerned with acquiring a quasi-autonomous art of clinical practice as with learning to apply research-based theory.

Beyond the confines of professional schools, there are other deviant traditions of education for practice. There are apprenticeships in industry and crafts. There is athletics coaching. And, perhaps most important, there are the conservatories of music and dance and the studios of the visual and plastic arts. The artistry of painters, sculptors, musicians, dancers, and designers bears a strong family resemblance to the artistry of extraordinary lawyers, physicians, managers, and teachers. It is no accident that professionals often refer to an "art" of teaching or management and use the term *artist* to refer to practitioners unusually adept at handling situations of uncertainty, uniqueness, and conflict.

In education for the fine arts, we find people learning to design, perform, and produce by engaging in design, performance, and production. Everything is practicum. Professional knowledge, in the sense of the propositional contents of applied science and scholarship, occupies a marginal place—if it is present at all—at the edges of the curriculum. Emphasis is placed on learning by doing, which John Dewey described long ago as the "primary or initial subject matter": "Recognition of the natural course of development . . . always sets out with situations which involve learning by doing. Arts and occupations form the initial stage of the curriculum, corresponding as they do to knowing how to go about the accomplishment of ends" (Dewey, 1974, p. 364).

Students learn by practicing the making or performing at which they seek to become adept, and they are helped to do so by senior practitioners who—again, in Dewey's terms—initiate them into the traditions of practice: "The customs, methods, and *working* standards of the calling constitute a 'tradition,' and . . . initiation into the tradition is the means by which the powers of learners are released and directed" (1974, p. 151).

The student cannot be *taught* what he needs to know, but he can be *coached:* "He has to *see* on his own behalf and in his own way the relations between means and methods employed and results achieved. Nobody else can see for him, and he can't see just by being 'told,' although the right kind of telling may guide his seeing and thus help him see what he needs to see" (1974, p. 151).

Often, there is a powerful sense of mystery and magic in the atmosphere—the magic of great performers, the mystery of talent that falls capriciously, like divine grace, now on one individual, now on another. There are the great performers who symbolize it and the child prodigies whose occasional appearance gives evidence of its continual renewal. In this rather magical environment, the function of coaching is controversial. In the absence of talent, some coaches believe, there is little to be done; and if there is talent in abundance, it is best to keep out of the student's way. Others believe that talented students can learn, by a kind of contagion, from exposure to master practitioners. And still others frame learning by doing as a disciplined initiation into the setting and solving of problems of production and performance.

Perhaps, then, learning *all* forms of professional artistry depends, at least in part, on conditions similar to those created in the studios and conservatories: freedom to learn by doing in a setting relatively low in risk, with access to coaches who initiate students into the "traditions of the calling" and help them, by "the right kind of telling," to see on their own behalf and in their own way what they need most to see. We ought, then, to study the experience of learning by doing and the artistry of good coaching. We should base our study on the working assumption that both processes are intelligent and—within limits to be discovered—intelligible. And we ought to search for examples wherever we can find them—in the dual curricula of the schools, the apprenticeships and practicums that aspiring practitioners find or create for themselves, and the deviant traditions of studio and conservatory.

Things to Come

In this book, I shall explore some of the deviant traditions
of education for artistry and develop from them a general view of
what I shall call a "reflective practicum"—a practicum aimed at
helping students acquire the kinds of artistry essential to competence in the indeterminate zones of practice. I shall argue that the
professional schools must rethink both the epistemology of
practice and the pedagogical assumptions on which their curricula are based and must bend their institutions to accommodate the
reflective practicum as a key element of professional education.

I shall begin with the architectural design studio. Schools of
architecture are interesting because they occupy a middle ground
between professional and art schools. Architecture is an established
profession charged with important social functions, but it is also a
fine art; and the arts tend to sit uneasily in the contemporary
research university. Although some schools of architecture are free-
standing institutions, most exist within a university, where they
tend to be marginal, isolated, and of dubious status—the more
prestigious the university, the more dubious the status. In their
curricula, some applied sciences may be taught, although the
status of such sciences is often ambiguous and controversial. For
the most part, however, these schools preserve a studio tradition
centered on the art of designing.

I have chosen to focus on the architectural design studio not
only because I have had the opportunity to study it at some length
but also because I have become convinced that architectural
designing is a prototype of the kind of artistry that other
professionals need most to acquire; and the design studio, with its
characteristic pattern of learning by doing and coaching, exemplifies the predicaments inherent in any reflective practicum and the
conditions and processes essential to its success. Thus, other
professional schools can learn from architecture.

In Part Two of this book, which will be devoted exclusively
to the design studio, I shall deal with the following themes:

• *Designing as a form of artistry.* What are the kinds of knowing
  at work in architectural designing?

- *Fundamental tasks and predicaments of a design studio.* How ought we to explain the sense of confusion and mystery that pervades the early stages of a design studio? In what sense are design competences teachable—or learnable? What are the characteristic roles and tasks of students and studio instructors?
- *Dialogue of student and coach.* If we think of the interaction of student and coach as one in which messages are sent, received, and interpreted, what are the forms of communication available to coach and student? On what factors does communicative efficacy depend?
- *Forms of dialogue.* What are some of the principal models of communicative interaction between coach and student? To what kinds of learning are they particularly suited?
- *Coach and student as practitioners.* Depending on the forms of dialogue at work in the studio, student and coach are subject to different sets of complementary demands. What are the characteristic problems they are called on to solve in their interactions with each other?
- *Coaching artistry.* Design coaches who are good at their work display a kind of artistry in their own right. What are its distinctive patterns of knowing?
- *Impediments to learning.* What are some of the ways in which the dialogue of student and coach can go wrong? What competences can overcome these impediments to learning?

Through the study of these themes in the context of architectural design studios, I shall outline the main features of a reflective practicum applicable to education for artistry in other professions.

In Parts Three and Four, I shall test and develop my interpretation of a reflective practicum by describing and analyzing four cases drawn from other fields: a master class in musical performance; examples of psychoanalytic supervision; the "theory of action" seminars that Chris Argyris and I have conducted over a period of seven years to help students learn skills of interpersonal and organizational consulting; and the introduction of a core curriculum in a department of city planning. In each of these cases, I shall show that students are seeking to acquire—and instructors, to help them acquire—a kind of artistry that is designlike. The characteristic predicaments and patterns of the design studio are also central to education for artistry in other fields. Students learn by doing, and instructors function more as coaches than as teachers. In the early stages of the practicum, confusion and mystery reign. The gradual passage to convergence of meaning is mediated—when it occurs—by a distinctive dialogue of student and coach in which description of practice is interwoven with performance; and the complex interactions of student and coach tend to conform to a few basic models, each suited to different contexts and kinds of learning. In these terms, I shall describe the practice of the practicum, the multiple demands placed on those who participate in it, and types of coaching artistry—including the artistry by which predictable impediments to learning may be overcome.

In addition, each of the examples to be analyzed in Parts Three and Four raises questions and considerations of its own.

The master class in musical performance is most closely related to the design studio. Both practicums exemplify deviant traditions of education for artistry, and they offer closely related examples of models of dialogue and forms of coaching competence. At the same time, they reveal important differences, attributable to their different substantive contents and media.

Psychoanalytic supervision is a large step away from either of the preceding examples, but it too is designlike. From a constructionist perspective, analysts are active listeners who construct the meanings of their patients' material and try to build a special relationship conducive to the distinctive psychoanalytic uses of the transference. Similarly, psychoanalytic supervision can be understood as a reflective practicum in which student therapist and supervisor create parallelisms—in each other's practice, inside and outside the practicum—on the basis of which they enhance or impede the work of learning and coaching.

These parallelisms, and the hall of mirrors they make possible, are also inherent in the "theory of action" seminars. Here, however, because we will have access to records of students' and coaches' experience over long periods of time, we will be able to study long-term cycles of learning and coaching. We will examine how students' "failure cycles" evolve and are sometimes transcended and how coaches can learn from the experience of many practicums.

Finally, in the case of the introduction of a new core curriculum in a department of city planning, we will be able to explore the ways in which the institutional context of a professional school resists the creation of a reflective practicum and, at the same time, holds potentials for its development.

From the study of these several examples and experiments, I shall assemble the outlines of a theory of the reflective practicum as a vehicle for education in artistry—a response to the predicament of professional schools increasingly aware of the need to prepare students for competence in the indeterminate zones of practice.

Before going on to Parts Two, Three, and Four, however, I shall present a more general analysis of artistry in practice and a more general description of the functions of a reflective practicum.

☙ Chapter Two ☙

Teaching Artistry Through
Reflection-in-Action

Knowing-in-Action

I have used the term *professional artistry* to refer to the kinds of competence practitioners sometimes display in unique, uncertain, and conflicted situations of practice. Note, however, that their artistry is a high-powered, esoteric variant of the more familiar sorts of competence all of us exhibit every day in countless acts of recognition, judgment, and skillful performance. What is striking about both kinds of competence is that they do not depend on our being able to describe what we know how to do or even to entertain in conscious thought the knowledge our actions reveal. As Gilbert Ryle observed, "What distinguishes sensible from silly operation is not their parentage but their procedure, and this holds no less for intellectual than for practical performances. 'Intelligent' cannot be defined in terms of 'intellectual' or 'knowing *how*' in terms of 'knowing *that*'; 'thinking what I am doing' does not connote 'both thinking what to do and doing it.' When I do something intelligently . . . I am doing one thing and not two. My performance has a special procedure or manner, not special antecedents" (1949, p. 32). For similar reasons, my late friend Raymond M. Hainer spoke of "knowing more than we can say," and Michael Polanyi, in *The Tacit Dimension* (1967), coined the term *tacit knowledge.*

Polanyi wrote, for example, about the remarkable virtuosity with which we recognize the faces of people we know. He pointed out that, when we notice a familiar face in a crowd, our experience of recognition is immediate. We are usually aware of no antecedent reasoning, no comparison of *this* face with images of other faces held in memory. We simply see the face of the person we know. And if someone should ask us how we do it, distinguishing one particular face from hundreds of others more or less similar to it, we are likely to discover that we cannot say. Usually we cannot construct a list of features particular to *this* face and distinct from the other faces around it; and even if we could do so, the immediacy of our recognition suggests that it does not proceed by a listing of features.

Polanyi has also described our ordinary tactile appreciation of the surfaces of materials. If we are asked what we feel when we explore the surface of a table with our hand, for example, we are apt to say that the table feels rough, smooth, cool, sticky, or slippery; but we are unlikely to say that we feel a certain compression or abrasion of our fingertips. Nevertheless, it must be from this kind of feeling that we get to our appreciation of the qualities of the table's surface. In Polanyi's words, we perceive *from* fingertip sensations *to* the qualities of the surface. Similarly, when we use a stick to probe, say, a hole in a stone wall, we focus, not on the impressions of the stick on the fingers and palm of our hand, but on the qualities of the hole—its size and shape, the surfaces of the stones around it—which we apprehend through these tacit impressions. To become skillful in the use of a tool is to learn to appreciate, directly and without intermediate reasoning, the qualities of the materials that we apprehend *through* the tacit sensations of the tool in our hand.

Often such processes of recognition or appreciation take the form of normative judgments. In the very act by which we recognize something, we also perceive it as "right" or "wrong." Chris Alexander (1968) has described how craftsmen recognize the mismatch of an element to an overall pattern—his most famous example is the making of Slovakian peasant shawls—without the slightest ability or need to describe in words the norms they see as violated. And Geoffrey Vickers (1978), commenting on Alexander's example, has gone on to observe that, not only in artistic judgment but in all our ordinary judgments of the qualities of things, we can recognize and describe deviations from a norm very much more clearly than we can describe the norm itself.

This capacity seems to have a great deal to do with the way we learn new skills. A tennis teacher of my acquaintance writes, for example, that he always begins by trying to help his students get the feeling of "hitting the ball right." Once they recognize this feeling, like it, and learn to distinguish it from the various feelings associated with "hitting the ball wrong," they begin to be able to detect and correct their own errors. But they usually cannot, and need not, describe what the feeling is like or by what means they produce it.

Skilled physicians speak of being able to recognize a particular disease, on occasion, the moment a person afflicted with it walks into their office. The recognition comes immediately and as a whole, and although the physician may later discover in his examination of the patient a full set of reasons for his diagnosis, he is often unable to say just what clues triggered his immediate judgment.

Chester Barnard wrote, in the appendix to *The Functions of the Executive* (1938/1968), about our "non-logical processes," by which he meant the skillful judgments, decisions, and actions we undertake spontaneously, without being able to state the rules or procedures we follow. A boy who has learned to throw a ball, for example, makes immediate judgments of distance and coordinates them with the bodily movements involved in the act of throwing, although he cannot say how he does so or perhaps even name the distance he estimates. A high school girl who has learned to solve quadratic equations can spontaneously perform a series of operations without being able to give an accurate description of the procedures she follows when she does so. A practiced account- ant of Barnard's acquaintance could "take a balance sheet of considerable complexity and within minutes or even seconds get a significant set of facts from it" (p. 306), although he could not describe in words the judgments and calculations that entered into his performance.

In similar fashion, we learn to execute such complex performances as crawling, walking, juggling, or riding a bicycle without being able to give a verbal description even roughly adequate to our actual performance. Indeed, if we are asked to say how we do such things, we tend to give wrong answers which, if we were to act according to them, would get us into trouble. When people who know how to ride a bicycle are asked, for example, how to keep from falling when the bicycle begins to tilt to their left, some of them say that they regain their balance by turning the wheel to their right. If they actually did so, they would be likely to fall; fortunately, however, the know-how implicit in their actions is incongruent with their description of it.

I shall use *knowing-in-action* to refer to the sorts of know-how we reveal in our intelligent action—publicly observable, physical performances like riding a bicycle and private operations like instant analysis of a balance sheet. In both cases, the knowing is *in* the action. We reveal it by our spontaneous, skillful execution of the performance; and we are characteristically unable to make it verbally explicit.

Nevertheless, it is sometimes possible, by observing and reflecting on our actions, to make a description of the tacit knowing implicit in them. Our descriptions are of different kinds, depending on our purposes and the languages of description available to us. We may refer, for example, to the sequences of operations and procedures we execute; the clues we observe and the rules we follow; or the values, strategies, and assumptions that make up our "theories" of action.

Whatever language we may employ, however, our descriptions of knowing-in-action are always *constructions*. They are always attempts to put into explicit, symbolic form a kind of intelligence that begins by being tacit and spontaneous. Our descriptions are conjectures that need to be tested against observation of their originals—which, in at least one respect, they are bound to distort. For knowing-in-action is dynamic, and "facts," "procedures," "rules," and "theories" are static. When we know how to catch a ball, for example, we anticipate the ball's coming by the way we extend and cup our hands and by the on-line adjustments we make as the ball approaches. Catching a ball is a continuous activity in which awareness, appreciation, and adjustment play their parts. Similarly, sawing along a penciled line requires a more or less continuous process of detecting and correcting deviations from the line. Indeed, it is this on-line anticipation and adjustment, this continuous detection and correction of error, that leads us, in the first place, to call activity "intelligent." Know*ing* suggests the dynamic quality of knowing-in-action, which, when we describe it, we convert to know*ledge*-in-action.

Reflection-in-Action

When we have learned how to do something, we can execute smooth sequences of activity, recognition, decision, and adjustment without having, as we say, to "think about it." Our spontaneous knowing-in-action usually gets us through the day. On occasion, however, it doesn't. A familiar routine produces an unexpected result; an error stubbornly resists correction; or, although the usual actions produce the usual outcomes, we find something odd about them because, for some reason, we have begun to look at them in a new way. All such experiences, pleasant and unpleasant, contain an element of *surprise*. Something fails to meet our expectations. In an attempt to preserve the constancy of our usual patterns of knowing-in-action, we may respond to surprise by brushing it aside, selectively inattending to the signals that produce it. Or we may respond to it by reflection, and we may do so in one of two ways.

We may reflect *on* action, thinking back on what we have done in order to discover how our knowing-in-action may have contributed to an unexpected outcome. We may do so after the fact, in tranquility, or we may pause in the midst of action to make what Hannah Arendt (1971) calls a "stop-and-think." In either case, our reflection has no direct connection to present action. Alternatively, we may reflect in the midst of action without interrupting it. In an *action-present*—a period of time, variable with the context, during which we can still make a difference to the situation at hand—our thinking serves to reshape what we are doing while we are doing it. I shall say, in cases like this, that we reflect-*in*-action.

Recently, for example, I built a gate out of wooden pickets and strapping. I had made a drawing and figured out the dimensions I wanted, but I had not reckoned with the problem of keeping the structure square. As I began to nail the strapping to the pickets, I noticed a wobble. I knew the structure would become rigid when I nailed in a diagonal piece, but how could I be sure it would be square? There came to mind a vague memory about diagonals: in a rectangle diagonals are equal. I took a yardstick, intending to measure the diagonals, but I found I could not use it without disturbing the structure. It occurred to me to use a piece of string. Then it became apparent that, in order to measure the diagonals, I needed a precise location at each corner. After several trials, I found I could locate the center point at each corner by constructing diagonals there (see illustration). I hammered in a nail at each of the four center points and used the nails as anchors for the measurement string. It took several minutes to figure out how to adjust the structure so as to correct the errors I found by measuring. And then, when I had the diagonals equal, I nailed in a piece of strapping to freeze the structure.

Here, in an example that must have its analogues in the experiences of amateur carpenters the world over, my intuitive way of going about the task led me to a surprise (the discovery of the wobble), which I interpreted as a problem. In the midst of action, I invented procedures to solve the problem, discovered further unpleasant surprises, and made further corrective inventions, including the several minor ones necessary to carry out the idea of using string to measure the diagonals. We might call such a process "trial and error." But the trials are not randomly related to one another; reflection on each trial and its results sets the stage for the next trial. Such a pattern of inquiry is better described as a sequence of "moments" in a process of reflection-in-action:

• There is, to begin with, a situation of action to which we bring spontaneous, routinized responses. These reveal knowing-in-action that may be described in terms of strategies, understandings of phenomena, and ways of framing a task or problem appropriate to the situation. The knowing-in-action is tacit, spontaneously delivered without conscious deliberation; and it works, yielding intended outcomes so long as the situation falls within the boundaries of what we have learned to treat as normal.

• Routine responses produce a surprise—an unexpected outcome, pleasant or unpleasant, that does not fit the categories of our knowing-in-action. Inherent in a surprise is the fact that it gets our attention. For example, I might not have been surprised by the wobble in my gate because I might not have attended to it; the structure might not have ended up square, and I might not have noticed.

• Surprise leads to reflection within an action-present. Reflection is at least in some measure conscious, although it need not occur in the medium of words. We consider both the unexpected event and the knowing-in-action that led up to it, asking ourselves, as it were, "What is this?" and, at the same time, "How have I been thinking about it?" Our thought turns back on the surprising phenomenon and, at the same time, back on itself.

• Reflection-in-action has a critical function, questioning the assumptional structure of knowing-in-action. We think critically about the thinking that got us into this fix or this opportunity; and we may, in the process, restructure strategies of action, understandings of phenomena, or ways of framing problems. In my example, the surprise triggered by my observation of the wobble led me to frame a new problem: "How to keep the gate square?"

• Reflection gives rise to on-the-spot experiment. We think up and try out new actions intended to explore the newly observed phenomena, test our tentative understandings of them, or affirm the moves we have invented to change things for the better. With my measuring-string experiment, I tested both my understanding of squareness as equality of diagonals and the effectiveness of the procedures I had invented for determining when diagonals are equal. On-the-spot experiment may work, again in the sense of yielding intended results, or it may produce surprises that call for further reflection and experiment.

The description I have given is, of course, an idealized one. The moments of reflection-in-action are rarely as distinct from one another as I have made them out to be. The experience of surprise may present itself in such a way as to seem already interpreted. The criticism and restructuring of knowing-in-action may be compressed into a single process. But regardless of the distinctness of its moments or the constancy of their sequence, what distinguishes reflection-in-action from other kinds of reflection is its immediate significance for action. In reflection-in-action, the rethinking of some part of our knowing-in-action leads to on-the-spot experiment and further thinking that affects what we do—in the situation at hand and perhaps also in others we shall see as similar to it.

The distinction between reflection- and knowing-in-action may be subtle. A skilled performer adjusts his responses to variations in phenomena. In his moment-by-moment appreciations of a process, he deploys a wide-ranging repertoire of images of contexts and actions. So a baseball pitcher adapts his pitching style to the peculiarities of a particular batter or situation in a game. In order to counter an opponent's changing strategies, a tennis player executes split-second variations in play. We can say, in cases like these, that the performer responds to *variation* rather than *surprise* because the changes in context and response never cross the boundaries of the familiar.

However, in a kind of process that may look from the outside like the ones described above, a skilled performer can integrate reflection-in-action into the smooth performance of an ongoing task. I recently heard the story of a cellist who had been called to join in performing a new piece of chamber music. Because of illness, he missed the first few rehearsals and finally put in an appearance the day before the performance was to take place. He sat down with the other musicians and sight-read his way through the difficult part, playing it so well that the conductor had no need to reschedule the performance. As the cellist sight-read the score, he could not have known for certain where the piece was heading. Yet he must have sensed at each moment the direction of its development, picking up in his own performance the lines of development already laid down by others. He must have encountered surprises in response to which he formed, on-line, an interpretation guided by his emerging sense of the whole. And the execution of this feat left him with a newly developed understanding of the piece and how to play it that he would reveal as knowing-in-action on the day of the performance.

When good jazz musicians improvise together, they similarly display reflection-in-action smoothly integrated into ongoing performance. Listening to one another, listening to themselves, they "feel" where the music is going and adjust their playing accordingly. A figure announced by one performer will be taken up by another, elaborated, turned into a new melody. Each player makes on-line inventions and responds to surprises triggered by the inventions of the other players. But the collective process of musical invention is organized around an underlying structure. There is a common schema of meter, melody, and harmonic development that gives the piece a predictable order. In addition, each player has at the ready a repertoire of musical figures around which he can weave variations as the opportunity arises. Improvisation consists in varying, combining, and recombining a set of figures within a schema that gives coherence to the whole piece. As the musicians feel the directions in which the music is developing, they make new sense of it. They reflect-in-action on the music they are collectively making—though not, of course, in the medium of words.

Their process resembles the familiar patterns of everyday conversation. In a good conversation—in some respects predictable and in others not—participants pick up and develop themes of talk, each spinning out variations on her repertoire of things to say. Conversation is collective verbal improvisation. At times it falls into conventional routines—the anecdote with side comments and reactions, for example, or the debate—which develop according to a pace and rhythm of interaction that the participants seem, without conscious deliberation, to work out in common within the framework of an evolving division of labor. At other times, there may be surprises, unexpected turns of phrase or directions of development to which participants invent on-the-spot responses.

In such examples, the participants are *making* something. Out of musical materials or themes of talk, they make a piece of music or a conversation, an artifact with its own meaning and coherence. Their reflection-in-action is a reflective conversation with the materials of a situation—"conversation," now, in a metaphorical sense. Each person carries out his own evolving role in the collective performance, "listens" to the surprises—or, as I shall say, "back talk"—that result from earlier moves, and responds through on-line production of new moves that give new meanings and directions to the development of the artifact. The process is reminiscent of Edmund Carpenter's description of the Eskimo sculptor patiently carving a reindeer bone, examining the gradually emerging shape, and finally exclaiming, "Ah, seal!"

Like knowing-in-action, reflection-in-action is a process we can deliver without being able to say what we are doing. Skillful improvisers often become tongue-tied or give obviously inadequate accounts when asked to say what they do. Clearly, it is one thing to be able to reflect-in-action and quite another to be able to reflect *on* our reflection-in-action so as to produce a good verbal description of it; and it is still another thing to be able to reflect on the resulting description.

But our reflection on our past reflection-in-action may indirectly shape our future action. The reflections of a Monday morning quarterback may be full of significance if the person reflecting is the quarterback who will play—and play differently because of his Monday morning quarterbacking—in next Saturday's game. As I think back on my experience with the wooden gate, I may consolidate my understanding of the problem or invent a better or more general solution to it. If I do, my present reflection on my earlier reflection-in-action begins a dialogue of thinking and doing through which I become a more skillful (though still amateur) carpenter. Indeed, as we shall see in later chapters, these several levels and kinds of reflection play important roles in the acquisition of artistry.

Practice

So far in this chapter, I have shifted focus from the specialized and esoteric artistry of professional practice to the more mundane—but no less remarkable—artistry of everyday life. I have done so in order to show that knowing-in-action and reflection-in-action enter into experiences of thinking and doing that everyone shares; when we learn the artistry of a professional practice—no matter how disjunct from ordinary life it may at first appear to be—we learn new ways of using *kinds* of competences we already possess.

Nevertheless, the context of a professional practice is significantly different from other contexts; and the roles of knowing- and reflection-in-action in professional artistry, correspondingly different.

Everett Hughes, as I have mentioned, defined a professional as one who makes a claim to extraordinary knowledge in matters of great human importance (Hughes, 1959). He saw the professional's claim to extraordinary knowledge as bound up in a paradigmatic bargain with society. In return for access to his special knowledge, the professional is accorded a special mandate for social control in matters of his expertise, a license to determine who shall enter his profession, and a relatively high degree of autonomy in the regulation of his practice. Thus, in close association with the very idea of a profession, we find the idea of a community of practitioners whose special knowledge sets them off from other individuals in relation to whom they hold special rights and privileges.

A professional practice is the province of a community of practitioners who share, in John Dewey's term, the traditions of a calling. They share conventions of action that include distinctive media, languages, and tools. They operate within particular kinds of institutional settings—the law court, the school, the hospital, and the business firm, for example. Their practices are structured in terms of particular kinds of units of activity—cases, patient visits, or lessons, for example—and they are socially and institutionally patterned so as to present repetitive occurrences of particular kinds of situations. A "practice" is made up of chunks of activity, divisible into more or less familiar types, each of which is seen as calling for the exercise of a certain kind of knowledge.

Practitioners of a profession differ from one another, of course, in their subspecialties, the particular experiences and perspectives they bring to their work, and their styles of operation. But they also share a common body of explicit, more or less systematically organized professional knowledge and what Geoffrey Vickers has called an "appreciative system"—the set of values, preferences, and norms in terms of which they make sense of practice situations, formulate goals and directions for action, and determine what constitutes acceptable professional conduct.

A professional's knowing-in-action is embedded in the socially and institutionally structured context shared by a community of practitioners. Knowing-in-*practice* is exercised in the institutional settings particular to the profession, organized in terms of its characteristic units of activity and its familiar types of practice situations, and constrained or facilitated by its common body of professional knowledge and its appreciative system.

So much we can say without making explicit reference to a particular epistemology of professional practice. Beyond this point, however, our view of a practitioner's knowing will greatly affect our descriptions of the functions and interactions of professional knowledge and professional artistry.

From the perspective of technical rationality, as I have already indicated, a competent practitioner is always concerned with instrumental problems. She searches for the means best suited to the achievement of fixed, unambiguous ends—in medicine, health; in law, success at litigation; in business, profit—and her effectiveness is measured by her success in finding, in each instance, the actions that produce the intended effects consistent with her objectives. In this view, *professional* competence consists in the application of theories and techniques derived from systematic, preferably scientific research to the solution of the instrumental problems of the practice.

From this perspective, we can distinguish two kinds of practice situations and two kinds of knowing appropriate to them.

There are familiar situations where the practitioner can solve the problem by routine application of facts, rules, and procedures derived from the body of professional knowledge. In city planning, for example, there are rules of thumb by which a planner can calculate, under a given zoning bylaw, the number of parking spaces required for each living unit in an apartment building. In medicine, there are routine diagnostic work-ups of patients and routine prescriptions for familiar, uncomplicated complaints.

There are also unfamiliar situations where the problem is not initially clear and there is no obvious fit between the characteristics of the situation and the available body of theories and techniques. It is common, in these types of situations, to speak of "thinking like a doctor"—or lawyer or manager—to refer to the kinds of inquiry by which competent practitioners bring available knowledge to bear on practice situations where its application is problematic. In this sense, the familiar law school drill takes students through a process that begins with a statement of "the facts of the case" and proceeds through characteristic patterns of reasoning to determine what legal questions are centrally at stake in the case and what judicial precedents are most pertinent to it. Similarly, medical students learn to "take a present illness" where, starting from standardized observations, physical examinations, interviews, and laboratory tests, the student must reason his way to a plausible diagnosis of the patient's illness and a proposed strategy of treatment.

From the perspective of technical rationality, "thinking like a _____" must be thought to consist in rule-governed inquiry. The competent practitioner is seen as following rules for data gathering, inference, and hypothesis testing, which allow him to make clear connections between presenting situations and the body of professional knowledge, where such connections are initially problematic. Such rules are presumed to be explicable, where they are not already explicit. The currently popular "expert systems," in clinical medicine as in other fields, are attempts to make explicit the information bases, rules, and procedures by which professional knowledge is applied to particular problematic cases (Kassirer and Gorry, 1970).

Within this framework, there is little room for professional artistry, except as a matter of style grafted onto technical expertise.

One might recognize the existence of professional artists capable of making sense of unique or uncertain situations, but there is no way to talk sensibly about their artistry—except, perhaps, to say that they are following rules that have not yet been made explicit.

On the alternative epistemology of practice suggested in this book, professional artistry is understood in terms of reflection-in-action, and it plays a central role in the description of professional competence.

On this view, we would recognize as a limiting case the situations in which it is possible to make a routine application of existing rules and procedures to the fact of particular problematic situations. Beyond these situations, familiar rules, theories, and techniques are put to work in concrete instances through the intermediary of an art that consists in a limited form of reflection-in-action. And beyond these, we would recognize cases of problematic diagnosis in which practitioners not only follow rules of inquiry but also sometimes respond to surprising findings by inventing new rules, on the spot. This kind of reflection-in-action is central to the artistry with which practitioners sometimes make new sense of uncertain, unique, or conflicted situations. For example:

- A physician, aware that about 85 percent of the cases that come into her office are not "in the book," responds to a patient's unique array of symptoms by inventing and testing a new diagnosis.
- A market researcher, monitoring consumers' reactions to a new product, discovers that they have seen in the product uses he never intended and responds by rethinking the product in terms of the consumers' discoveries.

In such cases, the practitioner experiences a surprise that leads her to rethink her knowing-in-action in ways that go beyond available rules, facts, theories, and operations. She responds to the unexpected or anomalous by restructuring some of her strategies of action, theories of phenomena, or ways of framing the problem; and she invents on-the-spot experiments to put her new understandings to the test. She behaves more like a researcher trying to model an expert system than like the "expert" whose behavior is modeled.

Underlying this view of the practitioner's reflection-in-action is a *constructionist* view of the reality with which the practitioner deals—a view that leads us to see the practitioner as constructing situations of his practice, not only in the exercise of professional artistry but also in all other modes of professional competence.

Technical rationality rests on an *objectivist* view of the relation of the knowing practitioner to the reality he knows. On this view, facts are what they are, and the truth of beliefs is strictly testable by reference to them. All meaningful disagreements are resolvable, at least in principle, by reference to the facts. And professional knowledge rests on a foundation of facts.

In the constructionist view, our perceptions, appreciations, and beliefs are rooted in worlds of our own making that we come to *accept* as reality. Communities of practitioners are continually engaged in what Nelson Goodman (1978) calls "worldmaking." Through countless acts of attention and inattention, naming, sensemaking, boundary setting, and control, they make and maintain the worlds matched to their professional knowledge and know-how. They are in transaction with their practice worlds, framing the problems that arise in practice situations and shaping the situations to fit the frames, framing their roles and constructing practice situations to make their role-frames operational. They have, in short, a particular, professional way of seeing their world and a way of constructing and maintaining the world as they see it. When practitioners respond to the indeterminate zones of practice by holding a reflective conversation with the materials of their situations, they remake a part of their practice world and thereby reveal the usually tacit processes of worldmaking that underlie all of their practice.

Practicum

When someone learns a practice, he is initiated into the traditions of a community of practitioners and the practice world they inhabit. He learns their conventions, constraints, languages, and appreciative systems, their repertoire of exemplars, systematic knowledge, and patterns of knowing-in-action.

He may do so in one of several ways. Rarely, he may learn the practice on his own, as people sometimes learn hunting, carpentry, or the criminal trades. He may become an apprentice to senior practitioners, as many craftsmen, industrial workers, and professionals still do. Or he may enter a practicum.

Picking up a practice on one's own has the advantage of freedom—freedom to experiment without the constraints of received views. But it also has the disadvantage of requiring each student to reinvent the wheel, gaining little or nothing from the accumulated experience of others. Apprenticeship offers direct exposure to real conditions of practice and patterns of work. But most offices, factories, firms, and clinics are not set up for the demanding tasks of initiation and education. Pressures for performance tend to be high; time, at a premium; and mistakes, costly. Senior professionals have learned, in addition, to expect apprentices to come equipped with rudimentary practice skills. Nevertheless, many novices still learn through apprenticeship, and many senior practitioners and critics of professional education still see it as the method of choice.

A practicum is a setting designed for the task of learning a practice. In a context that approximates a practice world, students learn by doing, although their doing usually falls short of real-world work. They learn by undertaking projects that simulate and simplify practice; or they take on real-world projects under close supervision. The practicum is a virtual world, relatively free of the pressures, distractions, and risks of the real one, to which, nevertheless, it refers. It stands in an intermediate space between the practice world, the "lay" world of ordinary life, and the esoteric world of the academy. It is also a collective world in its own right, with its own mix of materials, tools, languages, and appreciations. It embodies particular ways of seeing, thinking, and doing that tend, over time, as far as the student is concerned, to assert themselves with increasing authority.

When a student enters a practicum, she is presented, explicitly or implicitly, with certain fundamental tasks. She must learn to recognize competent practice. She must build an image of it, an appreciation of where she stands in relation to it, and a map of the path by which she can get from where she is to where she wants to be. She must come to terms with the claims implicit in the practicum: that a practice exists, worth learning, learnable by her, and represented in its essential features by the practicum. She must learn the "practice of the practicum"—its tools, methods, projects, and possibilities—and assimilate to it her emerging image of how she can best learn what she wants to learn.

The work of the practicum is accomplished through some combination of the student's learning by doing, her interactions with coaches and fellow students, and a more diffuse process of "background learning."

Students practice in a double sense. In simulated, partial, or protected form, they engage in the practice they wish to learn. But they also practice, as one practices the piano, the analogues in their fields of the pianist's scales and arpeggios. They do these things under the guidance of a senior practitioner—a studio master, supervising physician, or case instructor, for example. From time to time, these individuals may teach in the conventional sense, communicating information, advocating theories, describing examples of practice. Mainly, however, they function as coaches whose main activities are demonstrating, advising, questioning, and criticizing.

Most practicums involve groups of students who are often as important to one another as the coach. Sometimes they play the coach's role. And it is through the medium of the group that a student can immerse himself in the world of the practicum—the all-encompassing worlds of a design studio, a musical conservatory, or psychoanalytic supervision, for example—learning new habits of thought and action. Learning by exposure and immersion, *background* learning, often proceeds without conscious awareness, although a student may become aware of it later on, as he moves into a different setting.

Our view of the work of the practicum and the conditions and processes appropriate to it depends in part on our view of the kinds of knowing essential to professional competence. The types of knowing described in the previous section, and the different perspectives on them set forth there, suggest different conceptions of a practicum.

If we see professional knowledge in terms of facts, rules, and procedures applied nonproblematically to instrumental problems, we will see the practicum in its entirety as a form of technical training. It will be the business of the instructor to communicate and demonstrate the application of rules and operations to the facts of practice. One might imagine, on this view, a practicum for learning a computer language, techniques of analytic chemistry, or methods of statistical analysis. Students would be expected to acquire the material by reading, listening and watching, familiarizing themselves with examples of practice problems matched to the appropriate categories of theory and technique. Coaching would consist in observing student performance, detecting errors of application, pointing our correct responses.

If we see professional knowing in terms of "thinking like a" manager, lawyer, or teacher, students will still learn relevant facts and operations but will also learn the forms of inquiry by which competent practitioners reason their way, in problematic instances, to clear connections between general knowledge and particular cases. The standard drills of the law school classroom and the medical clinic exemplify this view. In a practicum of this kind, there is presumed to be a right answer for every situation, some item in the corpus of professional knowledge that can be seen, eventually, to fit the case at hand. But, depending on one's view of "thinking like a _____," coaches may emphasize either the *rules* of inquiry or the reflection-in-action by which, on occasion, students must develop new rules and methods of their own.

If we focus on the kinds of reflection-in-action through which practitioners sometimes make new sense of uncertain, unique or conflicted situations of practice, then we will assume neither that existing professional knowledge fits every case nor that every problem has a right answer. We will see students as having to learn a kind of reflection-in-action that goes beyond statable rules—not only by devising new methods of reasoning, as above, but also by constructing and testing new categories of understanding, strategies of action, and ways of framing problems.

Coaches will emphasize indeterminate zones of practice and reflective conversations with the materials of a situation.

It is important to add that the third kind of practicum need not obviate the work of the first and second. Perhaps we learn to reflect-in-action by learning first to recognize and apply standard rules, facts, and operations; then to reason from general rules to problematic cases, in ways characteristic of the profession; and only then to develop and test new forms of understanding and action where familiar categories and ways of thinking fail.*

Practicums of the third kind exist, in greater or lesser degree, in the deviant traditions of studio and conservatory. They are sometimes also found in association with apprenticeships or—less often, and usually without formal legitimacy or status—in the clinics, workshops, and internships of professional schools. These practicums are reflective in that they aim at helping students learn to become proficient at a kind of reflection-in-action. They are reflective, as we shall see, in the further sense that they depend for their effectiveness on a reciprocally reflective dialogue of coach and student. They and their design, conduct, conditions, and characteristic dilemmas are the concern of the following chapters.

*There are two points here, and they are of equal importance. The first is that the knowing-in-action characteristic of competent practitioners in a professional field is not the same as the professional knowledge taught in the schools; in any given case, the relationship of the two kinds of knowledge should be treated as an open question. Ordinary knowing-in-action may be an application of research-based professional knowledge taught in the schools, may be overlapping with it, or may have nothing to do with it. This point is similar to the one made by Charles Lindblom and David Cohen in *Usable Knowledge* (1979).

The second point is that competent professional practitioners often have the capacity to generate new knowing-in-action through reflection-in-action undertaken in the indeterminate zones of practice. The sources of knowing-in-action include this reflection-in-action and are not limited to research produced by university-based professional schools.

 *Part Two*

The Architectural Studio as Educational Model for Reflection-in-Action

Architectural artistry may not seem, at first glance, to be prototypical of reflection-in-action in other professions. The architectural studio may seem an odd choice to serve as the prototype of a reflective practicum. But architects are fundamentally concerned with designing—indeed, have as good a claim as anyone to epitomize the design professions—and designing, broadly conceived, is the process fundamental to the exercise of artistry in all professions.

In *The Sciences of the Artificial,* Herbert Simon (1976) made this very point; but his view of design there was very different from the one I shall take here. He saw designing as instrumental problem solving: in its best and purest form, a process of optimization. This view ignores the most important functions of designing in situations of uncertainty, uniqueness, and conflict where instrumental problem solving—and certainly optimization—occupy a secondary place, if they have a place at all. In contrast, I see designing as a kind of making.

Architects, landscape architects, interior or industrial or engineering designers, make physical objects that occupy space and have plastic and visual form. In a more general sense, a designer makes an image—a representation—of something to be brought to reality, whether conceived primarily in visual, spatial, plastic terms or not. Designing in its broader sense involves

41

complexity and synthesis. In contrast to analysts or critics, designers put things together and bring new things into being, dealing in the process with many variables and constraints, some initially known and some discovered through designing. Almost always, designers' moves have consequences other than those intended for them. Designers juggle variables, reconcile conflicting values, and maneuver around constraints—a process in which, although some design products may be superior to others, there are no unique right answers.

Among those who have considered the broader sense of designing, some have chosen to focus on the management of complexity; others, on imaging an ideal to be realized in practice; still others, on search within a field of constraints. Without ignoring any of these features, I prefer Dewey's view of the designer as one who converts indeterminate situations to determinate ones. Beginning with situations that are at least in part uncertain, ill defined, complex, and incoherent ("messes," as Russell Ackoff, 1979, has called them), designers *construct* and impose a coherence of their own. Subsequently they discover consequences and implications of their constructions—some unintended—which they appreciate and evaluate. Analysis and criticism play critical roles within their larger process. Their designing is a web of projected moves and discovered consequences and implications, sometimes leading to reconstruction of the initial coherence—a reflective conversation with the materials of a situation.

Artists make things and are, in this sense, designers. Indeed, the ancient Greeks used the term *poetics* to refer to the study of making things—poems being one category of things made. Professional practitioners are also makers of artifacts. Lawyers build cases, arguments, agreements, and pieces of legislation. Physicians construct diagnoses and regimens of testing and treatment. Planners construct spatial plans, policies, regulatory arrangements, and systems for the orchestration of contending interests. Practitioners are also makers in the more general constructionist sense introduced in the previous chapter. They frame problems and shape situations to match their professional understanding and methods, they construct situations suited to the roles they frame, and they shape the very practice worlds in which they live out their professional lives.

As makers of artifacts, all practitioners are design professionals; and from this perspective, architecture exemplifies professional artistry. Architecture, moreover, has a bimodality that gives it a special interest. On the one hand, it is a utilitarian profession concerned with the functional design and construction of settings for human activity; on the other, an art that uses the forms of buildings and the experience of passage through their spaces as media of esthetic expression. In architecture, then, we have access to a prototype of the designer's reflective conversation with his materials; and we can observe it in service both to functional and to esthetic values.

Architecture crystallized as a profession before the rise of technical rationality and carries the seeds of an earlier view of professional knowledge. Perhaps for this reason, it occupies a marginal place in the contemporary university. Its bimodality and implicit reliance on another epistemology of practice make the university uneasy. Even when architects are tempted to put on the university's lineaments of applied science, they cannot escape the profession's core of artistry; for architects are self-recognized designers, and although such ancillary sciences as soil mechanics, climatology, and structural engineering may contribute to specialized design tasks, there is no general usable science of design. So architectural education still embraces its studio traditions.

Studios are typically organized around manageable projects of design, individually or collectively undertaken, more or less closely patterned on projects drawn from actual practice. They have evolved their own rituals, such as master demonstrations, design reviews, desk crits, and design juries, all attached to a core process of learning by doing. And because studio instructors must try to make their approaches to design understandable to their students, the studio offers privileged access to designers' reflections on designing. It is at once a living and a traditional example of a reflective practicum.

🌿 Chapter Three 🌿

The Design Process as
Reflection-in-Action

In this chapter, I shall explore the designer's reflective conversation with his materials in the context of architectural designing. I have chosen to describe an event in an architectural studio—a "design review"—because it is in this kind of event that the outlines of the design process are most likely to be clearly visible.*

The setting is a loftlike studio space in which each of twenty students has arranged his or her drawing table, paper, books, pictures, and models. This is the space in which students spend much of their working lives, at times talking together but mostly engaged in private, parallel pursuit of the common design task. At the beginning of the semester, Quist, the studio master, gave all the students a "program"—a set of design specifications, in this case, for the design of an elementary school, and a graphic description of the site on which the school is to be built.

*The origins of this case study are in a review of architectural education in which I participated during the late 1970s. The study, supported by the Andrew Mellon Foundation, was directed by Dean William Porter of the M.I.T. School of Architecture and Planning and Dean Maurice Kilbridge of the Harvard Graduate School of Design. Several participant observation studies were conducted in design studios at universities at several locations in the United States. It is from one of these that I have drawn the protocol that follows. It was recorded by Roger Simmonds, then a graduate student of mine. I am grateful to Simmonds for his help in this, as well as to William Porter, Julian Beinart, Imre Halasz, and Florian Von Buttlar, with all of whom I had illuminating conversations. Dean Porter, especially, helped to initiate me into the world of architectural thinking.

In the course of the semester, each student is to develop her own version of the design, recording her results in preliminary sketches, working drawings, and models. At the end of the semester, there will be a "crit" at which the students present their designs to Quist and to a group of outside critics (the "jury"). At intervals throughout the semester, Quist holds a design review with each student, and it is just such a review that Quist, in our protocol, conducts with Petra.

For several weeks Petra has worked on the early phases of her design. She has prepared some drawings. Quist examines these while Petra describes how she is "stuck."

After a while, Quist places a sheet of tracing paper over her sketches and begins to draw over her drawing. As he draws, he talks. He says, for example:

> The kindergarten might go over here . . . then
> you might carry the gallery level through—and look
> down into here . . .

As Quist says these things, he also draws, placing the kindergarten "here" in the drawing, making the line that "carries the gallery level through." His words do not describe what is already there on paper but parallel the process by which he makes what is there. Drawing and talking are parallel ways of designing and together make up what I call the language of designing.

The language of designing is a language of doing architecture, a language game that Quist models for Petra, displaying for her the competences he would like her to acquire. But Quist's discourse is also punctuated by parentheses in which he talks *about* designing. He says, for example,

> You should begin with a discipline, even if it
> is arbitrary.
> The principle is that you work simultaneously
> from the unit and from the total and then go in
> cycles.

These are examples of a language about designing, a metalanguage by means of which Quist describes some features of the process he is demonstrating and by which he introduces Petra, however cursorily, to reflection on the action of designing.

In the protocol that follows, the two kinds of language are intertwined.

The Protocol

This design review lasts for about twenty minutes and may be divided into several phases. In the first of these, Petra presents her preliminary sketches and describes the problems she has encountered. Quist reframes the problems in his own terms and proceeds to demonstrate the working out of a design solution. There follows a brief interval of reflection on the demonstration so far. Quist then sets out the next steps Petra will have to undertake, including one (the calibration of the grid) that leads him to try to get her to look differently at the representation of the slopes. There is, finally, a coda of reflection on all that has gone before.

Petra's Presentation

> *Petra:* I am having trouble getting past the diagrammatic phase—I've written down the problems on this list.
>
> I've tried to butt the shape of the building into contours of the land there—but the shape doesn't fit into the slope. [She has a model with a slightly exaggerated slope; they discuss this.]
>
> I chose the site because it would relate to the field there, but the approach is here. So I decided the gym must be here—so [showing rough layout—see illustration, top of next page] I have the layout like this.
>
> *Quist:* What other big problems?
>
> *Petra:* I had six of these classroom units, but they were too small in scale to do much with. So I

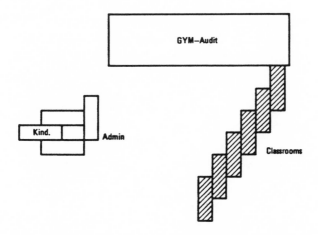

changed them to this more significant layout [the L-shapes]. It relates one to two, three to four, and five to six grades, which is more what I wanted to do educationally anyway. What I have here is a space in which is more of a home base. I'll have an outside/inside which can be used and an outside/inside which can be used—then that opens into your resource library/language thing.

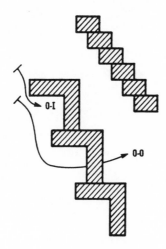

Q: This is to scale?

P: Yes.

Q: Okay, say we have introduced scale. But in the new setup, what about north-south? [He draws his orientation diagram.]

[Showing preferred orientation:]

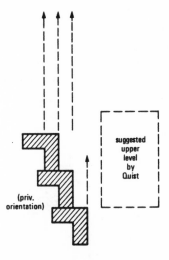

P: This is the road coming in here, and I figured the turning circle would be somewhat here—

Petra has taken the contours of the land seriously, accepting the norm that building shape and land contours must fit each other. In her sketches she has tried the experiment of "butting" the shape of her building into the contours of the slope, but the experiment failed; hence the problem.

Petra has also experimented with the size and arrangement of her classroom units. She has found that classrooms must reach a threshold of scale in order to be "significant" enough for design. By regrouping the six smaller classroom units into three large L-shaped ones, she has tried for "more significant scale." But in doing so, she has also put next to one another the spaces that contain the people who ought most to encounter one another, and she has created a "home base," which sounds like a good place to be, a private outer space that can be used by the kids, and an inner space that has to do, perhaps, with the circulation of the school.

Quist's Reframing of the Problem

> *Q:* Now this would allow you one private orienta-
> tion from here and it would generate geometry in this
> direction. It would be a parallel . . .
>
> *P:* Yes, I'd thought of twenty feet . . .
>
> *Q:* You should begin with a discipline, even if it is
> arbitrary, because the site is so screwy—you can
> always break it open later.

The main problem, in Quist's view, is not of fitting the shape of the building to the slope; the site is too "screwy" for that. Instead, coherence must be given to the site in the form of a geometry—a "discipline"—that can be imposed on it. In the remainder of this phase of the protocol, Quist plays out the consequences of such a move.

Quist's demonstration will now center on the new problem of coordinating the constructed geometry with the "screwy" contours of the slope. But the geometry can be "broken open" again. I think this means that you can dissolve the original discipline in order to try another one and that you can later make knowing violations of the initial geometry. In Quist's metaphor, the geometry is a sort of armor that, once constructed, can be broken open in places. Quist will speak often of the need to "soften" a consistent discipline by consciously departing from it.

Quist's Demonstration

> Q: Now, in this direction, that being the gully and
> that the hill, that could then be the bridge, which
> might generate an upper level which could drop
> down two ways.

> [One way from the classroom] We get a total differen-
> tial potential here from one end of the classroom to
> the far end of the other. There is fifteen feet max,
> right?—so we have as much as five-foot intervals,
> which for a kid is maximum height, right? The
> section through here could be one of nooks in here,
> and the differentiation between this unit and this
> would be at two levels.

The sketches in Figure 1 will help to make clear what is going on
in this passage. Quist now proceeds to play out the imposition of
the two-dimensional geometry of the L-shaped classroom on the
"screwy" three-dimensional contours of the slope. The L-shaped
classrooms are carved into the slope, as in sketch A. The "differential potential," as shown in the sectional sketch B, is the total
difference in height from the top of the classroom lying highest on
the slope to the bottom of the classroom that is lowest on the
slope. The "fifteen feet max" is given by the total drop in the slope
over the distance covered by the three classrooms. The slope is now
divided into three levels, one for each of the classrooms, as in B. C
shows the "interval" from the ground on one level to the roof of
the classroom that stands on the next lower level. The roof of the
classroom will rise five feet above the ground at the next level up,
and since five feet is "maximum height for a kid," kids will be able
to be in "nooks" (sketch C) that are approximately as high as the
tallest kid.

   A drawing experiment has been conducted, and its outcome
partially confirms Quist's way of setting the L-shaped classrooms
on the incoherent slope. Classrooms now flow down the slope in
three stages, creating protected spaces "maximum height for a kid"
at each level. These Quist sees as "nooks," something he could not

Figure 1. Sketches Illustrating Quist's Demonstration.

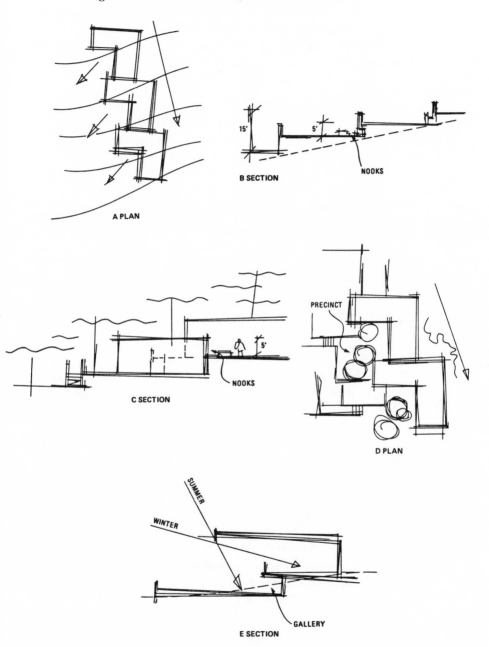

have done had the level difference come to very much less or more than five feet. To say that the section "could be one of nooks" is to invest these spaces with a special value made possible by the level differences, and it is this that partially confirms Quist's earlier move.

> *Q:* Now you would give preference to that as a precinct which opens out into here and into here, and then, of course, we'd have a wall—on the inside there could be a wall or steps to relate in downward. Well, that either happens here or here, and you'll have to investigate which way it should or can go. If it happens this way, the gallery is northwards—but I think the gallery might be a kind of garden—a sort of soft back area to these.

> The kindergarten might go over here—which might indicate that the administration over here—just sort of like what you have here—then this works slightly with the contours—

The "nooks" open out into "precincts" whose treatment is a new problem. Retaining walls are required for structural reasons at each level, as in sketch D, but they also mark the different levels. Walls or steps now function as punctuation, marking boundaries and relationships. Quist invites Petra to consider the gallery as a "soft back area," as in sketch D, which would go well with the "hard" classrooms. It can also be "a kind of garden."

   The resulting array—L-shaped classrooms, gallery, kindergarten, and administration—now "works slightly" with the contours of the slope. With this, Quist harks back to his reframing of Petra's original problem. When she couldn't butt the shape of the building into the screwy slope, Quist imposed on it a geometry of parallels suggested by the L-shaped classrooms. Now the resulting configuration "works slightly" with them. The fit is not very strong, but it is enough.

Q: Then you might carry the gallery level through—and look down into here—which is nice.

Let the land generate some subideas here, which could be very nice. Maybe the cafeteria needn't be such a formal function—maybe it could come into here to get summer sun here and winter here [sketch E].

P: Now, this gallery is more a general pass-through that anyone can use.

Q: It's a general pass-through that anyone has the liberty to pass through, but it is not a corridor. It marks a level difference from here to here—it might have steps or a ramp up to it.

P: My concern is that the circulation through this way—the gallery is generating something awfully cute, but how to pass through here [the library space].

[More examples of Quist's answering questions before they are asked.]

Q: So don't think of the auditorium as a hard-edged block there.

Quist draws the extension of the gallery as he voices its possibility, imagining the experience of a person who would be following such a path, and he finds the result "nice," once more creating a confirmation of the string of moves made so far.

Petra has not "let" the cafeteria diverge from its regular geometric shape. He invites her to "soften it" by taking advantage of the site's north-south orientation, which will cause sunlight to fall on the slope at different angles in summer and winter, as in sketch E. Similarly, he invites her to "soften" the auditorium by relating it to nearby spaces.

Intermediate Reflection

P: Where I was hung up was with the original shape; this here makes much more sense.

Q: Much more sense—so that what you have in gross terms is this [points to his gallery]. It is an artifice—the sort of thing Aalto would invent just to give it some order. He's done that on occasion. So in a very minor way, that is the major thing. This repetitive thing in an organized way—there is this which is not repetitive. It is very nice and just the right scale. It also has a sort of verbal order that you can explain to someone.

The gallery, which had begun in Petra's mind as a minor element of the design, a "general pass-through," has now become "in a minor way . . . the major thing." Quist's reframing and reworking of the problem have led to a reappreciation of the situation, which he now evaluates in terms of norms drawn from several domains—form, scale, and verbal explainability.

Next Steps

Q: Now you have to think about the size of this middle area. You should have the administration over here.

P: Well, that does sort of solve the problems I had with the administration blocking access to the gym.

Q: No good, horrible—it just ruins the whole idea—but if you move it over there, it is in a better location and opens up the space.

The size of the middle area (not its detailed design) can come up now that they have solved the big problem of adapting the geometry of the classrooms to the screwy slope. In the middle area, they are again concerned with the location of major programmatic elements in relation to one another. And with his criticism of the position of the administration, Quist implies that everything he has so far done—the construction of a basic geometry, the imposition of that geometry upon the slope, the creation of the gallery—constitutes an internally coherent whole, all moves having been made with fidelity to the implications set up by earlier moves.

> *Q:* Now the calibration of this becomes important. You just have to draw and draw and try out different grids.
>
> *P:* Well, there seemed to be a strange correlation between the two.
>
> *Q:* No—look at it sideways. It looks much steeper in section. You see, sections always seem much steeper in reality. Try driving up a ten-degree road— you think you would never make it [draws his slope diagram].

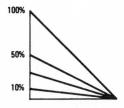

Coda

> *P:* Yes, this was the main thing to get down—how that basic unit—I was thinking in much closer terms coming through the thing—
>
> *Q:* [Cuts her off] Yeah, and the other thing is the subjection to a common set of geometry. You'll see that that will be a common problem which will come up with everyone, either too much constraint or not enough. How to do that, that is the problem of this problem.
>
> *P:* It's amazing—intuitively you look at the shape and you know it's wrong, but it's very hard to get down to the reason . . .

Q: Yeah, well, that is what you are here for. So—
I'd worry about the basic geometry of the site. I
wouldn't concentrate on the roof.

The principle is that you work simultaneously from
the unit and from the total and then go in cycles—
back and forth, back and forth—which is what you've
done a couple of times stutteringly. You have some
ideas of the whole, which is the grid thing, but you
don't know its dimensions. You've done something
about this by eliminating that idea, which I think is
a good decision. You keep going on—you are going
to make it.

Quist returns to his earlier theme ("You should begin with a
discipline, even if it is arbitrary") but now develops it. The basic
geometry should bind the designer, but under a norm of modera-
tion. And, in fact, Quist has continually urged Petra to "soften"
her "hard" geometric forms and to depart on occasion from the
basic geometry—but only after it has been established.

Quist has been able to give Petra reasons for her intuitions.
Now he makes a basic design principle explicit: attention must
oscillate between the "whole" and the "unit," the global and the
local. Under the metaphor of designing as speaking, Quist
contrasts her "stuttering" with his own smooth delivery.

Analysis of the Protocol

Quist's designing takes the form of a reflective conversation
with the situation.

At the beginning of the review, Petra is stuck:

I've tried to butt the shape of the building into
the contours of the land there—but the shape doesn't
fit into the slope.

Quist criticizes her framing of the problem, pointing out that she
has tried to fit the shapes of the buildings into the contours of a

"screwy" slope that offers no basis for coherence. Instead, he resets her problem:

> You should begin with a discipline, even if it
> is arbitrary . . . you can always break it open later.

Petra should make the screwy site coherent by imposing on it a discipline of her own, a "what if" to be adopted in order to discover its consequences. If these are unsatisfactory, she can always "break it open later."

From "you should begin with a discipline" to "this works slightly with the contours," Quist plays out the consequences of the new discipline by carving the geometry into the slope. In the media of sketch and spatial-action language, he represents buildings on the site through moves which are also experiments. Each move has consequences described and evaluated in terms drawn from one or more design domains. Each has implications binding on later moves. And each creates new problems to be described and solved. Quist designs by spinning out a web of moves, consequences, implications, appreciations, and further moves.

Once the smaller classroom units have been made into L-shaped aggregates, they are "more satisfactory in scale," "put grade one next to grade two," and imply ("generate") a "geometry of parallels in this direction." Given these changes, Quist invents a new move: "that being the gully and that the hill, that could then be the bridge." The bridge also generates something new, an upper level that "could drop down two ways."

Each move is a local experiment that contributes to the global experiment of reframing the problem. Some moves are resisted (the shapes cannot be made to fit the contours), while others generate new phenomena. As Quist reflects on the unexpected consequences and implications of his moves, he listens to the situation's back talk, forming new appreciations, which guide his further moves. Most significantly, he becomes aware that the gallery he has created, the "soft back area" to the L-shaped classrooms, has become "in a minor way . . . the major thing." Seizing on the gallery's potential, he "extends it here so as to look down into here." Later, he carefully avoids placing the administration building on the site in a way that would spoil "the whole idea."

Thus the global experiment in reframing the problem is also a reflective conversation with the situation in which Quist comes to appreciate and then to develop the implications of a new whole idea. The reframing of the problem is justified by the discovery that the new geometry "works slightly with the contours," yields pleasant nooks, views, and soft back areas, and evokes in the situation the potential for a new coherence. Out of reframing of Petra's problem, Quist derives a problem he can solve and a coherent organization of materials from which he can make something he likes.

Three dimensions of this process are particularly noteworthy: the domains of language in which the designer describes and appreciates the consequences of his moves, the implications he discovers and follows, and his changing stance toward the situation with which he converses.

Design Domains

Quist makes his moves in a language of designing that combines drawing and speaking. In this language, words have different roles. When Quist speaks of a cafeteria that could "come down into here to get summer sun here," "an upper level [that could] drop down two ways," "steps to relate in downward," he uses spatial-action language. He attributes actions to elements of the design as though they were creating form and organizing space. At the same time, he anticipates the experienced felt-path of a user of the building who could find that the upper level drops down or that the steps relate in downward. Quist also uses words to name elements of design ("steps," a "wall," and "administration"), to describe the consequences and implications of moves, and to reappreciate the situation.

Elements of the language of designing can be grouped into clusters, of which I have identified twelve (Table 1). These design domains contain the names of elements, features, relations, and actions and of norms used to evaluate problems, consequences, and

Table 1. Normative/Descriptive Design Domains.

Domain	Definition	Examples
Program/use	Functions of buildings or building components; uses of building or site; specification for use	"Gym," "auditorium," "classroom"; "5', which is maximum height for a kid"; "no city will plow a road that steep"
Siting	Features, elements, relations of the building site	"Land contour," "slope," "hill," "gully"
Building elements	Buildings or components of buildings	"Gym," "kindergarten," "ramp," "wall," "roof," "steps"
Organization of space	Kinds of spaces and relations of spaces to one another	"A general pass-through," "outside/outside," "layout"
Form	1. Shape of building or component 2. Geometry 3. Markings of organization of space 4. Experienced felt-path of movement through spaces	"Hard-edged block" "A geometry of parallels" "Marks a level difference from here to here" "Carry the gallery through and look down into here, which is nice"
Structure/technology	Structures, technologies, and processes used in building	"A construction module for these classrooms"
Scale	Magnitudes of building and elements in relation to one another	"A 20' parallel," "too small in scale to do much with," "just the right scale"
Cost	Dollar cost of construction	(None in this protocol)
Building character	Kind of building, as sign of style or mode of building	("Warehouse," "hangar," "beach cottage" —but not in this protocol)
Precedent	Reference to other kinds of buildings, styles, or architectural modes	"An artifice . . . the sort of thing Aalto would invent"
Representation	Languages and notations by which elements of other domains are represented	"Look at it in section," "1/16-scale model"
Explanation	Context of interaction between designer and others	"The sort of verbal order you could explain to someone"

implications. As he designs, Quist draws on a repertoire of design domains to fulfill a variety of constructive, descriptive, and normative functions.

In the domain of program/use, for example, such terms as "classroom," "administration," and "kindergarten" name buildings according to their uses. Phrases like "maximum height for a kid" and "how to pass through . . . the library space" describe the experience of using the buildings.

In the siting domain, Petra uses "contours of the land" to describe her problem, and Quist uses "hill," "gully," and "slope" to construct some of the early steps by which he carves the geometry into the slope.

In the domain of organization of space, Petra speaks of the "outside/outside" created by her L-shaped classrooms, and Quist characterizes the gallery as "a general pass-through that anyone has the liberty to pass through, but . . . not a corridor."

The domain of form has four meanings, distinct but related. First, there are the geometrical shapes of buildings, like Petra's "hard-edged block." There is also the sense of global geometry, as in "the geometry of parallels generated by the L-shaped classrooms." There is form as a visible sign of the organization of space, as in Quist's observation that the gallery marks level differences in the slope. And finally, there are frequent references to the felt-paths of those who will travel through the organized space, apprehending the figures, qualities, and relations that arise in the experience of movement from place to place.

In their appreciations of the situation they are shaping, Quist and Petra employ feelingful or associative terms such as "home base," "nook," "garden," and "soft back area." "A kind of garden" is not literally a garden, and the "soft back area" is not literally soft, but the metaphors of "garden" and "soft" are used to convey particular values of experience.

Often moves are found to have consequences and implications that cut across design domains. The retaining walls are necessary to the structural soundness of the buildings carved into the slope, but they also mark off formal differences in the levels of the slope. The gallery, which Petra finds "awfully cute," also creates problems of circulation. When design terms are ambiguous in this way, they may create confusion, but they also call attention to multiple consequences. Terms like "stair," "ramp," and "wall" refer both to particular building elements and to formal functions such as "marking" and "relating in." "Gallery" refers both to an organization of space and to a particular precedent ("the sort of thing Aalto would invent"). Aspiring members of the linguistic community of design learn to detect multiple references, distinguish particular meanings in context, and use multiple references as an aid to vision across design domains.

The designer's repertoire of domains has a structure of priorities for attending to features of situations. In our protocol, there are many references to organization of space, especially to the location of major building elements such as the gym, turning circle, bridge, and kindergarten. There are several references to scale, building elements, program/use, and the several senses of form. But there are only single references in each of the domain of precedent, structure/technology, and explanation. The domains cost and building character do not appear in the protocol at all. The relative frequencies of references to the various design domains reveal Quist's priorities for attention at this early stage of the process.

Implications

When Petra says, "This is the road coming in here, and I figured the turning circle would be somewhere here," and when Quist later remarks that "the kindergarten might go over here— which might indicate that the administration [goes] over here," they are noting the implications of earlier moves for later ones, on the basis of a system of norms that governs the relative placement of major building elements. This system includes norms for access (the administration building's central accessibility to all other units), circulation (ease and clarity of movement from one unit to another), and use ("opening up the space"). Thus a decision to locate a road or a kindergarten "here" has implications for the location of a turning circle or an administration "there." In this sense, there is a literal logic of design, a pattern of "if . . . then" propositions that relates the cumulative sequence of prior moves to the choices now confronting the designer.

Because of the contextual relatedness of norms drawn from the domains of site, program, geometry, felt-path, structure, and the like, the designer's moves yield systems of implications. These constitute a discipline. If Petra chooses to "locate the site here because it would relate to the field there . . . [and] the approach is here," *then* "the gym must be here." As Quist says, however, a discipline can always be broken open later. The implications of prior moves must generally be honored but may be violated in a knowledgeable way.

The web of moves has many branchings, and this complicates the problem by creating many implications to be discovered and honored. Given the layering of the classrooms on the slope, for example, there could be "a wall or steps to relate in downwards," which might "happen here or here." These are choice points. As the designer reflects-in-action on the situation created by his earlier moves, he must consider not only the present choice but the tree of further choices to which it leads, each of which has different meanings in relation to the systems of implications set up by earlier moves. Quist's virtuosity lies in his ability to string out design webs of great complexity. But even he cannot hold in mind an indefinitely expanding web. At some point, he must move from a "what if?" to a decision, which then becomes a design node with binding implications for further moves. Thus there is a continually evolving system of implications within which the designer reflects-in-action.

The testing of local moves is partly linked to, and partly independent of, this system of implications. Quist discovers that the three classroom levels carved into the slope yield a "total differential potential" of "fifteen feet max" which would permit "as much as five-foot intervals," and he subsequently notices that these spaces, seen in section, could be made into "nooks." Here he affirms a local move because he finds that it has produced a situation out of which he can make something he likes. In this he makes use of his knowledge of the relations between slopes of various grades and their uses. But he finds further support for the dimensions of the geometry he has carved into the slope when he discovers that the resulting configuration "works slightly with the contours." His method of carving the geometry of the classrooms into the slope is affirmed in one way when he sees it as a local experiment and in another way when he sees it as part of a global experiment.

Moves also lead to the apprehension of new problems, such as the treatment of the "precincts" that flow out from the nooks, and they lead to new potentials for the creation of desirable artifacts, such as the softening of the hard-edged shape of the cafeteria by allowing it to "come down into here to get summer sun here and winter sun here." In the designer's conversation with the materials of his design, he can never make a move that has only the effects intended for it. His materials are continually talking back to him, causing him to apprehend unexpected problems and potentials. As he appreciates such new and unexpected phenomena, he also evaluates the moves that have created them.

Thus the designer evaluates his moves in a threefold way: in terms of the desirability of their consequences judged in categories drawn from the normative design domains, in terms of their conformity to or violation of implications set up by earlier moves, and in terms of his appreciation of the new problems or potentials they have created.

Shifts in Stance

As Quist spins out his web of moves, his stance toward the design situation undergoes a series of changes.

Sometimes he speaks of what "can" or "might" happen and sometimes of what "should" or "must" happen. He shifts from a recognition of possibility and freedom of choice to an acceptance of the imperatives that follow from choice. He urges Petra to step into the problem freely, imposing her own constructs on it. Without this freedom, there can be no "what if?" But he also calls attention to the discipline of implications generated by her moves. The geometry of the L-shaped classrooms must be followed. Degrees of slope imply constraints on possible uses of the site. Implications for access to sun, circulation, boundary markings, nook-ness, street plowing, consistency of scale, access to gym or administration, fate of trees are at stake in a relatively uncomplicated series of moves. As Quist draws out these implications, he demonstrates fidelity to the "musts" by which the freely chosen "what ifs?" are to be judged.

He also demonstrates how the whole is at stake in every partial move. Once a whole idea has been created, a bad placement of the administration can ruin it. Hence the designer must oscillate between the unit and the total, and—as Quist points out in one of his infrequent metacomments—he must oscillate between involvement and detachment. Quist becomes at times so involved in the local development of forms that the design appears to be making itself. But he also steps back from the projected experience of passage through the space in order to take note of the larger relationships on which the qualities of the whole idea will depend.

Finally, as he cycles through iteration of moves and appreciations of the outcomes of moves, Quist shifts from tentative adoption of a strategy to eventual commitment. This shift enables him to achieve economy of design, simplifying the evolving web of moves to make his thought experiment manageable.

The Underlying Process of Reflection-in-Action

Petra's problem solving has led her to a dead end. Quist reflects critically on the main problem she has set, reframes it, and proceeds to work out the consequences of the new geometry he has imposed on the screwy site. The ensuing inquiry is a global experiment, a reflection-in-action on the restructured problem. Quist spins out a web of moves, subjecting each cluster of moves to multiple evaluations drawn from his repertoire of design domains. As he does so, he shifts from embracing freedom of choice to accepting implications, from involvement in the local units to a distanced consideration of the resulting whole, and from a stance of tentative exploration to one of commitment. He discovers in the situation's back talk a whole new idea, which generates a system of implications for further moves. His global experiment is also a reflective conversation with the situation.

It is not difficult to see how a design process of this form might underlie differences of language and style associated with the various schools of architecture. Designers might differ, for example, in the priorities they assign to design domains at various stages of the process. They might focus less on the global geometry of buildings, as Quist does, than on the site or on the properties and potentials of materials. They might let the design depend more heavily on the formal implications of construction modules. Their governing images might be framed in terms of building character, and they might allow particular precedents to influence more frankly the order they impose on the site. But whatever their differences of languages, priorities, images, styles, and precedents, they are likely to find themselves, like Quist, in a situation of complexity and uncertainty which demands the imposition of an order. From whatever sources they draw such an initial discipline, they will treat its imposition on the site as a global experiment whose results will be only dimly apparent in the early stages of the process. They will need to discover its consequences and implications. And although they may differ from Quist in their way of appreciating these, they will, like him, engage in a conversation with the situation they are shaping. Although their repertoire of meaning may differ from Quist's, they are likely to find new and unexpected meanings in the changes they produce and to redirect their moves in response to such discoveries. And if they are good designers, they will reflect-in-action on the situation's back talk, shifting stance as they do so from "what if?" to recognition of implications, from involvement in the unit to consideration of the total, and from exploration to commitment.

Such is the skeleton of the process. It suggests two further questions:

1. When the practitioner takes seriously the uniqueness of the present situation, how does he make use of the experience he has accumulated in his earlier practice? When he cannot apply familiar categories of theory or technique, how does he bring prior knowledge to bear on the invention of new frames, theories, and strategies of action?

2.   Reflection-in-action is a kind of experimenting. But practice
     situations are notoriously resistant to controlled experiment.
     How does the practitioner escape or compensate for the
     practical limits to controlled experiment? In what sense, if
     any, is there rigor in his experimentation?

Our exploration of these questions will lead to a further elaboration of reflection-in-action as an epistemology of practice.

Bringing Past Experience to Bear on a Unique Situation

Quist recognizes many familiar things in Petra's situation,
and he places them within familiar, named categories, such as
"parallels," "classrooms," "slope," and "wall." But he does not
similarly subsume the situation as a whole under a familiar
category. Quist has very likely seen other screwy sites, but his
initial description of this one does not place it within a design
category that calls for a standard solution. Rather, it sets in motion
an inquiry into the peculiar features of these slopes, which
respond in very special ways to the imposition of a geometry of
parallels, creating a particular set of problems and a particular
coherence.

It is in relation to the unique features of his problematic
situation that he undertakes the problem-setting experiment we
have just discussed. But just this is puzzling. How can an inquirer
use what he already knows in a situation that he takes to be
unique?

He cannot apply a rule drawn from past experience, like the
rule Quist gives for uses appropriate to slopes of various grades;
for he would then ignore the uniqueness of the situation, treating
it as an instance of a class of familiar things. Nor does he invent
a new description out of whole cloth, without any reference to
what he already knows. It is clear that Quist uses a great deal of his
experience and knowledge, and it is far from clear what might be
meant by the spontaneous generation of a description.

What I want to propose is this: Quist has built up a
repertoire of examples, images, understandings, and actions. His
repertoire ranges across the design domains. It includes sites he has

seen, buildings he has known, design problems he has encountered, and solutions he has devised. All these things are parts of Quist's repertoire insofar as they are accessible to him for understanding and action.

When a practitioner makes sense of a situation he perceives to be unique, he *sees* it as something already present in his repertoire. To see *this* site as *that* one is not to subsume the first under a familiar category or rule. It is, rather, to see the unfamiliar situation as both similar to and different from the familiar one, without at first being able to say similar or different with respect to what. The familiar situation functions as a precedent, or a metaphor, or—in Thomas Kuhn's (1977) phrase—an exemplar for the unfamiliar one.

Seeing *this* situation as *that* one, a practitioner may also *do* in this situation *as* in that one. When a beginning physics student sees a pendulum problem as a familiar inclined-plane problem, he can set up the new problem and solve it, using procedures both similar to and different from those he has used before. Just as he sees the new problem as a variation on the old one, so his new problem-solving behavior is a variation on the old. Just as he is unable at first to articulate the relevant similarities and differences of the problems, so he is unable at first to articulate the similarities and differences of his problem-solving procedures. Indeed, the whole process of *seeing-as* and *doing-as* may proceed without conscious articulation.

However, the inquirer may reflect on the similarities and differences he has perceived or enacted. He may do this by consciously comparing the two situations or by describing the present situation in the light of a tacit reference to the other. When Quist immediately calls Petra's site "screwy" and says that she must impose a discipline on it, which can always be broken open later, I believe he is seeing her situation as one or more others with which he is familiar and carrying over to her problem variations of strategies he has used before. The later descriptions of the situation are reflections on and elaborations of the first, unarticulated perceptions of similarity and difference.

It would be a mistake to attribute to the inquirer at the beginning of such a process the articulated description that he achieves later on—to say, for example, that Quist must have known unconsciously at the beginning just how this site is screwy and just how the geometry of parallels can be succcessfully imposed on it. To do so would be to engage in instant historical revisionism. The perception of similarity and difference implicit in Quist's initial description of the situation is, as Kuhn says, both logically and psychologically prior to his later articulation of it.

It is our capacity to see unfamiliar situations as familiar ones, and to do in the former as we have done in the latter, that enables us to bring our past experience to bear on the unique case. It is our capacity to *see-as* and *do-as* that allows us to have a feel for problems that do not fit existing rules.

The artistry of a practitioner like Quist hinges on the range and variety of the repertoire that he brings to unfamiliar situations. Because he is able to make sense of their uniqueness, he need not reduce them to instances of standard categories.

Moreover, each new experience of reflection-in-action enriches his repertoire. Petra's case may function as an exemplar for new situations. Reflection-in-action in a unique case may be generalized to other cases, not by giving rise to general principles, but by contributing to the practitioner's repertoire of exemplary themes from which, in the subsequent cases of his practice, he may compose new variations.

Rigor in On-the-Spot Experiment

Seeing-as is not enough, however. When a practitioner sees a new situation as some element of his repertoire, he gets a new way of seeing it and a new possibility for action in it, but the adequacy and utility of his new view must still be discovered in action. Reflection-in-action necessarily involves experiment.

Indeed, as we have seen, Quist conducts a reflective conversation with his situation which is an experiment in reframing. From his repertoire of examples, images, descriptions, he has derived (by seeing-as) a way of framing the present, unique situation. He tries, then, to shape the situation to the frame; and he evaluates the entire process by criteria I have described earlier in this chapter—whether he can solve the problem he has set; whether he values what he gets when he solves it (or what he can make of what he gets); whether he achieves in the situation a coherence of artifact and idea, a congruence with his fundamental theories and values; whether he can keep inquiry moving. Nested within the larger problem-setting experiment are also local experiments of various sorts.

But in what sense is this really *experimenting?*

The question arises because there is another sense of experiment that is central to the model of professional knowledge as technical rationality, one that Quist's inquiry does not seem to exemplify at all. In this sense, experimenting is an activity by which a researcher confirms or refutes a hypothesis. Its logic is roughly as follows: The researcher wants to account for a puzzling phenomenon, Q. He entertains several hypotheses (A, B, C) about Q, each of which explains it. That is, from each hypothesis, if true, Q would follow. How does the researcher determine which of the hypotheses is correct? He must employ some version of Mill's "method of difference," showing that if A (or B or C) is absent, then Q is also absent.* For if he *only* shows that A (or B or C) is present along with Q, there may be some other factor which is also copresent and is the cause of Q. This method of hypothesis testing follows a process of elimination. The experimenter tries to produce conditions that disconfirm each of the competing hypotheses, showing that the conditions that would follow from each of these are not observed. The hypothesis that most successfully resists refutation is the one the experimenter accepts—only tentatively, however, because some other factor, as yet undiscovered, may turn out to be the actual cause of Q.

In order to stage such a competition of hypotheses, the experimenter must be able to achieve selective variation of the factors named by competing hypotheses, and he must be able to isolate the experimental situation from confounding changes in the environment. By his control of the experimental process, he is thought to achieve objectivity, so that other inquirers who use the

---

*Mill's method of difference, along with his methods of agreement and concomitant variations, is described in *A System of Logic* (Mill, 1843/ 1949).

same methods will get the same results. And to this end, he is expected to preserve his distance from experimental phenomena, keeping his biases from the object of study.

Under conditions of everyday professional practice, the norms of controlled experiment are achievable only in a very limited way. The practitioner is usually unable to shield his experiments from the effects of confounding changes in the environment. The practice situation often changes rapidly and may change out from under the experiment. Variables are often locked into one another, so that the inquirer cannot separate them. The practice situation is often uncertain, in the sense that one doesn't know what the relevant variables are. And the very act of experimenting is often risky.

In what, then, does Quist's experimenting consist? What is his logic of experimental inference? In what sense, if any, can we see his reflection-in-action as rigorous experimentation?

Let us step back to consider what *experimenting* means. I want to show that hypothesis testing is only one of several kinds of experiments, each of which has its own logic and its own criteria of success and failure. In practice these several kinds of experiments are mixed up together.

In the most generic sense, to experiment is to act in order to see what follows.

When action is undertaken *only* to see what follows, without accompanying predictions or expectations, I call it *exploratory*. This is much of what an infant does when he explores the world around him, what an artist does when she juxtaposes colors to see what effect they make, and what a newcomer does when he wanders around a strange neighborhood. It is also what a scientist often does when she first encounters and probes a strange substance to see how it will respond. Exploratory experiment is the probing, playful activity by which we get a feel for things. It succeeds when it leads to the discovery of something there.

There is another way in which we sometimes do things in order to produce an intended change. A carpenter who wants to make a structure stable tries fastening a board across the angle of a corner. A chess player advances her pawn in order to protect her queen. A parent gives his child a quarter to keep the child from crying. I shall call these *move-testing experiments.* Any deliberate action undertaken with an end in mind is, in this sense, an experiment. In the simple case, where there are no unintended outcomes and one either gets the intended consequence or does not, I shall say the move is *affirmed* when it produces what is intended and is *negated* when it does not. In more complicated cases, however, moves produce effects beyond those intended. One can get very good things without intending them, and very bad things may accompany the achievement of intended results. Here the test of the affirmation of a move is not only Do you get what you intend? but Do you like what you get? In chess, when you accidentally checkmate your opponent, the move is good and you do not take it back because its results are unexpected. However, giving a child a quarter may not only get him to stop crying but also teach him to make money by crying—and the unintended effect is not so good. In these cases a better description of the logic of move-testing experiments is this: Do you like what you get from the action, taking its consequences as a whole? If you do, then the move is affirmed. If you do not, it is negated.

A third kind of experimenting, *hypothesis testing,* I have already described. Hypothesis-testing experiment succeeds when it effects an intended discrimination among competing hypotheses. If the consequences predicted on the basis of a given hypothesis, H, fit what is observed, and the predictions derived from alternative hypotheses do not, then H has been tentatively *confirmed* and the others *disconfirmed.*

In practice, the hypothesis subjected to experiment may be one that has been implicit in the pattern of one's moves. In the on-the-spot experimenting characteristic of reflection-in-action, the *logic* of hypothesis testing is essentially the same as it is in the research context. If the carpenter asks himself, What makes this structure stable?, and begins to experiment to find out—trying now one device, now another—he is basically in the same business as the research scientist. He puts forward hypotheses and, within the constraints set by the practice context, tries to discriminate among them—taking as disconfirmation of a hypothesis the failure to get the consequences predicted from it. The logic of his experimental inference is the same as that of the researcher's.

What is it, then, that is distinctive about the experimenting that goes on in practice?

The practice context is different from the research context in several important ways, all of which have to do with the relationship between changing things and understanding them. The practitioner has an interest in transforming the situation from what it is to something he likes better. He also has an interest in understanding the situation, but it is in the service of his interest in change.

When the practitioner reflects-in-action in a case he perceives as unique, paying attention to phenomena and surfacing his intuitive understanding of them, his experimenting is at once exploratory, move testing, and hypothesis testing. The three functions are fulfilled by the very same actions. And from this fact follows the distinctive character of experimenting in practice.

Let us consider, in this light, Quist's reflection-in-action. When Quist imposes his geometry of parallels on the screwy slope, he undertakes a global sequence of moves whose intent is to transform the situation into one that fits the geometry. His move-testing experiment succeeds because he solves the problem he has set and because, in addition, he likes what he can make of what he gets. The global move is affirmed.

His moves also function as exploratory probes of his situation. His moves stimulate the situation's back talk, which causes him to appreciate things in the situation that go beyond his initial perception of the problem. For example, he perceives a new whole idea, created unexpectedly by the gallery's appearance as centerpiece of the design.

Further, Quist's reframing of the problem of the situation carries with it a hypothesis about the situation. He surfaces the model of the phenomena associated with his student's framing of the problem, which he rejects. He proposes a new problem and, with it, a new model of the phenomena, which he proceeds to treat as a hypothesis to be tested. The hypothesis is that this slope and this geometry of parallels can be made to fit each other.

When we compare the practitioner's hypothesis-testing experiment with the method of controlled experiment, however, there are several notable differences.

The practitioner makes his hypothesis come true, thereby violating the canons of controlled experiment—dear to technical rationality—that call for "objectivity" and "distance." He says, in effect "Let it be the case that X . . .," and shapes the situation so that X becomes true. Quist *carves* his geometry into the slope. His hypothesis testing consists of moves that change the phenomena to make the hypothesis fit. Nevertheless, his situation is not wholly manipulable. It may resist his attempts to shape it and, in so doing, yield the unintended effects of the manipulation. Quist might have found that the slope could *not* be made to conform to his geometry of parallels. As it is, he sets the criterion of fit so that "slightly" is enough.

His hypothesis-testing experiment is not wholly self-fulfilling. Rather, it is a game with the situation in which he seeks to make the situation conform to his hypothesis but remains open to the possibility that it will not. Quist's relation to this situation is *transactional* (Dewey and Bentley, 1949). He shapes the situation, but in conversation with it, so that his own methods and appreciations are also shaped by the situation. The phenomena that he seeks to understand are partly of his own making; he is in the situation that he seeks to understand.

This is another way of saying that the action by which he tests his hypothesis is also a move by which he tries to effect a desired change in the situation and a probe by which he explores it. He understands the situation by trying to change it, and he considers the resulting change to be not a defect of experimental method but the essence of its success.

This fact has an important bearing on the practitioner's answer to the question, When should I stop experimenting?

In the context of controlled experiment, the experimenter might keep on experimenting indefinitely—as long as he is able to invent new, plausible hypotheses that might resist refutation more effectively than those he has already tried. But in a practice situation like Quist's—where experimental action is also a move and a probe, where the inquirer's interest in changing the

situation takes precedence over his interest in understanding it—
hypothesis testing is bounded by appreciations. It is initiated by
the perception of something troubling or promising, and it is
terminated by the production of changes one finds, on the whole,
satisfactory or by the discovery of new features that give the
situation new meaning and change the nature of the questions to
be explored. Such events bring hypothesis testing to a close even
when the inquirer has not exhausted his store of plausible
alternative hypotheses.

In our case study, Quist has made the geometry of parallels
work slightly with the contours of the slope. But other geometries
might also have been made to do so. Why does he stop here?
Because he has produced changes he found satisfactory, has made
of unintended outcomes something he likes, and has produced an
unintended artifact that creates a new whole idea.

It is true that the larger inquiry continues beyond these
findings, its further directions set by them. But the experimenter
need discriminate among contending hypotheses only to the point
where his moves are affirmed or yield new appreciations of the
situation. Thus hypothesis-testing experiment has a more limited
function in practice than in research; and consequently, constraints on controlled experiment in the practice situation are less
disruptive of inquiry than they would otherwise be.

Conversely, the practice context places demands on the
hypothesis testing that are not present in the context of research.
The hypothesis must lend itself to embodiment in a move. Quist
has no interest in a hypothesis about the site that he cannot
immediately translate into design.

These distinctive features of experimenting in practice carry
with them distinctive norms for rigor. The inquirer who reflects-
in-action plays a game with the situation in which he is bound by
considerations pertaining to the three levels of experiment—
exploration, move testing, and hypothesis testing. His primary
interest is in changing the situation. But if he ignores its
resistances to change, he falls into mere self-fulfilling prophecy.
He experiments rigorously when he strives to make the situation
conform to his view of it while remaining open to evidence of his
failure to do so. He must be open to learning, by reflection on the

situation's resistance, that his hypothesis is inadequate and in what way. Moreover, he plays his game in relation to a moving target, changing the phenomena as he experiments.

Virtual Worlds

Quist's situation is, in an important way, not the real thing. He is not moving earth on the site. He operates in a virtual world, a constructed representation of the real world of practice.

This fact is significant for the question of rigor in experimenting. In his virtual world, the practitioner can manage some of the constraints on hypothesis-testing experiment that are inherent in the world of his practice. Hence his ability to construct and manipulate virtual worlds is a crucial component of his ability not only to perform artistically but to experiment rigorously.

For Quist and Petra, the graphic world of the sketchpad is the medium of reflection-in-action. Here they can draw and talk their moves in spatial-action language, leaving traces that represent the forms of buildings on the site. Because the drawing reveals qualities and relations unimagined beforehand, moves can function as experiments. Petra can discover that her building shapes do not fit the slope and that her classrooms are too small in scale to do much with. Quist can find nooks in the intervals he has created and can see that his geometry works slightly with the contours of the site. Considering the gallery he has made, he can observe that "there is this which is repetitive and this again which is not repetitive."

Constraints that would prevent or inhibit experiment in the built world are greatly reduced in the virtual world of the drawing.

The act of drawing can be rapid and spontaneous, but the residual traces are stable. The designer can examine them at leisure.

The pace of action can be varied at will. The designer can slow down to think about what he is doing; and events that would take a long time in the built world—the carving of a slope, the "shaving" of trees—can be made to "happen" immediately in the drawing.

No move is irreversible. The designer can try, look, and by shifting to another sheet of paper, try again. As a consequence, he can perform learning sequences in which he corrects his errors and takes account of previously unexpected results of his moves. Petra can explore the size and shape of her classroom units and the placement of the administration building. Quist can propose that she "draw and draw" to determine the proper dimensions of her grid, figure out how to treat the "middle area," and "shave off the trees." Moves that would be costly in the built world can be tried at little or no risk in the world of drawing.

In the virtual world, one eliminates changes in the environment that would disrupt or confound the experiment. In the drawing, there are no work stoppages, breakdowns of equipment, or soil conditions that preclude sinking a foundation.

Some variables that are interlocking in the built world can be separated from each other in the world of the drawing. A global geometry of buildings on the site can be explored without any reference to particular construction methods. A building shape can be considered while deferring the question of the material from which the shape is to be made.

In order to capture the benefits of the drawn world as a context for experiment, the designer must acquire certain competences and understandings. He needs to learn the traditions of graphic media, languages, and notations. Quist, for example, has a repertoire of media that enables him to choose the graphic system best suited to exploration of particular phenomena. Sketches enable him to explore global geometries; cross-sectional drawings, to examine three-dimensional effects; drawings to scale, to experiment with the dimensions of design; models, to examine relations among building mass, comparative volumes, and sun and shade. He uses media selectively to address the issues to which he gives priority at each stage of the design process.

Quist also has learned to use graphic language transparently. When he represents a contour of the site by a set of concentric lines, he sees *through* it to the actual shapes of the slope, just as practiced readers can see through the letters on a page to words and meanings. Hence he is able to move in the drawing as though he were moving through buildings on the site, exploring the felt-paths as a user of the buildings would experience them.

But the virtual world of the drawing can function reliably as a context for experiment only insofar as the results of experiment can be transferred to the built world. The validity of the transfer depends on the fidelity with which the drawn world represents the built one. As an architect's practice enables him to move back and forth between drawings and buildings, he learns how his drawings will "build" and develops a capacity for accurate rehearsal. He learns to recognize the representational limits of graphic media. He learns, for example, how drawings fail to capture qualities of materials, surfaces, and technologies. He learns to remember that drawings cannot represent soil conditions, wind, costs of materials and labor, breakdowns of equipment, and man-made changes in the environment. Drawing functions as a context for experiment precisely because it enables the designer to eliminate features of the real-world situation that might confound or disrupt his experiments, but when he comes to interpret the results of his experiments, he must remember the factors that have been eliminated.

The architect's sketchpad is an example of the variety of virtual worlds on which all the professions are dependent. A sculptor learns to infer from the feel of a maquette in her hand the qualities of a monumental figure that will be built from it. Engineers become adept at the uses of scale models, wind tunnels, and computer simulations. In an orchestra rehearsal, conductors experiment with tempo, phrasing, and instrumental balance. A roleplay is an improvised game in which the participants learn to discover properties of an interpersonal situation and to reflect-in-action on their intuitive responses to it. In improvisation, musical or dramatic, participants can conduct on-the-spot experiments in which, as improvisation tends to lead toward performance, the boundaries between virtual and real worlds may become blurred.

Virtual worlds are contexts for experiment within which practitioners can suspend or control some of the everyday impediments to rigorous reflection-in-action. They are representative worlds of practice in the double sense of "practice." And practice in the construction, maintenance, and use of virtual worlds develops the capacity for reflection-in-action that we call artistry.

Technical Rationality and Reflection-in-Action Compared

As we have described Quist's designing, we have also begun to describe an alternative epistemology of practice within which technical problem solving occupies a limited place. From the perspective of an inquirer's reflective conversation with his situation, the model of technical rationality appears radically incomplete.

The positivist epistemology of practice rests on three dichotomies. Given the separation of means from ends, instrumental problem solving can be seen as a technical procedure to be measured by its effectiveness in achieving a preestablished objective. Given the separation of research from practice, rigorous practice can be seen as an application to instrumental problems of research-based theories and techniques whose objectivity and generality derive from the method of controlled experiment. Given the separation of knowing from doing, action is only an implementation and a test of technical decision.

In Quist's reflective conversation, these dichotomies do not hold. For him, practice is researchlike. Means and ends are framed interdependently in his problem setting. And his inquiry is a transaction with the situation in which knowing and doing are inseparable.

As Quist frames the problem of his problematic situation, he determines the features he will notice, the order he will try to impose, the directions in which he will try to effect change. In so doing, he identifies both the ends to be sought and the means to be employed. In the ensuing inquiry, his problem solving is part of a larger experiment in problem setting. For example, his rules of thumb about the uses of various slopes play a subordinate role in the larger experiment in which he imposes a geometry of parallels on the screwy site.

He reflects on Petra's intuitive understanding of her design situation and constructs a new problem. He derives it, however, not from research-based theory but from his repertoire of themes and examples. By seeing- and doing-as, he makes a new model of the situation. But the on-the-spot experiments by which he tests that model, in the virtual world of the sketchpad, also function as transforming moves and exploratory probes. His hypothesis testing functions mainly to guide his further moves and to surface phenomena that lead him to reframe the situation.

In a reflective conversation, the values of control, distance, and objectivity—central to technical rationality—take on new meanings. The practitioner tries, within the limits of his virtual world, to control variables for the sake of hypothesis-testing experiment. But his hypotheses are about the situation's potential for transformation, and as he tests them, he inevitably steps into the situation. He produces knowledge that is objective in the sense that he can discover error—for example, that he has not produced the change he intended. But his knowledge is also personal; its validity is relative to his commitments to a particular appreciative system and overarching theory. His results will be compelling only for those who share his commitments.

❦ Chapter Four ❦

Paradoxes and Predicaments in Learning to Design

So far, we have considered the dialogue of Quist and Petra for what it reveals about the design process. What would we notice if we took it as an example of design *education?*

Petra, who has been trying to do something on her own, has got stuck. She seems unclear just what she should be doing, or she has ideas about it that are incongruent with Quist's. Quist, after listening to her "big problems," takes charge of the desk crit. Using the drawing/talking language to make his process accessible to Petra, he demonstrates the kind of process he believes she should be carrying out, punctuating his demonstration with reflections on designing.

What does Petra make of all this? Quist does not ask her, and she does not tell him. If she remains confused about the meaning of "designing," in spite of Quist's demonstrations and reflections, neither we nor Quist can know it from the data available. But there is considerable evidence that many students at Petra's stage of development *are* thoroughly confused about designing; indeed, they sometimes find the whole experience of the studio mysterious.

In Petra's studio, for example, in spite of the students' general admiration for Quist as practitioner and teacher, fully half the group find it hard to grasp what he means by "thinking architecturally." Judith, a colleague of Petra's, has a jury in which the critic finally tells her:

> Unless you can begin to think of the problem architecturally, you aren't going to find any way to proceed.

And Judith herself says, in a later interview,

> I began to realize that my approach wasn't architectural at all.

In another studio, the studio master, Leftwich, says of a student,

> Lauda is the hardest guy to deal with. Intelligent, articulate, comes up with something that works, but architecturally, it's horrible. Now, what do I do? In a way, it's the kind of case which precipitates the weakest responses, because he has not internalized some of the covert things . . . I think he should do something else. He is bright but totally unvisual. Within the frame of reference of a designing architect, he is totally misplaced . . . I wouldn't know what to do with him.*

Leftwich argues that, because Lauda has not picked up the "covert things," he does not know what to do with him. As for Lauda, he accepts but is rather bewildered by the demand that he perform according to standards that he finds alien and mysterious:

> I think that at times, Leftwich assumed a greater awareness on my part than I had . . . I wasn't doing it around my own standards. My standards were far surpassed. . . . That's probably the key thing.

So he says,

> I want to go out and learn first. I want to know what it is we are arguing about.

*"Leftwich" and "Lauda" are fictitious names assigned by Florian Von Buttlar to a master and a student in a design studio where he observed as part of the Harvard/M.I.T. Review of Architectural Education.

In yet another studio, a student who has not been singled out by
his teachers as a problem makes this poignant observation:

> What we have is a very Kafkaesque situation
> where you really don't know where you are, and you
> have no basis for evaluation. You hang on the
> inflection of the tone of voice in your crit to discover
> if something is really wrong.

So, in addition to the features of design education I have
already mentioned—the student trying to do something on her
own, being unclear about just what she is supposed to do, and
getting stuck; the studio master offering demonstration, instruction, and reflection—we must add, at least in the early phase of the
studio, the student's experience of mystery and confusion. These
phenomena are not unique to Quist's dialogue with Petra or even
to Quist's studio as a whole. They are characteristic of architectural studios. To make sense of them, we must begin with a certain
paradox inherent in design education.

The Paradox of Learning to Design

Initially, the student does not and cannot understand what
designing means. He finds the artistry of thinking like an architect
to be elusive, obscure, alien, and mysterious. Moreover, even if he
were able to give a plausible verbal description of designing—to
intellectualize about it—he would still be unable to meet the
requirement that he demonstrate an understanding of designing *in
the doing.*

From his observation of the students' performance, the
studio master realizes that they do not at first understand the
essential things. He sees, further, that he cannot explain these
things with any hope of being understood, at least at the outset,
because they can be grasped only through the experience of actual
designing. Indeed, many studio masters believe, along with
Leftwich, that there are essential "covert things" that can never be
explained; either the student gets them in the doing, or he does not
get them at all. Hence the Kafkaesque situation in which the

student must "hang on the inflection of the tone of voice . . . to discover if something is really wrong."

The design studio shares in a general paradox attendant on the teaching and learning of any really new competence or understanding; for the student seeks to learn things whose meaning and importance she cannot grasp ahead of time. She is caught in the paradox Plato describes so vividly in his dialogue the *Meno*. There, just as Socrates induces Meno to admit that he hasn't the least idea what virtue is, Meno bursts out with this question:

> But how will you look for something when you don't in the least know what it is? How on earth are you going to set up something you don't know as the object of your search? To put it another way, even if you come right up against it, how will you know that what you have found is the thing you didn't know? [Plato, 1956, p. 128.]

Like Meno, the design student knows she needs to look for something but does not know what that something is. She seeks to learn it, moreover, in the sense of coming to know it *in action*. Yet, at the beginning, she can neither do it nor recognize it when she sees it. Hence, she is caught up in a self-contradiction: "looking for something" implies a capacity to recognize the thing one looks for, but the student lacks at first the capacity to recognize the object of her search. The instructor is caught up in the same paradox: he cannot tell the student what she needs to know, even if he has words for it, because the student would not at that point understand him.

The logical paradox of the *Meno* accurately describes the experience of learning to design. It captures the very feelings of mystery, confusion, frustration, and futility that many students experience in their early months or years of architectural study. Yet most students do attempt to carry out the paradoxical task.

The student discovers that she is expected to learn, by doing, both what designing is and how to do it. The studio seems to rest on the assumption that it is only in this way that she can learn. Others may help her, but they can do so only as she begins to understand for herself the process she finds initially mysterious. And although they may help her, *she* is the essential self-educator. In this respect, the studio tradition of design education is consistent with an older and broader tradition of educational thought and practice, according to which the most important things—artistry, wisdom, virtue—can only be learned for oneself.

In the *Meno,* to return to that deceptively simple text, Plato has Socrates argue that one person cannot teach virtue to another. The evidence is that good men, who have certainly wished to teach virtue to their sons, have manifestly failed to do so.

> *Socrates:*   . . . there are plenty of good statesmen here in Athens and have been as good in the past. The question is, have they also been good teachers of their own virtue? That is the point we are discussing . . . whether virtue can be taught. It amounts to the question whether the good men of this and former times have known how to hand on to someone else the goodness that was in themselves, or whether, on the contrary, it is not something that can be handed over, or that one man can receive from another [Plato, 1956, p. 148].

And in answer to this question, having considered the cases of a number of celebrated statesmen and their sons, Socrates finally concludes,

> I am afraid it is something that cannot be done by teaching [p. 149].

How, then, do human beings become good? For that some do, Socrates leaves no doubt. On this point, the *Meno* offers two perhaps conflicting and certainly disconnected answers. In the final section of the dialogue, Socrates concludes that virtue is a matter of "divine dispensation":

> If all we have said in this discussion and the questions we have asked have been right, virtue will

be acquired neither by nature nor by teaching. Whoever has it gets it by divine dispensation, without taking thought, unless he be the kind of statesman who can create another like himself [pp. 156–157].

But earlier in his discussion of the implications of his paradox, Socrates suggests a different view:

One thing I am ready to fight for as long as I can, in word and act: that is, that we shall be better, braver, and more active men if we believe it right to look for what we don't know than if we believe there is no point in looking because what we don't know we can never discover [p. 139].

Indeed, in his parable of the slave boy from whom he elicits the statement of a geometrical theorem, Socrates goes so far as to suggest the nature of the process by which we may "look for what we don't know." It is, in its essence, a process of *recollection;* the learner "spontaneously recovers knowledge that is in him but forgotten."

This knowledge will not come from teaching but from questioning. He [the slave boy] will recover it for himself [p. 138].

And the beginning of this process of recovery depends on Socrates, the epistemological gadfly and midwife, who goads the boy into discovering that he does not know what he thought the knew:

Socrates: Do you suppose, then, that he would have attempted to look for, or learn, what he thought he knew (although he did not), before he was thrown into perplexity, became aware of this ignorance, and felt a desire to know?

Meno: No.

Socrates: Then the numbing process was good for him?

Meno: I agree [p. 135].

Perhaps we can reconcile the two Platonic views of the process by which human beings learn something new. The earlier view is the general one: we can learn something new by recovering forgotten knowledge with the help of a Socratic gadfly whose questioning numbs us into perplexity. When it comes to really important things like virtue, however, the recovery of forgotten knowledge also depends on a talent given, as though by divine dispensation, to only a few.

Some contemporary authors have tried to dissolve the paradox of the *Meno* by arguments similar to Plato's. Just as Plato argued that the slave boy had once known and then forgotten the geometrical theorem and could therefore, when properly numbed and awakened, *recognize* it, so other writers have attributed to those who seek to learn something new an implicit capacity to recognize it when they find it.

Polanyi proposed that we already know *tacitly* the things we seek to learn. Socrates' dialogue with the slave boy is, for Polanyi, a parable of reflection on tacit knowledge:

> The *Meno* shows conclusively that if all knowledge is explicit, that is, capable of being clearly stated, then we cannot know a problem or look for its solution. And the *Meno* also shows, therefore, that if problems nevertheless exist, and discoveries can be made by solving them, we can know things, and important things, that we cannot tell.
>
> The kind of tacit knowledge that solves the paradox of the *Meno* consists in the intimation of something hidden which we may yet discover [Polanyi, 1967, pp. 22–23].

Herbert Simon (1969), who thinks of designing as converting a situation from its actual state to a preferred one, proposes to solve the paradox of the *Meno* by distinguishing between "state" and "process." Surely, he argues, we can describe the change of state that occurs when we solve a problem—climb a hill or win a game of chess—even though we cannot at first describe the process that would produce it. Problem solving is search for the values of the process variables that would produce a desired change of state; we regulate our search for the former by our capacity to recognize the latter.

Israel Scheffler has suggested in informal conversation that the paradox of the *Meno* can be dissolved by distinguishing between "inside" and "outside" views of the activity we are trying to learn. As he sees it, the architectural students know, from the very beginning of their studies, that they want a diploma; and they want to be on the inside of the practice they see at first only from the outside. Extending Scheffler's view, we might say that the students can recognize, from the very beginning, the external signs of a competent design performance. The problem they try to solve in the studio is to learn the internal cues that correspond to these external signs. They try to discover what it feels like to do the things they have seen the studio master do. And they regulate their search by the external signs of competence they already know how to recognize.

Each of these proposals—based, as it is, on a distinction between tacit and explicit, state and process, or outside and inside—captures something important about the process of learning to design.

If we were to apply Polanyi's view to the experience of students in the design studio, we would say, correctly, that learning to design sometimes takes the form of making explicit what one already knows how to do. As Petra says, "Intuitively you look at the shape and you know it is wrong, but it's hard to get down to the reason." And students do seem to experience, at one time or another, Polanyi's "intimation of something hidden." However, most students do not *begin* with a tacit knowledge of competent designing. If anything, they are more likely at the outset to be able to give verbal descriptions of designing that they cannot produce. Only later, when they have learned some aspects of designing, can they advance their learning by reflecting on the tacit knowledge implicit in their own performance.

Simon's resolution of the paradox holds for a limited number of design problems where the student *can* recognize the change of state that would constitute a solution—for example, "In a space of a given size and shape, arrange certain specified items of furniture so that the space holds the furniture comfortably and allows for its ordinary use." But not all design problems are of this kind; indeed, the most important ones are not. At the beginning of her dialogue with Quist, Petra has not yet arrived at a satisfactory formulation of the problem to be solved—"the problem of this problem," as Quist calls it. She does not begin with a capacity to recognize either the problem or its solution. In the course of the dialogue, however, it is quite possible that she begins to understand the problem of establishing the global configuration of the buildings on the site and to identify a direction in which to search for solutions to it. It is by learning to work on the problem that she may also learn to recognize when she has solved it. About this kind of learning, however, Simon's account tells us nothing.

Scheffler is clearly right when he says that the first-year design students know they want to get a diploma and become insiders to the profession. But this does not cut very deeply into the paradox of learning to design, for many students who hold such aspirations still haven't the faintest idea what it means to think like an architect. It is true that students do often come to recognize and appreciate the qualities of competent designing, which they then try to learn to produce. One way of learning to design does seem to consist in coordinating the inner feelings of performance with the external signs of competent designing. What is important, however, is that students must *come* to be able to do this. In our effort to account for this way of learning, we cannot avoid the problem of explaining how, in the first place, they come to recognize good designing when they see it.

In the early stages of the design studio, most students do experience the paradox of the *Meno;* they feel like people looking for something they could not recognize even if they stumbled across it. Hence, their initial learning process bears a double burden: they must learn both to execute design performances and to recognize their competent execution. But these two components of the learning task support each other: as the student begins to perform, she also begins to recognize competent performance and to regulate her search by reference to the qualities she recognizes. *How* she comes to be able to do this is quite another matter, to which we will return in our discussion of the dialogue between student and coach.

In 1952 a Socratic figure of our own times, Carl Rogers, presented some personal reflections on teaching and learning to a group of teachers assembled at Harvard University. What he said on that occasion closely parallels the line of thought I have been developing here:

a. My experience has been that I cannot teach another person how to teach. To attempt it is for me, in the long run, futile.

b. It seems to me that anything that can be taught to another is relatively inconsequential and has little or no significant influence on behavior. That sounds so ridiculous that I can't help but question it at the same time I present it.

c. I realize increasingly that I am only interested in learnings which significantly influence behavior. Quite possibly this is simply a personal idiosyncrasy.

d. I have come to feel that only learning which significantly influences behavior is self-discovered, self-appropriated learning.

e. Such self-discovered learning, truth that has been personally appropriated and assimilated in experience, cannot be directly communicated to another. As soon as an individual tries to communicate such experience directly, often with a quite natural enthusiasm, it becomes teaching, and its results are inconsequential. It was some relief recently to discover that Sören Kierkegaard, the Danish philosopher, has found this, too, in his own experience, and stated it very clearly a century ago. It made it seem less absurd.

f.   As a consequence of the above, I realize that I have lost interest in being a teacher.

g.   When I try to teach, as I do sometimes, I am appalled by the results, which seem a little more than inconsequential, because sometimes the teaching appears to succeed. When this happens, I find that the results are damaging. It seems to cause the individual to distrust his own experience and to stifle significant learning. Hence I have come to feel that the outcomes of teaching are either unimportant or hurtful.

h.   When I look back at the results of my past teaching, the real results seem the same—either damage was done, or nothing significant occurred. This is frankly troubling.

i.   As a consequence, I realize that I am only interested in being a learner, preferably learning things that matter, that have some significant influence on my own behavior.

j.   I find it very rewarding to learn, in groups, in relationship with one person as in therapy, or by myself.

k.   I find that one of the best, but most difficult, ways for me to learn is to drop my own defensiveness, at least temporarily, and to try to understand the way in which this experience seems and feels to the other person.

l.   I find that another way of learning for me is to state my own uncertainties, to try to clarify my puzzlement, and thus get closer to the meaning that my experience actually seems to have.

m.   The whole train of experiencing, and the meanings that I have thus far discovered in it, seem to have launched me on a process which is both fascinating and at times a little frightening. It seems to mean letting my experience carry me

> on, in a direction which appears to be forward,
> toward that I can but dimly define, as I try to
> understand at least the current meaning of that
> experience. The sensation is that of floating with
> a complex stream of experience, with the fasci-
> nating possibility of trying to comprehend its
> ever-changing reality [Rogers, 1969, p. 277].

In the remaining few moments of his talk, Rogers drew some
further inferences. If others' experience agreed with his own, he
thought, we would do away with teaching, examinations, grades,
credits, "the exposition of conclusions," and the whole apparatus
of formal education.

His words had a profound effect on the assembled teachers.
As he describes it,

> Feelings ran high. It seemed I was threatening
> their jobs. I was obviously saying things I didn't
> mean, etc., etc. And occasionally a quiet voice of
> appreciation arose from a teacher who had felt these
> things but never dared to say them . . . I refused to
> defend myself by replying to the questions and
> attacks which came from every quarter. I endeavored
> to accept and empathize with the indignation, the
> frustration, the criticisms which they felt. I pointed
> out that I had merely expressed some very personal
> views of my own. I had not asked nor expected others
> to agree. After much storm, members of the group
> began expressing, more and more frankly, their own
> significant feelings about teaching—often feelings
> divergent from mine, often feelings divergent from
> each other. It was a very thought-provoking session.
> I question whether any participant in that session
> has ever forgotten it [Rogers, 1969, p. 277].

There is something odd about Rogers's account. He tells the
teachers that, having come to believe in the futility of trying to
teach anything of significance for behavior, he has lost interest in

being a teacher. Yet clearly he believes that his conduct of the session contributed to a climate of self-expression and self-discovery that few of the participants will ever forget. From the evidence of this example, I would say, not that Rogers has lost all interest in being a teacher, but that he has *reframed teaching* in a way that gives central importance to his own role as a learner. He elicits self-discovery in others, first by modeling for others, as a learner, the open expression of his own deepest reflections (however absurd they may seem) and then, when others criticize him, by refusing to become defensive. As he expresses his own uncertainties and convictions, emphasizes the "merely personal" nature of his views, and invites and listens to the reactions of others, he seeks to be literally thought-provoking. He believes that the very expression of thoughts and feelings usually withheld, manifestly divergent from one another, has the potential to promote self-discovery.

Like Socrates in the *Meno*, Rogers believes that the most important things cannot be taught but must be discovered and appropriated for oneself. Like Socrates, he attributes to himself and others a capacity for self-discovery and functions as a paradoxical teacher who does not teach but serves as gadfly and midwife to others' self-discovery—provoking in his interlocutors, like Socrates, a storm of anger and confusion.

More recently still, a friend of mine, Professor Thomas Cowan of the University of Pennsylvania, put the same point of view very succinctly in a letter to me, as follows:

> I like old Carl Gustav Jung best on education. You know that, unlike Freud, for whom psychoanalysis is a branch of the healing arts, Jung always insisted that it is a propadeutic, a branch of education. For him, education is what one does to and for oneself. Hence, the universal irrelevance of all systems of education. . . . This view forced me to distinguish education from training: education—the self-learning process; training—what others make you do. . . . What are educational systems (so-called) *really* doing? For example, law school, I discovered,

primarily trains students to listen . . . to think and talk the way the rest of the profession does. What is its educational function, then? To drive you mad with its incessant drill to educate yourself. The process is or appears terribly wasteful, yet some do get educated. If the teacher had a big stick and hit you over the head every time you tried to get him to educate you, the thing would be done in less than a semester. It seems to me that this is the Zen method of education, so of course I can't claim to have invented it [personal communication, 1979].

The Predicament of Learning to Design

The paradox of learning a really new competence is this: that a student cannot at first understand what he needs to learn, can learn it only by educating himself, and can educate himself only by beginning to do what he does not yet understand.

In the architectural studio, the paradox inherent in learning to design places the student in a predicament. He is expected to plunge into designing, trying from the very outset to do what he does not yet know how to do, in order to get the sort of experience that will help him learn what designing means. He cannot make an informed choice to take this plunge because he does not yet grasp its essential meanings, and his instructors cannot convey these to him until he has had the requisite experience. Thus, he must jump in without knowing—indeed, in order to discover— what he needs to learn.

It is as though the studio master had said to him, "I can tell you that there is something you need to know, and with my help you may be able to learn it. But I cannot tell you what it is in a way you can now understand. I can only arrange for you to have the right sorts of experiences for yourself. You must be willing, therefore, to have these experiences. Then you will be able to make an informed choice about whether you wish to continue. If you are unwilling to step into this new experience without knowing ahead of time what it will be like, I cannot help you. You must trust me."

As Quist said in an interview, the studio master asks his students to make a "willing suspension of disbelief":

> It has to be a kind of contract between the two. The teacher must be open to challenge and must be able to defend his position. The student, in turn, must be willing to suspend his disbelief, to give the teacher's suggestion a chance—to try the suggestion out. The student must be willing to trust that the faculty member has a programmatic intention which will be preempted or ruined by his requiring full justification and explanation before anything is done. . . . A good student is capable of the willing suspension of disbelief.

Quist's phrase originated with Samuel Taylor Coleridge, who used it to describe the stance essential to an understanding of poetry (Coleridge, 1817/1983). In order to allow a poem to do its work, Coleridge thought, the reader must enter into a kind of contract with the poet, willingly suspending his disbelief in utterances that seem false or even absurd. The reader is not asked to will "belief," because he cannot be expected to make an informed choice to believe until he understands, which depends, in turn, on his having the right sort of experience. Disbelief must be suspended until the reader (or student) has access to the information on which to base a good decision. But in order to get that information, he must commit to the enterprise that yields the experience.

What makes this situation into a predicament for the student is that he or she is likely to find the costs of commitment greater than its expected rewards. Perhaps the least of these costs is the opportunity cost of remaining in the studio. More important is the sense of being at risk. Swimming in unfamiliar waters, the student risks the loss of his sense of competence, control, and confidence. He must temporarily abandon much that he already values. If he comes to the studio with knowledge he considers useful, he may be asked to unlearn it. If he comes with a perspective on what is valuable for design, he may be asked to put it aside. Later in his studio education, or after it, he may judge for himself what he wishes to keep, discard, or combine, but he is at first unable to make such a judgment. And he may fear that, by a kind of insidious coercion, he may permanently lose what he already knows and values.

He becomes dependent on his instructors. He must look to them for help in acquiring understanding, direction, and competence. As he willingly suspends disbelief, he also suspends autonomy—as though he were becoming a child again. In such a predicament, he is more or less vulnerable to anxiety, depending on the strengths and weaknesses he brings to the studio. If he is easily threatened by the temporary surrender of his sense of competence, then the risk of loss will seem to be high. If he comes with a distrust of those in authority, a readiness to see them as manipulating him, especially if he is unaware of his dispositions to perceive, then the willing suspension of disbelief may seem difficult or even impossible.

The studio master has a predicament complementary to the student's. He knows that he cannot at first communicate to the student what he understands about designing. He knows that the student, like a postulant asked to make a leap of faith in order to attain understanding, can get good reasons for acting only by beginning to act. However much the master may dislike asking the student to give up his autonomy, he must invite him to enter into a temporary relationship of trust and dependency.

To be sure, the learning contract between student and instructor is seldom made explicit. Quist is exceptional in the degree to which he reflects on it. More frequently, the two parties simply find themselves in the relationship described by the contract. And if they should happen to think about it later on, their attempts to talk about it will be embedded in the complex, multileveled discourse in which the main work of the studio consists.

Communication Between Student and Studio Master

We can think of this process as one of sending and receiving messages. However, it is not a kind of telegraphy in which meaningful signals are directly transmitted from one participant to the other.* Rather, each participant must construct for himself the meaning of the other's messages and must design messages whose meanings the other can decipher. When the process works well, it is a kind of reciprocal construction that results in convergence of meaning. So much the studio shares with all human communication.

But communication between student and studio master is in several ways problematic.

Messages often refer both to the process of designing and to the process of learning to design. An event like Petra's desk crit, pertaining to both processes, holds a potential for two-tiered confusion.

Messages are conveyed primarily through actions—the studio master's demonstrations and the student's efforts at design. This is useful, because successful communication is measured, after all, not by the student's ability to talk about design but by her ability to do it. Nevertheless, communication through action poses problems. The student must construct the meanings of the studio master's actions even though his meanings are likely to conflict with her own (the likelihood of their conflict underlies the need for an initial suspension of disbelief); and the student's own action-messages make her vulnerable to feelings of confusion and failure.

The studio master wants to convey essential things, some of which go beyond statable rules even if he is good at reflecting on his own tacit knowledge. He can alert his students to the desirability of attending to the situation's surprising back talk, for example, but he cannot give them rules for doing so. His feeling for drawing—to represent contours of the site, cross-sectional views of buildings, or perspective—cannot be conveyed by a verbal description of rules for drawing. This is true, first, because drawing depends on seeing, and words are very poor approximations to visual things, but also because skillful drawing depends on a feeling for the use of line that is not reducible to verbally

*Michael Reddy (1979) has described this way of looking at interpersonal communication in terms of the "conduit metaphor."

described procedures. And designing, like other forms of artistry, demands authenticity. A designer must *mean* what she does. If she works from a generative metaphor, for example, she must take it seriously, enter into it, and treat it as her own. The studio master cannot give rules for authenticity; even if he could imagine them, the student would still need to apply them in an authentic way!

Not everything important about designing escapes verbal description. There are many things the studio master can put into words. But his attempts to clarify, specify, and differentiate meanings are vulnerable to the very ambiguities he would like to dispel.

Quist, for example, devotes much effort to demonstrating and describing the variety of design domains that ought to be considered in spinning out and evaluating the consequences of a designer's moves. He advises Petra to see the cafeteria not only as a "formal function" but also in terms of access to summer and winter sun, and he treats the gallery not only as circulation but as a way of marking differences in level. Nowhere, however, does he make explicit reference to the system of design domains on which he draws. And even if he were to do so, some students would find it confusing. A student like Lauda can understand designing only in terms of structure and technology; Judith, in terms of program and use. For them, other domains are vague or nonexistent.

When Quist tells Petra that she must "draw and draw" in order to calibrate her grid, he means drawing in the sense of drawing experiment. She must draw in order to discover the consequences of the various possible grids. Students who understood drawing only as the visual presentation of an idea, however, would probably take Quist's advice to mean that their delineations lacked polish. Quist uses *metaphor* to mean the image generative of a design. But a student like Judith, for whom the term seems to mean embellishment of an existing design, can say that in order to please her instructors she will "put in some metaphors."

The subprocesses of design—making a site plan, for example, or analyzing a program—can be demonstrated and described. But designing is a holistic process, and the studio master cannot explain "thinking architecturally" by listing component design skills. A student cannot understand and acquire each component skill, in the sense in which "thinking architecturally" requires it, until he has experienced that component in the context of a whole process. Hence, he may be confused about what he has learned—or he may believe he has learned more than the studio master thinks he has.

There are potential sources of unclarity in the studio master's implicit claims about his approach to design. Quist makes clearly positive judgments about nooks and soft back areas, and he expresses negative judgments by such terms as "screwy," "no good," and "spoils the whole idea." Suppose, however, that Petra had happened not to share his judgments. In the one case where she raises a question of this kind—the calibration of the grid—he invites her to look at it in section. But if she were to persist in her point of view, would he try to argue her out of it or simply give up, as though she had missed the point of a joke? Certainly, Quist acts as though his judgments had objective validity. The site *is* screwy, he seems to say; the auditorium *is* too much of a hard-edged block. But students like Petra, exposed to many different schools of contemporary architecture, may wonder. When Quist expresses such judgments, is he also conveying the message that they are normatively binding on everyone? Or is he saying only that she must invest her design with values of her own, regardless of their fit with his? Are the differences among schools of architecture objectively grounded, or are they matters of taste or ideology? On such issues even Quist is silent. As one student says, "One of the things that really bug me about architectural education is that a lot of things are really implicit, remain under the surface and are not talked about."

The studio master's silence about his implicit claims becomes a projective test for the student. Petra is free to think, for example:

"These things are obvious to everyone but me."
"Quist cannot say what he means."
"What he means is inexpressible in words."
"I have not learned to ask the right questions."

The issue becomes crucial just at the point when a student, seeking to interpret an instructor's criticism of her work, cannot grasp the view of designing that underlies the criticism. Then her questions about the error she has failed to see may be joined to confusion about the perspective that allows the studio master to see it and the ambiguity of his implicit claims to objectivity. How she resolves these questions has much to do with her further learning.

The architectural studio rests on an implicit response to the paradox and predicament of learning to design: the student must begin to design before she knows what she is doing, so that the studio master's demonstrations and descriptions can take on meanings useful to her further designing. But this "virtuous circle" depends on the capacity of student and studio master to communicate effectively with each other, in spite of the potential for vagueness, ambiguity, or obscurity inherent in the things about which they try to communicate. Their search for convergence of meaning will be the subject of the next chapter.

👑 Chapter Five 👑

The Dialogue Between
Coach and Student

In the early phases of architectural education, many students who have taken the plunge begin to try to design even though they do not yet know what designing means and cannot recognize it when they see it. At first, their coaches cannot make things easier for them. They cannot tell them what designing is, because they have a limited ability to say what they know, because some essential features of designing escape clearly statable rules, and because much of what they *can* say is graspable by a student only as he begins to design. Even if coaches could produce good, clear, and compelling descriptions of designing, students, with their very different systems of understanding, would be likely to find them confusing and mysterious.

At this stage, communication between student and coach seems very nearly impossible. Yet in a matter of a few years or even months, students and coaches begin to talk with each other elliptically, using shorthand in word and gesture to convey ideas that to an outsider seem complex or obscure. They communicate easily, finishing each other's sentences or leaving sentences unfinished, confident that the listener has grasped their essential meaning.

To be sure, not everyone achieves this state of communicative grace. Some students never do understand what the coach is talking about—or they believe they understand when the coach is sure they do not—and some coaches never get through to their students. Many succeed, nevertheless, in crossing over an apparently unbridgeable communication gap to a seeming convergence of meaning. How do they do it?

Student and coach bring to the experience of the studio a capacity for a particular kind of dialogue about the thing—designing—that they see at first in such divergent ways. Their dialogue has three essential features: it takes place in the context of the student's attempts to design; it makes use of actions as well as words; and it depends on reciprocal reflection-in-action.

The coach tries to discern what the student understands, what her peculiar difficulties are about, what she already knows how to do, mainly from the evidence of the student's initial efforts at design. In response, the coach can show or tell. He can demonstrate some part or aspect of the process he thinks the student needs to learn, offering it as a model to be imitated; and he can, with questions, instructions, advice, or criticism, describe some feature of designing. Coaches vary in their predilections for showing and telling. Some refuse to draw, out of fear that the student's imitation will be blind and mechanical. Others *only* draw, distrusting mere words to convey something as inherently visual as designing. Some, like Quist, combine the two strategies. Whatever he chooses to do, the coach experiments in communication, testing with each of his interventions both his diagnosis of a student's understandings and problems and the effectiveness of his own strategies of communication. In this sense, he reflects-in-action.

The student tries to decipher the coach's demonstrations and descriptions, testing the meanings she has constructed by applying them to her further designing—revealing in this way what she has made of things heard or seen. In this sense, the student reflects-in-action.

Reflection-in-action becomes reciprocal when the coach treats the student's further designing as an utterance, a carrier of meanings like "This is what I take you to mean" or "This is what I really meant to say," and responds to her interpretations with further showing or telling, which the student may, in turn, decipher anew and translate into new design performance. The process continues throughout the sequence of design projects that make up the studio, moving—though not necessarily in a straight line—toward convergence of meaning and toward the student's increasing capacity to produce what she and her coach regard as competent designing.

In this process, several kinds of learning are interwoven. The student learns to recognize and appreciate the qualities of good design and competent designing, in the same process by which she also learns to produce those qualities. She learns the meanings of technical operations in the same process by which she learns to carry them out. And as she learns to design, she also learns to learn to design—that is, she learns the practice of the practicum.

Given this brief and idealized description of the dialogue of student and coach, I shall turn in the rest of this chapter to the component processes of telling and listening, demonstrating and imitating.

Telling and Listening

A coach has many ways of "telling." He can give specific instructions, telling, for example, how to prepare a site plan, assign uses to slopes of different grades, or produce cross-sectional drawings, elevations, or plans. He can criticize a student's product or process, suggesting things the student needs to do, like "Work on the size of the middle area" or "Calibrate the dimensions of the grid." He can tell the student how to set priorities, as in "Work on the overall geometry of the buildings on the site; I wouldn't worry about the shapes of the roofs." He can propose experiments the student might consider trying, analyze or reformulate problems, and deliver reflections about the process he has demonstrated.

Whatever the coach may choose to say, it is important that he say it, for the most part, in the context of the student's *doing*. He must talk to the student while she is in the midst of a task (and perhaps stuck in it), or is about to begin a new task, or thinks back on a task she has just completed, or rehearses in imagination a task she may perform in the future.

There is no magical dividing line between the world of the studio and the world outside it. The student does not suddenly understand, when she steps into the studio, what in the outside world she would have found obscure. But in the context of her attempts to design, both the coach's telling and her listening have a heightened potential for efficacy. When Petra is trying, with difficulty, to place administration, gym, and kindergarten on her screwy site, and Quist talks to her about her problem, she listens to him with operative attention—that is, with a special readiness to translate what she hears into action, as we might listen to someone giving us directions to an unfamiliar place when we are the ones who will have to drive. With this attitude of operative attention, Petra is likely to place special demands on Quist's advice, and he is likely to try to respond to her demands.

Instructions are always and inevitably incomplete. Unless we already know how to do the thing in question, there is always a gap between the instruction and the action it describes—a gap we are unlikely to detect except when we listen in the mode of operative attention. This instructional gap may be of several kinds.

The instruction may contain a description that is not specific enough or may not have the kind of specificity that matches the student's need to know. In order to follow Quist's "Draw and draw in order to calibrate the grid," for example, Petra must know how to test a particular choice of dimension for its effects on such factors as access to buildings, circulation, and fit with the contours of the slope. Quist might try to help her by adducing examples of these kinds of effects, which might or might not suit the particular difficulties she experiences as she tries to act on his advice. He cannot foresee all the difficulties she might possibly experience, and if he tried to do so, he would surely overwhelm her with information. He must try to produce descriptions suited to her present know-how and sense of the problem, aware, as he does so, that some things likely to cause her the greatest difficulty are just the ones he takes most for granted.

Instructions may be ambiguous; most instructions are. "Take the first left after the lights" could mean, in a particular context, "Take the dirt road, which is the first left" or "Take the first *paved* road on the left." Because the giver of directions knows what he means, it does not occur to him that "the first left" may be ambiguous. For the listener who tries to decipher the instruction in order to act on it, however, the ambiguity readily presents itself as a problem to be solved—by inference or experiment or both. If the giver of instructions takes his task seriously, he must first reflect on the thing he already knows how to do, trying to make explicit to himself the procedures he follows more or less spontaneously, and then he must try to anticipate and clarify the ambiguities the listener may discover in his description. Because of ambiguities peculiar to the language of designing, as noted earlier, a design student, listening with operative attention, is likely to experience a special need for clarification.

Instructions may be strange, referring to things, procedures, or qualities unfamiliar to the listener or incongruent with meanings she already holds. So it is with Judith's understanding of such directives as "Think architecturally," "Draw to scale," "Base your work on an organizing metaphor." Either these commands hold no meaning at all for her, or she constructs a meaning for them that is entirely incongruent with the one her instructor intends.

When a student enacts an instruction, she reveals the meanings she has constructed for it, indicating how she may have filled a gap of specificity, ambiguity, or strangeness. Observing what she draws, the coach may realize that she thinks "drawing to scale" means using a ruler or that she does not know what it means to calibrate a grid. He may be surprised by the evidence of a gap previously unsuspected or a problem different from the one he had in mind. And he may invent, in response, what he ought to say or do next. Every attempt to produce an instruction is an experiment that tests both the coach's reflection on his own knowing-in-action and his understanding of the student's difficulty. Every attempt to act on an instruction reveals and tests the student's understanding of its meaning and, at the same time, the quality of the instruction itself. The student asks, in effect, Do I understand what he's talking about? Does it make sense to me? Can I do it? Have I got it right? And the coach, observing and reading the student's performance, asks similar questions about both his own instructions and the student's attempt to make sense of them.

In a different context—teaching the rudiments of reading— Leo Tolstoy described the reflection-in-action of a coach who tries to craft instructions matched to the capacities and difficulties of particular students:

> Every individual must, in order to acquire the art of reading in the shortest possible time, be taught quite apart from any other, and therefore there must be a separate method for each. That which forms an insuperable difficulty to one does not in the least keep back another, and vice versa. One pupil has a good memory, and it is easier for him to memorize the syllables than to comprehend the vowellessness of the consonants; another reflects calmly and will comprehend a most rational sound method; another has a fine instinct, and he grasps the law of word combination by reading whole words at a time.
>
> The best teacher will be he who has at his tongue's end the explanation of what it is that is bothering the pupil. These explanations give the teacher the knowledge of the greatest possible number of methods, the ability of inventing new methods and, above all, not a blind adherence to one method but the conviction that all methods are one-sided, and that the best method would be the one which would answer best to all the possible difficulties incurred by a pupil, that is, not a method but an art and talent. . . .
>
> . . . Every teacher must . . . by regarding every imperfection in the pupil's comprehension, not as a defect of the pupil but as a defect in his own instruction, endeavor to develop in himself the ability of discovering new methods [1861/1967, pp. 57–58].

Like Tolstoy's teacher of reading, a good design coach has at his disposal and is capable of inventing on the spot many strategies of instructing, questioning, and describing—all aimed at responding to the difficulties and potentials of a particular student who is trying to do something.

For example, the coach may frame a question that directs the student's attention to a new aspect of the design situation: "Why does the administration belong here?" "What if you opened up the space here?" His question may advance an idea the student has not yet entertained; he may ask, "How will you mark the difference in level?" for example, when the student has not yet noticed the irregularity of the slope.

He may give the student a very concrete operational instruction that contains an implicit, deeper meaning. Quist might ask Petra, for example, "Why don't you see what the gallery looks like in cross-section?," hoping she will notice that it is more than a vehicle for circulation. Similarly, a piano teacher might say, "You should change the fingering here," meaning "This should mark the end of one phrase and the beginning of another." In such cases the coach tries to get the student to perform a particular operation in order to become aware of its function in the situation—performing a technical operation, as Wittgenstein observed, in order to learn its meaning (1953).

The coach may pick up the exact words a student uses to describe her intention—developing them, however, in a direction different from the one she had in mind. Thus, Quist echoes Petra's description of the gallery: "It is a general pass-through that anyone has the liberty to pass through," but adds, "It is not a corridor."

He may try to find a concrete image, accessible to his student, that carries a complex network of associations. Thus, Quist speaks of "a garden, a soft back area [to these hard-edged forms]"; he talks, somewhat disparagingly, of "shaving the trees."

He may make a judgment about his student's need to know something now or her readiness to hear it. Quist notices that Petra is disposed to deal with individual building elements (to "work closely," as she puts it), and so he focuses on establishing the basic geometry of the buildings on the site. He sees that she hesitates to make apparently arbitrary choices that could invest her design with meaning from which a basic idea might follow, and so he tells her to impose a discipline, however arbitrary—"you can always break it open later." Seeing that she is not adept at stringing out a long and complex sequence of conditional moves and consequences, he talks her through such a string of moves. Seeing that she is limited in the domains of norms by which she allows herself to be influenced, he talks about the formal implications of chosen geometries, the use-related idea of being one with the trees, the effects of orientation on the site, the meanings that may be attached to building elements, the uses compatible with different grades of slope. When Petra seems interested only in the purity of her hard-edged forms, Quist speaks of "softening them and breaking them up" by accommodation to norms derived from other domains.

Just as the coach can vary his strategy of description, depending on his present reading of a particular student, so he varies the manner in which he gives a description. He may treat one student with gentleness and indirection, barely hinting at issues that call for change; with another, he may be direct and challenging. In Quist's studio, some of the variations in students' responses to him may reflect the different sides of himself he chooses to present to them.

Demonstrating and Imitating

In Quist's dialogue with Petra, after he has heard her "big problems," he demonstrates a version of the global process she has already tried (stutteringly, as he says) to carry out.

How shall we describe his intention? He wants her to understand his demonstration so that she can go on to do something like it. "You keep going on," he says, "you are going to make it." He has shown her a way of designing the geometry of the buildings on the site so that she can proceed to imitate it—not in its details but in its essential features. And she seems to accept the demonstration in the spirit of his intention, feeling that he has helped her see where she was stuck and given her an alternative approach that she will be able to develop for herself.

A coach demonstrates parts or aspects of designing in order to help his student grasp what he believes she needs to learn and, in doing so, attributes to her a capacity for imitation.

At first glance, there is nothing in this process of demonstration and imitation that merits extraordinary attention.

Children often learn to play by imitating other children and learn to function in an adult world by imitating the adults around them. We learn new physical skills, games, ways of working, practices of everyday life, in part by imitating others who are already good at these things. We may not like the *idea* of imitation (I shall have more to say about this later on), but we are continually doing it— and usually without feeling that we are doing anything remarkable. The obviousness of imitation dissolves, howevei, when we examine it more closely.

Consider a mother who sits facing her baby, clapping her hands. The baby begins to clap too, mimicking its mother. The mother begins to clap at a faster pace; the baby responds by clapping faster as well. The mother claps slowly again, this time beating out a steady rhythm. The baby does likewise. The mother speeds up the beat and makes the rhythm more complicated. The baby responds by producing a lot of little, fast claps. The mother begins to play pat-a-cake with the baby, first extending her two palms to touch the baby's two palms, then touching the baby's right palm with her right, the baby's left palm with her left. Confused at first, the baby soon responds by extending right hand to meet mother's right hand, left hand to meet her left.

Even so "simple" an example shows extraordinary complexity. The baby does as it has seen its mother do, reproducing her global gestures. But in order to do so, it must be able to produce and control, from internal cues of feeling, what it apprehends through visual observation of external cues. Somehow, it manages to coordinate inner and outer cues to produce actions that conform, in some essential respects, to the actions observed.

Even in this "simple" example, imitation presents itself as a process of selective construction. The features of the performance to be reproduced are not *given* with the demonstration. The baby selects and integrates in its own performance what it takes to be essential in the things it sees the mother do. Or perhaps we ought to say, there is already in its perception of its mother's action a construction of the essential and inessential things, which it then translates into its own performance.

When the baby claps, for example, it sits facing its mother; its mimicry does not include turning around to sit facing in the same direction as the mother. The baby detects certain variations in the mother's clapping—slowing down, for example—and responds by reproducing them. When the mother claps a more complex rhythm, however, the baby produces a lot of little claps—which may represent what the baby hears or perhaps reflects its limited ability to produce the more complex rhythm it hears.

Imitative reconstruction of an observed action is a kind of problem solving—indicated especially, in our example, by the baby's gradual success in "getting" the alternating pat-a-cake motions. Problem solving may take the form of successive differentiations of a global gesture or of learning to string together component actions. The imitator has access to observation of the process (in this case, the clapping) and of the product (the sounds of the claps) and may regulate his selective construction by reference to either or both of these. When the process of imitation is interactive, as in our example, the demonstrator's reactions can also regulate the constructive process. When the baby claps, the mother smiles and nods, rewarding its performance.

The baby's imitative construction does not depend on its ability to make a verbal description of what it sees, hears, or does. The problem solving involved in imitation—doing as it has seen and heard its mother do—does not depend on an explicit verbal formulation of similarities perceived and enacted. The baby can produce an action similar to the action it has perceived without being able to say "similar with respect to what." Its constructive process is nonetheless a form of reflection-in-action—an on-the-spot inquiry in which the imitator constructs and tests, in its own action, the essential features of the action it has observed.

As an infant matures, its capacity for this sort of reflection-in-action develops. Its imitative reconstructions become increasingly complex, undoubtedly playing a major role in all the processes we associate with skill acquisition. In learning to ski, juggle, or draw, for example, observation and imitation of skillful performances are crucially important. In these sorts of examples, as in the baby's clapping, we have access to observations of both product and process and may give priority to either or both of these. I can see the movements of a skiing instructor as she goes into a parallel turn. I can also see (and hear) the actual turning with which she completes the maneuver, skis held tightly together, facing slightly uphill, making a noise like sandpaper as the skis skid over the snow. I can watch an expert draftsman as he makes a freehand drawing of a fern. I can observe his gestures, see how he guides his pen over the paper, and see, finally, the finished drawing left by the traces of his pen.

Insofar as I pay attention to the product—the parallel turn or the drawing—I have something to *copy*. Here I am free of the need to reproduce an observed process of action; I work against the constraint of producing something like the original product, something I can perceive as similar to it—again before I can say "similar with respect to what." As I set myself the problem of copying the product, I regulate my on-line experiments by my perceptions of similarities and differences between the original and my copy of it. I may be limited, of course, by my ability to perceive the product—a master performer might see it very differently—but the very act of copying may lead me to see the original in new ways.

Insofar as I attend to the *process* of action, trying to do as I have seen a skillful performer do, I reflect-in-action both on the original process I have observed and on my attempts to reproduce it. I ask, "What is he really doing?" and as I try to do as he has done, I ask, "What am I really doing?" I can break the whole gesture I have imitated into parts, trying to see what in each part makes my attempt at reproduction right or wrong. Because I can detect this "rightness" or "wrongness" more readily than I can state the norms that underlie my judgments, I can reflect on the criteria that underlie my perceptions of match or mismatch. I can experiment with different ways of correcting the errors I detect. I can examine the "joints" that connect parts of the performance I try to reproduce, recognize intermediate stages of the task of construction, differentiate aspects of my performance—noting, for example, what happens when my skis bite more sharply into the snow or my pen moves more slowly over the surface of the paper. Often in this process I discover new meanings in the operations I try to reproduce. Leaning into the slope as I have seen an expert skier do, I may discover how this gives me a feeling of solid balance and purchase for the turn. Imitating the observed performance, I put myself into a new situation of action and from its vantage point get a new view of and feeling for the performance I am trying to imitate.

I may coordinate the two strategies of imitation: reproducing a process and copying its product. I may use each as a test of the other, judging that I have finally got it right, for example, when I detect in my own action a fit to the process I have observed and in my own result a fit to the original product. At this point, I may try to do it again, now directing my effort at imitation to my own just-completed action. I progress from imitating the other to imitating myself.

Combining Telling/Listening and Demonstrating/Imitating

In the design studio, as in other kinds of reflective practicums, the coach's showing and telling are interwoven, as are the student's listening and imitating. Through their combination, students can learn what they cannot learn by imitation or following instructions alone. Each process can help to fill communication gaps inherent in the other.

Instructions are always incomplete, as we have seen, and are often read as ambiguous, strange, or incongruent with the listener's understandings. Similarly, every demonstration is ambiguous, always open to the question "Just what in this is to be imitated?" Whatever a coach may see as the essential features of his demonstration, students must construct their own versions of it, and these are often incongruent with the coach's intentions.

In addition, there are several ways in which a demonstration may present obstacles to imitation. It may be too refined, containing differences that escape the observer's attention. A cello teacher may demonstrate the touch of a bow on a string that makes the tone more brilliant, for example, and his student may hear and reproduce it as simply louder. The demonstration may go by too quickly for the student to detect what is going on. Its complexity may elude the student's grasp. For example, the demonstration may consist of a string of moves too long and subtly interconnected for the student to hold in mind, or it may consist of a coordination of many concurrent moves. It may vary over time in a way that seems unpredictable to the novice although it reveals to the initiated an understanding of a complex system—like the sequence of moves by which a skilled mechanic probes an engine.

Verbal description can provide clues to the essential features of a demonstration, and demonstration can make clear the kind of performance denoted by a description that at first seems vague or obscure. A tennis coach might advise a student to hit the ball on the rise, for example, and a student might find this advice impenetrable until he observes how the coach approaches and attacks the ball. When the student tries to do this for himself, the coach observes him and says, "Get your racket back!" calling attention to a feature of the demonstration the student had missed.

The coach's or student's reflection on his own or the other's performance can yield a description that highlights subtle differences, distinguishes the joints in a long and rapid string of moves, or reveals the understanding that informs surface variations. The tennis coach Timothy Gallwey asks his students to tell him where their rackets are when they hit the ball. Attending to the position of the racket at the precise moment of impact, the student learns what he is doing wrong, and his efforts to correct his errors become more reliable. Seymour Papert used to teach juggling by informing would-be jugglers that they are susceptible to a variety of typical mistakes, or "bugs"—throwing the ball too far forward, for example. Asking them from time to time to describe the "bug" they had just illustrated, he would give them a language with which to reflect on their own performance. He would name parts of the juggling process—distinguishing a "pass" from a "toss," for example—thus helping the student break into manageable parts what had at first appeared to be a seamless flow of movement.

Quist's drawing and talking—his language of designing—seems to help Petra make sense of his rather long and complex demonstration. And his occasional comments about designing, like "Work back and forth between unit and total," seem to help her attend to essential features. His descriptions indicate what Petra is meant to imitate, both in the particular task at hand and in the generic process it illustrates. His demonstrations clarify descriptions that might otherwise strike her as vague or obscure.

We can identify the "moments" of the process in which Petra responds reflectively to Quist's demonstrations and descriptions:

Initially, she watches and listens and gives operative attention to his drawing and talking, asking herself what its essential elements are.

She does as she has seen him do, enacting the verbal description he has given. She constructs in her own performance what she has seen as essential in his, experiencing from the inside the patterns of action she had observed from the outside, and she produces a new product that may be compared with the one Quist has made.

She can now reflect on her own process, asking what rules, operations, and understandings she has enacted, comparing these with Quist's earlier descriptions. How, for example, has she "worked back and forth between unit and total"? She can reflect on her new product, comparing it with Quist's, asking herself whether she has "got it" and what she has got.

As she repeats this process, both the component actions and the reflections on action, she may at some point discover that she has internalized the performance. What began as an imitative reconstruction of Quist's action, she now experiences as something of her own, a new element of her own repertoire available for use, through seeing- and doing-as, in the next design situation.

What Petra learns in this process depends on the content and quality of her reflection-in-action. She may pick up some of Quist's mechanical operations (for example, his way of representing how "summer sun comes in here"), his language, or his mannerisms. She may learn that a soft back garden area is nice or, on the contrary, that she must make appreciative judgments of her own. She may learn only to impose this particular geometry of parallels on this screwy slope or, instead, to step into any initially incoherent situation by imposing on it a coherence of her own devising. Whatever she learns, she will reveal in her further designing, creating a new object of possible reflection.

The Ladder of Reflection

When telling/listening and demonstrating/imitating are combined, as they usually are, they offer a great variety of possible objects and modes of reflection that can be coordinated to fill the gaps inherent in each subprocess. Questioning, answering, advising, listening, demonstrating, observing, imitating, criticizing—all are chained together so that one intervention or response can trigger or build on another.

The chain of reciprocal actions and reflections that makes up the dialogue of student and coach can be analyzed in several ways.

We can begin with a straightforward map of interventions and responses, for example:

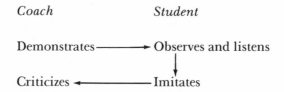

Such a picture simply displays a sequence of actions, arrows indicating assumed causal links between elements of the sequence.

We can also introduce another dimension of analysis, a vertical dimension according to which higher levels of activity are "meta" to those below. To move "up," in this sense, is to move from an activity to reflection *on* that activity; to move "down" is to move from reflection to an action that enacts reflection. The levels of action and reflection on action can be seen as the rungs of a ladder. Climbing up the ladder, one makes what has happened at the rung below into an object of reflection. For example, a coach may reflect on the message implicit in his own performance; a student may reflect on the problems inherent in her own drawings. Climbing down the ladder, one acts on the basis of a previous reflection. Having reflected on an earlier performance, the coach may offer a new demonstration, or the student may try a new drawing.

Diagonal moves along the ladder of reflection occur when one party's action triggers the other's reflection or when one party's reflection triggers the other's action. For example:

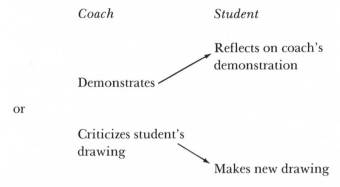

Coach   *Student*

                                  Reflects on coach's demonstration

Demonstrates

or

Criticizes student's drawing

                                  Makes new drawing

When things go wrong at one level of activity—when one party is stuck or does not understand or feels misunderstood—then it is possible, by climbing up a rung on the ladder of reflection, to communicate about the stalemate or misunderstanding the person has experienced at the level below.

We can think of the rungs of the ladder of reflection in the following way:

4. Reflection on reflection on description of designing.
3. Reflection on description of designing.
2. Description of designing.
1. Designing.

At the base, designing is (as we have seen), in its own way, a process of reflection-in-action. One level up, reflection on designing takes the form of a description—for example, "I have aggregated these smaller shapes into the larger, L-shaped classrooms." Description may be combined with appreciation: "It relates [grades] one to two . . . which is more what I wanted to do educationally anyway." Description may be incorporated into advice or criticism: "I wouldn't worry at this point about the shapes of the roofs," "Horrible—it just ruins the whole idea." Description may refer to knowing-in-action implicit in designing—for example, "You have tried to fit the shapes of the buildings to the contours of the slope, but the slope is screwy."

Two levels up, in reflection on description, the coach might ask, for example, "What does she mean when she says, 'Larger in scale, more satisfying'?" or "What does her 'big problem' say about her way of framing the design task at this point?" The student might ask, "What does he mean by describing the gallery as 'in a minor way the major thing'?" She might put her reflections into a question or try out a new drawing that she sees as following Quist's advice. Coach or student may reflect on the meaning the other has constructed for a description he or she has given. Quist might ask himself, for example, what Petra has got out of his whole demonstration, wondering whether she has grasped the idea of imposing a discipline that can be broken open later.

At the fourth level, finally, the parties to the dialogue might reflect on the dialogue itself. They might ask, privately or publicly, whether they have come any closer to a shared under-standing of the problem or tested their understandings of each other's meanings. If, on reflection, they are dissatisfied with their efforts at communication, they might experiment with new strategies or media: "Perhaps it is time to visit the site," "Perhaps it would be helpful to try a different kind of drawing."

Progress in learning need not take the form of climbing up the ladder of reflection. The work of reciprocal reflection-in-action inherent in telling and listening, demonstrating and imitating, may go very well without recourse to higher levels of reflection. But when coach and student are stuck, their ability to move up or down the ladder opens up new possibilities in the search for convergence of meaning.

Not least important, negotiation of the ladder of reflection offers possible responses to a student's doubts about the value of her instructor's message. A successful dialogue of student and coach need not end in the student's compliance with the coach's intentions. On the contrary, the more she understands what he means, the more she may discover that she does not want to learn what he has to teach. Conversely, when a student fails to under-stand through apparent incapacity or unwillingness to learn, the coach ought to consider the possibility that the "failure" is attributable not to her shortcomings or even to his inadequate coaching but to her refusal to give up something she sees as valuable. Such discoveries are reliably made, however, only when student or coach can be reasonably sure of having constructed an accurate picture of the other's meanings. Negotiating the ladder of reflection is a way of submitting such private constructions to public testing.

Conclusion

Through what sort of process, then, can a student begin to educate herself in designing when, at the outset, she does not understand what designing means and can neither recognize nor produce it? What enables a coach to help her undertake such a process when, at the outset, he cannot communicate to her what she needs to learn?

Design studios are premised on a particular kind of learning by doing. The student is asked to start designing before she knows what designing means. If she accepts this challenge and the perceived risks it entails, entering, tacitly or explicitly, into a contract with the coach that carries with it a willing suspension of disbelief, she begins to have the sorts of experiences to which the coach's language refers. She puts herself into a mode of operative attention, intensifying her demands on the coach's descriptions and demonstrations and on her own listening and observation.

Her initial efforts at design provide the coach with evidence from which to infer her difficulties and understandings and a basis for the framing of questions, criticisms, and suggestions.

Within limits variable from person to person, the student comes to the studio with a capacity to follow instructions so as to carry out technical operations whose meaning she does not yet understand. Similarly, she comes to the studio equipped with a capacity for imitation, an ability to do as she sees another person doing, so as to reproduce elements of an activity whose meaning she does not yet understand. Executing such performances, she experiences them, feeling what they are like and discovering in them, by reflection, meanings she had not previously suspected.

When coach and student coordinate demonstrating and imitating, telling and listening, each component process fills gaps of meaning inherent in the other. The coach's demonstrations and self-descriptions, the student's efforts at performance and self-descriptions, the comparisons of process and product, provide material for reciprocal reflection-in-action. Learning and coaching to design become experiments in the work of designing and in communication about design.

When experimentation generates new problems, puzzles, and confusions, these, too, can become material for reciprocal reflection. Communicative dead ends can yield to movement up or down the ladder of reflection.

For both student and coach, effective search for convergence of meaning depends on learning to become proficient at the practice of the practicum—and this may seem to imply a vicious learning circle. The coach must learn ways of showing and telling matched to the peculiar qualities of the student before him, learn how to read her particular difficulties and potentials from her efforts at performance, and discover and test what she makes of his interventions. The student must learn operative listening, reflective imitation, reflection on her own knowing-in-action, and the coach's meanings.

Does it not seem that she must be capable of reflecting-in-action in order to learn to reflect-in-action? But the reflection-in-action essential to the practice of the practicum is not the same as the reflection-in-action essential to designing. Students bring to the studio, in greater or lesser degree, generic competences for communication, experimentation, and imitation on which they can build, in dialogue with the coach, in order to learn to do the cognitive work of learning to design.

It is not enough, however, for student and coach to have these competences; they must also choose to exercise them, adopting a kind of stance toward each other that we shall explore in the next chapter.

❦ Chapter Six ❦

How the Teaching and Learning Processes Can Go Wrong

In this chapter, I shall examine some of the contextual features on which the success of the dialogue of student and coach may depend: the stances adopted by the two parties toward their joint effort at communication, the theories-in-use they bring to their patterns of interaction, and the qualities of the behavioral world they create for each other. I shall show how these features are interrelated and how they can facilitate or hinder the work of reciprocal reflection-in-action.

Stance

Some studio masters feel a need to protect their special artistry. Fearing that students may misunderstand, misuse, or misappropriate it, these instructors tend, sometimes unconsciously, under the guise of teaching, to actually withhold what they know. Some students feel threatened by the studio master's aura of expertise and respond to their learning predicament by becoming defensive. Under the guise of learning, they actually protect themselves against learning anything new.

When either party sees and feels about the studio situation in this way, he or she can spoil the search for convergence of meaning. That party's *stance* toward the interaction impedes the exercise and development of competences for reciprocal reflection-in-action. Indeed, one might think of "stance" as itself a kind of competence, since it involves not only attitudes and feelings but ways of perceiving and understanding. At the very least, we should recognize stance, in this sense, as a condition for the acquisition of competence: being willing to try something is a condition for acquiring an ability to do it.

Let us begin, then, by considering how the student's stance toward studio experience can impede or facilitate her self-education in design.

Earlier, concerning the willing suspension of disbelief, we noted that the student is called on to plunge into the experience of the studio without really knowing what it will entail. She is asked to let go of earlier understandings and know-how, along with the sense of control and confidence that accompanies them. She is expected to experience confusion and puzzlement. She is asked to trust the studio master and become temporarily dependent on him, while still retaining a sense of responsibility for self-education.

Once she has entered into an initial contract with the studio master, the demands on her do not come to an end. She must be willing to try out his approach to designing and conduct an active search for the essential meanings of his instructions and demonstrations, even when these conflict with her own prior understandings. In order to discover how her existing tacit knowledge conflicts with what she wishes to learn, she must be willing to reflect on it.

When it comes to the studio master's demonstration, she is asked to take up a stance of reflective imitation—even though she is very likely to feel an abhorrence of imitation, especially if she belongs to a culture (like the American one) that espouses independence of thought and action. Negative feelings toward imitation may take any of the following forms:

> "I do not want to become dependent on you; I want to preserve my own identity."
> "I do not want to give up my freedom of action; I don't like to be constrained by you."
> "If I imitate you, I accept your authority and become your subordinate."
> "If I imitate you, I lose my originality; I merely reproduce your actions without real feeling or understanding of my own."

"If I imitate you, I give up my right to govern myself."

Such inhibitions seem linked to our idea of being grown up, which we conceive in terms of independence, freedom of choice, and fully vested selfhood. They are also linked to an ideology of education that advocates thinking for oneself (consider the withering epithet "Copycat!"). But inhibitions against the *idea* of imitation are very much at odds with the almost universal *practice* of imitation. Students in American culture, especially those fresh from an experience of adolescent rebellion, are likely to be profoundly ambivalent toward imitation, despising it in theory but embracing it in practice.

It is possible that this ambivalence is a phenomenon peculiar to certain national, or even class, cultures. In my experience, students from Far Eastern countries seem to be unconflicted about imitation; they expect to imitate their teachers and may be disconcerted by the prospect of doing anything else. Even in the United States, an apprentice machinist usually learns his trade by imitating just what he sees the master machinist do.

In any case, the willingness to imitate is a willingness to put oneself, at least for a while, in a position associated with a child's dependent role. Given the ambivalence of many students toward imitation, they may be willing to enter into that role only at the price of hiding from themselves the fact that they are doing so. Their ambivalence may drive them paradoxically, toward imitation of the blindly mechanical variety. Reflective imitation demands, on the contrary, a willingness to do as the studio master is doing and, at the same time, reflect on what one does. Consciously entering into the master's way of designing, the student adds to her range of possible performance and extends her freedom of choice.

There is a student in Quist's studio—we shall call her Johanna*—who, in all the respects outlined above, manifests to a very high degree a stance conducive to reciprocal reflection-in-

---

*"Johanna," like "Judith" and "Northover," "Quist" and "Petra," is a fictitious name asigned by Roger Simmonds to a participant in the design studio he observed.

action. Of all the students in that studio, she seems uniquely gifted with a capacity to learn from her interactions with Quist, and she is regarded by students and faculty alike as the best designer in the group.

Faced with the very conditions that drive some students to desperation and leave others with the feeling that they are caught in a Kafkaesque guessing game, Johanna describes Quist's instructions as "top notch." She seems, from the very beginning, to have grasped something that remains elusive to the others.

Quist is a strong advocate of a particular approach to designing. All the students react, in one way or another, to his powerful presence. All of them are, at least in some measure, afraid of it. But Johanna, alone among the students, reflects on her own ambivalence toward Quist. In one of her interviews, she offers the following comments:

> In a way, I completely trusted Quist's judgment, and worried about it. But in looking at it now, he doesn't work that way—he works with your own ideas and never imposes his own except in the most positive way of helping you to extend and see the implications of your own ideas. I don't think we are getting that doctrinaire a line. But in a way, it is laziness. You want a quicker way to get there. *I feel that even if someone is very dominant now, I will always be able to undo it later.* I feel many of the best people learned in that old Beaux Arts tradition where they got a very authoritarian line but later were able to get out of it.

Her words recall Quist's,

> You should begin with a discipline, even if it is arbitrary . . . you can always break it open later.

Just as Quist points out that designing depends on an initial imposition of an order which one can always break open later, so

Johanna accepts her initial dependence on an authoritative structure of meaning imposed by another because she feels confident that she will always be able to undo it later. She can will the suspension of disbelief in Quist's approach and also the suspension of her earlier beliefs, because she feels confident of her ability to evaluate it *once she has understood it,* to look back on it, and to break it apart. She can relinquish control for a time and leave the direction of her development open-ended because she feels confident in her ability to control the larger process that includes this temporary loss of control.

Similarly, Johanna reveals in her notebooks a preoccupation with the twin issues of freedom and discipline, issues central to the predicament in which she finds herself. She is conscious of the paradoxical requirement that she give up freedom, in designing as in learning, in order to gain the freedom that comes with new levels of understanding and control.

> Freedom is discipline—the step beyond progressive education . . . freedom *from* something is not freedom.

She is articulate about the oscillations, implicit in Quist's view of designing, between commitment and detachment.

> These are paradoxes and need a dual response, one simultaneously of detachment and commitment, the freedom of the first *allowing* the second.

Her ability to hold her ideas "loosely" gives her the freedom to perceive, compare, and coordinate many different meanings and sets the stage for an eventual commitment based on richer understanding.

Her attitude toward the entire studio experience, as she describes in her notebooks, shows up more concretely in her account of her approach to a particular task, the design of the school. Here, she begins with the idea that there must be a "skeleton, a core that all else nods to":

> The experience of the spine must be varied,
> must be exciting, must be sequential, must have
> climax, must be able to be used for other purposes,
> must sort out circulation activities, must have sur-
> prises and not give itself away. Direction is from top
> to bottom—must be a clue to the whole building.

She concerns herself with the relation of this core idea to the site:

> I went back to the site after the first idea and
> there was no way in which I could put it there. It is
> a totally wooded area, a beautiful area. People were
> using it just to walk in. . . . I said, "There must be
> some reason I can justify putting it there." Then I
> decided that that was the point when an architect has
> to say no! At base, it was wrong.

When her first idea collides with her respect for what is valuable in
the site, she is able to let that idea go.

The germ for her second idea comes as she draws the
contours for the new location—

> The contours coming in on the north side
> close together hit the building broadside and, when
> released through the stretched area of the building,
> are looser, freer.

The spine remains but no longer as the dominant theme. In the
new idea, classroom walls are at right angles to the changing
direction of slope, their angles determined by the slope. Of her new
approach, she says,

> Nestled into the hill—change in levels—home
> bases centered around resource center at angle to
> allow access to outside—positioned to get morning
> sun from the east.

Johanna is able to entertain multiple perspectives on a new experience with the confidence that she will be able, later, to choose among them and to coordinate them. In the studio as a whole, as in a particular design task, she can accept an initial discipline, confident that she will be able to break it open later. She can make an initial, as-if commitment to a point of view—her own or Quist's—and, later, distance herself from it. Her capacity to hold ideas loosely is a kind of "disciplined freedom," a "detached commitment."

If Johanna feels relatively little anxiety at the prospect of temporarily relinquishing control to Quist, it is because she has confidence in her own capacity to entertain, compare, coordinate, and restructure her own meanings. If she is not frightened by a temporary surrender of independence as she enters into Quist's view, it is because she can articulate to herself the cognitive work she can and must do and the situational predicament within which it must be done.

Quist's stance toward Johanna is, at least as she perceives it, very well matched to her own. He is prepared to advocate and demonstrate his view of designing. He is also prepared, as she says, to avoid imposing his own ideas on her. He is willing, as his dialogue with Petra shows, to reflect on his own designing. He says, in the interview quoted in Chapter Four, that he is open to the student's challenge and confrontations. We have seen how, in his dialogue with Petra, Quist does not reach out to test the impact of his words or actions on her. With Johanna, however, Quist's failure to test what the student makes of his interventions seems to have little or no negative effect. Her willingness to try to enter into his way of seeing things and her active search for his meanings seem to be sufficient to enable her to make very effective use of Quist for her self-education in designing.

Behavioral Worlds and Learning Binds

Other students in Quist's studio—more than a few of them—profess to find Quist problematic, threatening, and domineering. They have difficulty in learning anything from him. These are students who do not initially share the complex of attitudes that enables Johanna, in interaction with Quist, to make the experience of learning productive. One of these students, Judith, exhibits an initial stance that is in many ways the opposite of Johanna's.

Judith comes to the studio already armed with a strongly held view of architecture. What is required, she believes, is "a technology through which the user becomes largely the creator of his or her own environment." She recognizes only one programmatic need, namely, "flexibility . . . and that has no formal implications." Not surprisingly, her teachers find her work wanting; they accuse her of failing to think architecturally. But Judith is well defended. She construes her disagreements with her teachers as ideological ones; the teachers are simply on the wrong side of the fence.

> They've had their day in court, they can't handle the problem anymore . . . Their buildings can't be adapted to future use. . . .
>
> Because they believe in universals, they ignore the client. They even say so. They also ignore the user for the same reason.

Thus, Judith refuses to enter into a willing suspension of disbelief in her teachers' perspective and of belief in her own. Instead, she sees herself as a partisan who must engage her teachers in combat.

As she enters the studio, Judith could be described as confronting, partisan, defensive, ideological, and frozen in her own view. But this is her *initial* stance. What happens to her as the studio unfolds?

What happens to her is recorded, painfully, in the protocol of her dialogue with Northover, one of Quist's assistants—a dialogue typical of her interactions with her instructors. Like Petra's dialogue with Quist, this is a desk crit, and it occurs at about the same stage of her work on the problem of the school. It reveals a process of systematic miscommunication. Not only do the two parties fail to achieve convergence of meaning, each fails almost completely to understand what the other is talking about. And the process by which they fail shows how a student's initially resistant and defensive stance and a complementary stance by the instructor lead both parties to create a behavioral world (an interrelated context that shapes their views of their own and the other's actions) in which it is impossible for either to break through their mutual misunderstanding. They create for each other what I shall call a "learning bind."

Judith begins the dialogue with a comment on her plans for siting the school:

> *Judith:*   I haven't decided yet whether it's going to
> be sited right here or right here—I have the feeling
> it's going to be here and I'm going to make it level.

She describes the choice of site as a matter of "feeling," as though to say, "If I feel it's right, then it is!"

> *Northover:*   Do you have this to a large scale
> somewhere?

From our experience of other instances in which studio masters ask this question, we can infer that Northover asks for a scale drawing because he believes it to be essential to design experimentation. At this point, however, he does not state the thought behind his question.

> *J:*   Not right now, no. But it works as far as south-
> ern orientation—being far enough from here so I
> don't get drainage problems, being near enough to
> this flat area so I can set up playgrounds. . . .
> *N:*   So you don't have it on a site plan at all!

Judith shows her awareness of some of the norms relevant to siting the school, but Northover does not respond to these. He focuses on her omission of a site plan, again without saying why that omission is crucial. At this point, Judith launches into a long defense of her approach to the problem:

J: No, that didn't seem necessary, because it will be
flat. I've concerned myself with the building. We've
talked about the whole notion of progressive and
experimental schools, and I've stayed with this
decagon shape because it really is appropriate for the
number of classrooms I need. . . . Also you have
fewer windows and less surface area, so that I am
conserving energy.

But let me start with the plans . . . the main entrance
would be over here . . . when you walk in, there are
administration and health offices—there is this long
lobby for exhibits—this leads through to the gym—
I'm going to put seating in here and a stage here.
Here is a ramp which spirals up. The classrooms
begin here, and every portion of the decadon goes up
two feet. . . . It begins with the kindergarten and
preschool areas—across from this is the rest of their
play area plugged under the spiral, which has risen
to sixteen feet by then. I took an acoustics class last
term, and I'm designing this so that it will be very
nice acoustically.

She has decided that the decagon will do, because it fits the
number of classrooms and conserves energy. She has hit on a shape
for the building as a whole, a spiral, and has found a way to plug
in the necessary spaces. Elsewhere, she calls her spiral a
"Guggenheim."

She seems to have a very sparse repertoire of features drawn
from a few design domains. She says, in effect, "If I have *some*
feature on which to make a decision, then I'm OK!" But she is
unaware of this sparseness. She seems not to know that there are
many relevant domains, nor does she know how to draw out the
consequences and implications of her moves across multiple
domains.

Northover asks where the next floor plan is. Judith replies
that she has not thought it necessary to make one. She proposes to
put "art and cafeteria" on the main level and asks whether he

thinks this a good idea. He says, "That is possible, I guess." Then he asks about level changes and circulation. "Most people will use the ramp," she hopes.

> *N:*   Why do you want this stepping up?
>
> *J:*   Well, when I visited open schools, the one thing they complained about was the warehouse quality— of being able to see for miles. It would visually and acoustically break up the volume.

Again she has in mind one norm, building character, and one problem, "warehouse quality."

> *N:*   I think you have got to really discipline yourself to draw it up to scale and draw a section through it— let's just assume that these ramps do work, that access—if so, this ramp will cut off the views to and from the library.

That is, "You cannot really tell whether the ramp solution to circulation will work or whether you have solved the problem of warehouse quality until you draw it to scale and in section. And you must accept the discipline of doing it." Northover then gives her an example of a flaw in her design which she might discover by means of this discipline.

> *J:*   No, this ramp is really just a porch.
>
> *N:*   Yes, but it has a thickness which must be considered. It is difficult to read, you really need a section.
>
> *J:*   No, I need a model.
>
> *N:*   No, a section will really be sufficient.
>
> *J:*   But do you understand it even if it is poorly drawn?
>
> *N:*   Why was the gym left out of the whole schema?

She intends the ramp to be just a porch, to have no thickness that needs worrying about, but Northover points out that it will be thick whether she wants it to or not. She might discover this through a sectional drawing, but she may not know how to do such a drawing. In any case, she takes Northover's comments as a criticism of her drawing, yet it is clear that she sees drawing not as thought-experimenting but as a way of presenting ideas.

Northover seems to be saying, "You are not really designing at all. You are simply having 'ideas' and putting them down on paper. The moves you make have consequences that are testable, but you must draw to scale and in section in order to test them. The whole process of designing is lost to you because you will not do these things."

Judith, in contrast, thinks of designing in terms of simple shapes like the decagon or the spiral, which will allow users the freedom to construct their own forms. At most, such shapes need to be coupled with attention to such considerations as acoustics, energy conservation, or avoidance of warehouse quality. A basic idea, once discovered, can be decided on once and for all, and it can always be made to work. It is as though Judith understood the notion of arbitrary imposition of a geometry but not the discovery and testing of its consequences.

Judith and Northover bring to their dialogue two widely discrepant models of designing. The main difference between them is not the conflict over "form" versus "user participation"; it is, rather, that Judith simply has no idea what Northover means by drawing, conceived as a process of trying out design moves and discovering their consequences and implications. Nor does she grasp what he means by "knowing what something will look like." Similarly, Northover seems to have an inadequate picture of the perspectives and priorities Judith brings to her task and the image of designing that informs her responses.

If Judith wanted to discover the meaning of Northover's criticisms, she would have to focus on the gaps and mistakes he points out, trying to construct and test for herself the model of designing that makes these stand out for him. But she is very far from wanting to do this work. On the contrary, she sees the crit as a new battle in her continuing war with her teachers. She tries to ward off Northover's criticisms, which she sees as attacks, by getting him to admit that he understands and likes her big idea. To this end, she adopts several strategies. She brushes aside his probing questions, and when Northover points out a mistake he cannot help noticing, she dismisses it by making a perfunctory admission of error.

> *J:*   Once you are there, the whole thing is at the same level.
>
> *N:*   No, it's not, because there is a level change here.
>
> *J:*   OK, you're right.

At other times, she clings tenaciously to her view in spite of everything Northover can say to the contrary.

> *N:*   Don't you feel there were other rooms that didn't fit also—rooms that needed to define their own shape?
>
> *J:*   Well, I don't find the system that restrictive.
>
> *N:*   It is true of the classrooms, I won't argue, but what about other spaces? You say everything is possible but don't give reasons.
>
> *J:*   No, it's possible—it works, it really does.

She does not inquire into the basis for his questions and criticisms, nor does she seek to reflect on or test her own assertions. When she occasionally seems to be asking for criticism, her words suggest that it is really approval she wants:

> *J:*   What I need to know is what you feel about the scheme. Is it too complex? —I think it's fairly simple as a school.

With increasing desperation, she ignores Northover's questions and bids for his approbation. Yet she does not express her feelings directly, nor does she surface her view of this interaction as an episode in her continuing ideological struggle with Northover.

Northover, meanwhile, follows a strategy of "mystery and mastery." He asks many questions—"Where is the next floor plan?" "At what elevation is that?" "What is the main circulation system?" "How do you get from here to there?"—but keeps to himself the meanings underlying his questions. From time to time, he puts her answers together in his mind and comes up with a negative attribution, which he springs on her:

> So you don't have it on a site plan at all!

And from time to time, he advocates what he thinks she should do:

> I think you have got to really discipline
> yourself to draw it up to scale.

But he does not connect such prescriptions to the view of designing from which they flow.

Northover does not invite Judith's inquiry into his meanings, nor does he inquire into hers. He does not respond to her increasingly urgent bids for approval:

> *J:* But do you understand it even if it is poorly drawn?
>
> *N:* Why was the gym left out of the whole schema?

It may be that throughout the dialogue he feels caught in a dilemma that he voices only at the end—that he would like to respond to her questions but cannot do so because she is so far from having presented him with a scheme that makes her ideas understandable. And when he finally expresses that dilemma, he seems mostly to be trying to soften the blow:

> *N:* I'm not saying that you should be discouraged
> but that you should do more detailed work—the
> reason I can't give strong opinions is that I honestly
> can't feel what it will look like yet.

Judith and Northover seem to be playing a kind of game in which they drive each other round in circles.

Judith presents her grand scheme, for which she seeks Northover's understanding and approval. Northover sends out questions, criticisms, and prescriptions, all aimed at getting Judith to realize that she has not been designing at all. She perceives these interventions as attacks. She defends against them. She returns with increasing desperation to her own objective. Northover pursues his point, telling her that she must draw, she must really work it out in detail, until he seems to be afraid that he may have demoralized her completely. At this point, he tells her not to be discouraged.

Within their game of attack and defense, both Judith and Northover fail to notice that they have missed each other's meaning. Judith thinks the idea is there in the drawing; Northover says he can't feel what it will look like. He tells her to draw; she takes him to mean that she presents her ideas poorly. What he means, however, is that, without drawing in detail and to scale, she cannot experiment to discover the consequences of her moves. Judith pleads for his reactions to her idea; for Northover, there is as yet no idea.

If Judith were aware that Northover means something very different by designing than she does, she would find his meaning mysterious. Northover, who seems to think she shares his view of designing, regards her refusal to make detailed scale drawings as a sign of sheer stubbornness. He must feel frustrated because he cannot get her to carry out elementary design procedures. For Judith, the skirmish with Northover must reinforce her sense that she is engaged in an ideological battle with all her teachers.

Each of them constructs views of designing, meanings of key terms, and interpretations of the entire interaction that are incongruent with the views, meanings, and interpretations held by the other—and both seem unaware of this fact. The possibility of reciprocal work toward convergence of meaning depends on their discovering their present incongruity. But this they are unlikely to do, for each of them perceives the interaction as a conflict rather than as a failure of understanding. Nor is the game of attack and defense conducive, for either of them, to reciprocal reflection.

Later in the year, Judith will succumb to what she regards as superior force. As she says in an interview,

> After a particularly aggressive session with Quist . . . [I decided that] I must give my critics what they want.

But from the background of her experiences in the studio, she will not be able to understand what her critics mean when they say what they want, much less give it to them. She will try to lay on "metaphors," "scale drawings," and "formal functions." But since she has never grasped the meaning of these elements within Quist's view of designing, she will succeed only in grafting them onto what her critics regard as a nondesign. She will not be able to produce anything they can accept as architecture.

If we consider the dialogue of Judith and Northover from the point of view of the general conceptual issues that it raises, we can describe their process as one in which student and instructor succeed in creating a behavioral world in which the learning predicament becomes a learning bind. Moreover, as they create their behavioral world, they employ a shared pattern of behavior toward each other.

Judith's initial stance, toward the studio in general and this interaction in particular, is combative, hostile, rigid, and defensive. Yet she also wants something from her interaction with Northover: appreciation for what she has done. Thus, she seeks both to defend herself against his "attacks" and to secure his approval. From this point of view, we can describe the interpersonal theory of action—the values, strategies, and underlying assumptions—that she brings to the dialogue. She seeks to achieve her objective—defense of herself, appreciation for her accomplishments—as *she* defines it; she does not seek out Northover's goals for the interaction. She sees herself as involved in a win/lose game that she tries to win through strategies of unilateral control and defense—brushing aside questions she does not wish to answer, clinging tenaciously to her position, asking for criticisms in such a way as to elicit approval. At the same time, she tries to avoid the negative consequences of winning. She withholds her negative feelings—she does not accuse Northover of the hostility that, in a private interview, she attributes to all her teachers. She preserves a surface of cool reason. She appears to ask real questions, she gives some justification for her positions, and when Northover drives her into a corner with his arguments, she gives in to him in a perfunctory way.

Northover employs a very similar theory-in-use. He, too, has an objective for the interaction: to get Judith to see the inadequacy of her design and carry out (his view of) the fundamental procedures of good designing. He tries to achieve this objective unilaterally; he does not try to understand what she may want from the interaction. He, too, sees himself as involved in a win/lose game, and he tries to win. He seeks unilaterally to control the dialogue, shifting from one target of opportunity to another. He asks questions to which he already knows the answers ("Don't you feel there were other rooms that didn't fit also?"), uses argumentation to convince her of his position, tries to drive her into corners. At the same time, he withholds the intellectual basis of his questions and the negative feelings—irritation and frustration—that he is very likely experiencing. Finally, when he says, "I'm not saying you should be discouraged" and "I honestly can't feel what it will look like yet," he tries to soften the negative effects of his efforts to penetrate her defenses and win the argument.

The theory-in-use that Judith and Northover share conforms to a model of interpersonal theories of action that Chris Argyris and I have called Model I (Argyris and Schön, 1974). It is a model of unilateral control, win/lose strategies of mystery and mastery, withholding of negative feelings, and surface rationality. It is a model in which individuals make negative attributions to others which they test only in the privacy of their own minds—never publicly, out loud, with the other person.

When the parties to a pattern of interactions sustain Model I theories-in-use, they tend to create a certain kind of behavioral world, that is, a certain kind of communicative context which they perceive as reality. This is a win/lose world in which defensiveness and unilateral self-protection are the norms. Characteristically, however, within this world each perceives the other, and not himself, as defensive and as unilaterally bent on winning. It is a model in which each tends to see himself as caught in a dilemma, which he keeps to himself; negative attributions about the other are not publicly tested but are simply taken at face value. It is also a model of mutual deception, in which each party tries to win, exercise control, penetrate the other's defenses, while preserving an impression of cool rationality and concern for the other's feelings.

Such a behavioral world inhibits reflection—and therefore learning—at several levels. When each party is caught up in an effort to achieve his own objectives and win at the other's expense, he is unlikely to reflect on his underlying value assumptions, invite the other's challenges, test what the other makes of his utterances, or surface the dilemmas he experiences. Each participant constructs meanings for the interaction that inhibit reciprocal reflection. Neither one seeks out information that could disconfirm his view of the other or strives to make his assumptions confrontable by the other.

The meshing of these theories-in-use produces a behavioral world within which it is not possible to isolate troublesome phenomena so as to discover and juxtapose the different descriptions that each participant would construct for those phenomena. Rather, each party strives to persuade the other or to fend off the other's attacks. Each strives to impose his or her way of seeing on the other rather than enter the other's world so as to understand vicariously how a statement previously opaque could seem an explanation. Each demonstrates for the other the very norms and strategies (private testing and judging, suppression of feelings that might signal openness to inquiry, unilateral self-protection by speaking in inferred categories far removed from directly observable data) that are likely to keep their win/lose game from surfacing as an object of shared inquiry. Hence the behavioral world of the interaction becomes, for all practical purposes, self-sealing—a disease that prevents its own cure.

Judith and Northover are as unlikely to reflect on their incongruent views of designing as on their miscommunications. Far from being willing to suspend her disbelief in Northover's view of designing, Judith persists in fending off his attacks, at the same time pleading for his approval. It does not occur to her to explore his view of designing. She thinks she knows what it is; and in any case, she could not do so without seeming to make herself vulnerable in a battle she is determined to win. Northover cannot explore her understandings of his statements as long as he strives only to convince her of her mistakes, nor can he invite her confrontation of him or engage her in reflection on their dialogue without making himself vulnerable.

Here, student and studio master create for each other a behavioral world in which the learning predicament becomes a learning bind: Judith, locked into a view of designing from which she cannot discover what Northover thinks she needs to learn; Northover, locked into a mode of interaction in which he cannot help her discover it. They are stalemated at the lowest level of the ladder of reflection.

Unbinding

Although the case of Judith and Northover is certainly extreme, it is by no means unique. Any student's learning predicament can easily become a learning bind.

The potentials for this transformation are present in every design studio. Communication about designing is always subject to the impediments of ambiguity, vagueness, and inexpressibility. The understandings of student and instructor are always initially more or less incongruent. Under these circumstances, miscommunication is highly probable. Its correction depends on student's and studio master's being able and willing to search actively for convergence of meaning through a dialogue of reciprocal reflection-in-action. But this depends, in turn, on the creation of a behavioral world conducive to such a dialogue, and several factors may work against its creation. The student's early experience of loss of control, competence, and confidence—always present to some degree—can readily produce a sense of vulnerability that leads the student to become defensive. And the instructor may respond to the student's defensiveness, as Northover did, by strategies of unilateral control that increase defensiveness and reduce the chances for reciprocal reflection. Then the stage is set for a win/lose game. Once such a game has begun, moreover, the participants' Model I theories-in-use are likely to keep it going.

If the instructor tries to maintain unilateral control of the dialogue and the student resists him, then in the ensuing rounds of attack and defense it is unlikely that either party will stop to reflect on his or her own meaning or inquire into the other's. If the instructor tries to maintain unilateral control of the dialogue and the student submits to him, then it becomes difficult for the student to make a public test of her own understandings or explore the instructor's meanings, for this might undermine his unilateral control. If a student is confused and unable to articulate her confusion, then she needs to be helped to see that questions are possible and encouraged to ask them; but such encouragement is incompatible with a theory-in-use like Northover's that is based on mystery and mastery.

Once a learning bind is created, the search for convergence of meaning requires that student and studio master try to enter not only into each other's way of seeing design but into each other's ways of framing the interaction in which they are engaged. Northover would have to reflect on his way of designing and on Judith's, on his way of framing the interaction and on her's. And she would have to do likewise. They would have to test their reflections by on-the-spot experiments that would be impossible unless each could get valid information from the other. Judith would have to be able to tell Northover how she was seeing her interaction with him and how she understood the meaning of his questions and criticisms; Northover would have to be able to do the same for her.

These, then, are some of the elements of reciprocal reflection-in-action essential to unbinding a learning bind:

- Focus of attention on the present interaction as an object of reflection in its own right.
- Getting in touch with and describing one's own largely tacit knowing-in-action.
- Reflection on the other's understandings of the substantive material that the instructor wants to convey and the student wants to learn.
- Testing what one has understood of the other's knowing-in-

action and framing of the interaction; testing what the other has made of one's own attempts at communication.

* Reflection on the interpersonal theories-in-use brought to the communicative process.

In effect, student and studio master would have to extend their ladder of reflection, adding to it a "rung" of reflection on their own interaction, their behavioral world, and the theories-in-use by which they create and sustain it. They would have recourse to this level of reflection when things were not working and were locked in at the lower levels.

But in order to participate in this process, the student must already be able to get in touch with and describe her own intuitive understandings and enter into the studio master's, both in the domain of designing and in the domain of her interaction with the master. She must be able to put aside what she knows in order to enter into the as yet unknown world of someone else, to experience a zone of uncertainty where, having given up for the moment her usual ways of seeing, she is still unconnected to the other's ways of seeing. For this, she needs a capacity for cognitive risktaking. Rarely, a student—like Johanna—brings to the studio the strong sense of self on which this capacity depends. For most students, the wish to avoid uncertainty, coupled either to a win/lose theory-in-use or to an unreflective deference to the instructor's authority, makes it impossible to participate in such a process. A demand that they do so would place them in a vicious learning circle— asking them to exhibit, in order to learn, that which they most need to learn.

Responsibility for initiating a breaking of the learning bind must lie, in the first instance, with the instructor, who is presumably better equipped to do what the student cannot as yet do.

Let us explore, for example, how Northover might have dealt differently with Judith. What might he have done? And what competences would he have needed in order to do it?

Suppose Northover were to surface at the beginning of the interaction the dilemma he suggests at the very end,

> The reason I can't give strong opinions is that
> I honestly can't feel what it will look like yet.

If he were to do this, he would begin from a position that might (in a win/lose context) be perceived as one of weakness. He would start now from his inability to respond, but in a way that invites a question of the following kind:

> What do I have to do so that you can feel what
> it will look like?

The way would then be paved for Northover to describe what he means by a design idea or, better yet, to demonstrate, starting from a feature of Judith's approach, how by "drawing in scale" she might evolve a design idea.

If he were to start by surfacing a dilemma he feels, Northover would be encouraging Judith to explore his meanings rather than only clinging to her own. And Judith's exploration would increase the likelihood that Northover would open up for her inspection the system of understandings and know-how essential to his view of designing.

Or we can imagine a different approach that might take off from the ending of the dialogue we have already read. Northover might say something like:

> This discussion leaves me frustrated and wor-
> ried. Frustrated, because I don't think I'm helping
> you get at what lies behind my judgments and advice.
> Worried, because I may have discouraged you. I'd
> like to know whether these things are true.

Northover's expression of these feelings might encourage Judith to express her own feelings of anger and frustration at having been unable to get through to Northover or to pry out of him some appreciation of her work. His public reflection on their dialogue might encourage Judith to surface her own perception of it as a battle. The way would then be open for any of several lines of inquiry. Northover might say, for example,

It may be, as you say, that you attach more importance than I to the user's changing needs and less importance than I to the formal qualities of the building. But it seems to me that I haven't communicated or you haven't grasped what I mean by designing—even where the designer puts highest priority on use of the building.

He might then describe to Judith some of the things that lead him to this inference, asking for her agreement or disagreement. If Judith were to agree that she does not grasp what he means by designing, he might then propose that she join him in exploring an example of a design process in which considerations of building use and flexibility are joined to norms drawn from other design domains. Or, if she were to disagree, he might ask her to show him, in relation to her own drawings, what she means by designing. Or again, he might ask her to make explicit, by description and illustration, how her own understanding of designing differs from his.

Each of these interventions suggest a theory-in-use very different from the one Judith and Northover illustrate in the actual dialogue. The interactions I have suggested emphasize surfacing private attributions for public testing, giving directly observable data for one's judgments, revealing the private dilemmas with which one is grappling, actively exploring the other's meaning, and inviting the other's confrontation of one's own. These are elements of the interpersonal theory of action that Chris Argyris and I have described as Model II (Argyris and Schön, 1974). Its values, as we have described it, are those of valid information, free and informed choice, and internal (rather than externally generated) commitment. Its strategies include advocacy of one's views and interests coupled with inquiry into the views and interests of others. It is a theory-in-use built on a recognition of the fact that in every statement of ours we convey a twofold message. There is, first of all, the message conveyed directly—for example, "Let us test whether we have understood each other." But there is also the message conveyed by the theory-in-use that, intentionally or unintentionally, we model for each other. Students share with all human beings a great capacity for attention to messages at both levels and, especially, to their incongruity. If Northover were to espouse the reciprocal testing of meanings—even uttering sentences like the ones I have suggested—but were, at the same time, to convey to Judith a sense that this was simply a new stratagem for "winning," then she would be likely to pick up and play back to him, not the theory of action he espoused, but the tacit intention he conveyed.

In order to be able to recast his approach to interaction with Judith along the lines I have proposed, Northover would have to make a significant change in his theory-in-use, one that would cause him both to reflect on what he does in interactions like this one and to become proficient at inventing and producing alternatives to it. Not only would this require a new sort of reflection-in-action, it would also very likely require help from someone else.

In Chapter Ten I will discuss such transformations and the help appropriate to them. At this point, it is perhaps sufficient to observe that Northover is caught, at least for the time being, in a learning circle of his own—unable to engage Judith in reflection on their stalemated interaction because he is as yet unable to reflect on and restructure the theory-in-use he brings to it.

The Story of Dani and Michal

This discussion should not end with the impression that there is only one right approach to the learning predicament and the learning binds that may result from it. I believe, on the contrary, that there are many possibly effective approaches. Each of these makes special demands on its proponents; it suits some participants and learning contexts and not others. Counterintuitive as it may seem, for example, students may respond positively and openly to the basketball coach who yells at them mercilessly— but yells at *everyone,* under the same predictable conditions.

The story of Dani and Michal illustrates an approach very different from Quist's or Northover's or my suggested alternative to Northover's. The story was told and discussed at a workshop on the design studio, held at the School of Architecture and Planning at the Technion, in Israel, in November 1983. Dani, a practicing architect and studio master, had asked Michal, who had been a first-year student of his eight years before, to be present. In addition to Dani, participants at the workshop included several members of the architecture faculty and me.

I shall begin by telling the story in the words of Dani and Michal—their initial descriptions of the events and their responses to questions asked along the way.

> *Dani:*   I recalled the work that Michal Z. did when she was a first-year student, eight years ago. Even though it has been a long time since then, I remember the events and the feel of the project pretty well. I was teaching, and . . . it was "Introduction to Design," your first semester in the Technion. . . .
>
> In any case, I suddenly remembered this event, which was very unusual for me. Toward the end of the semester, I saw Michal was struggling with her work, and her project did not look at all like this [refers to drawings on the wall]. I asked her to show me her work, and I saw something like this [draws]—some buildings . . . and a corridor and rooms. It was uninspired, institutionalized, and the whole thing looked a little like a motel. I did not like it, but I did not say so. I just asked Michal if she liked what she was doing.
>
> *Participant:*   What was she supposed to design here?
>
> *Dani:*   I forgot to mention that—a field school. Maybe Michal should continue from here.
>
> *Michal:*   First of all, there were three projects in the semester, and this was the third and last one. We had about a month, and the subject was living quarters in a field school.
>
> What else would you like me to say?
>
> *Dani:*   Whatever seems important to you.
>
> *Michal:*   The evening before the session with Dani,

I remember thinking, This is not what I want. It really looked like what Dani drew over there.

There were also some buildings that I tried to have winding with the topography, or something like that. One story. And I remember that on the previous evening I more or less came to the conclusion by myself that I wanted something else. I could even define what I wanted.

Now Dani, in the session the next day, was supposed to instruct us what to prepare for the presentation, how to draft, etc. It was the last session a week before the end of the semester. I remember we even spoke about the elevation—I want such and such a type of windows and I don't want it to be symmetrical, or I do want it to be symmetrical, etc. We spoke about what to draw and how to build the model. And then he asked, "What do you think? Do you like it? What do you feel about it?" Then I was able to tell him the truth, that it really was not at all what I wanted and that, actually, I wanted . . . three things. . . .

First, I said, if it is a field school, then the "field" comes before the "school," before the house. I want nature to be dominant. I also told him, I want it to be a social experience for the groups that visit the field school. Usually classes visit and the kids all know each other, and I want it to be a social experience for them. And the third thing is, I want it to be a place that will develop their senses—that will sensitize them to changes, to feel. An unknown place will make you more aware of everything.

So Dani said to me, "Look, the semester is over already. But don't give up. Maybe during the vacation you will be able to do what you wanted. If you do, come to me and show me what you did." We spoke about how, maybe during the vacation, I would sit down and try to accomplish what I wanted. But the same evening, I came home and sat down and did it. That evening, I was very focused and I finished the building layout.

The next day, I came to Dani and said, "Look, I did this." Oh!—there is another important stage. When I told him the three things I wanted, he took a pen and started to sketch, "Maybe this way . . . or that." He very freely went over all kinds of possibilities, various designs. I think he made a kind of jump, and from that stage it was only [a little way] to the stage where it was really possible to actualize it [Figure 2]. . . .

Figure 2. Plan of Building in Field School.

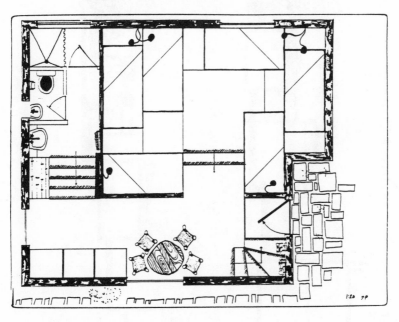

Dani: . . . We tried to clarify how to go about doing all that. How to make it hidden, what is the meaning of a "social experience." . . . Could you tell a bit about the social experience, some events or scenarios of social experience that were later expressed in your work?

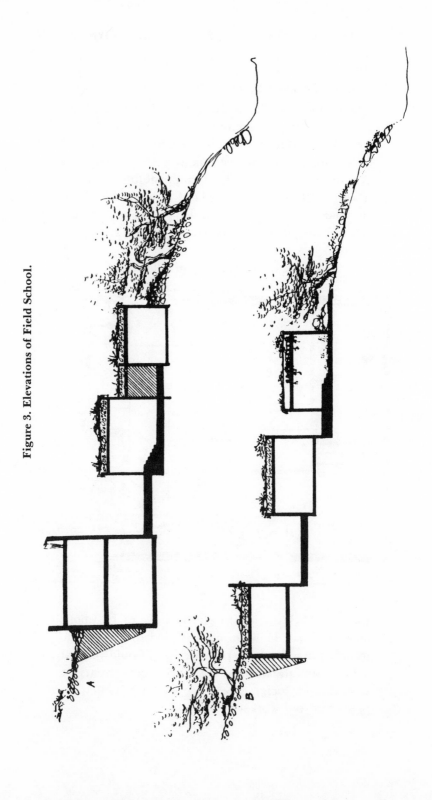

Figure 3. Elevations of Field School.

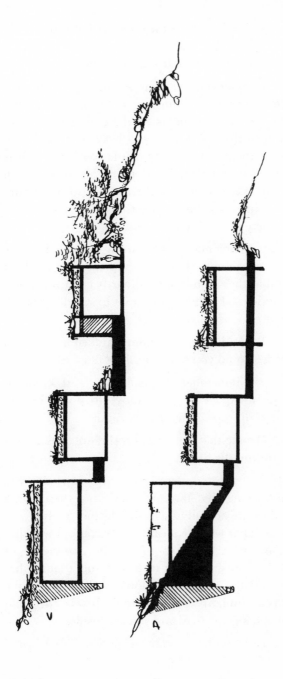

Michal: I don't remember all the details.

Dani: I remember. For example, you should be able to enter the room without exactly being inside. That is, to peek in, see who is in there, and be able to decide to join or not after you have seen what and who is in there. You can see if it is your gang that is in there, what they are doing, if you feel like joining them, etc. . . . I remember there was also something about surprises—chance meetings that could take place where people's paths cross. . . .

Michal: I remember another thing. I wanted to give excuses to people to look into and enter all kinds of rooms that they would not ordinarily enter because it was not theirs. I remember excuses to wander around, different reasons to come to a certain spot. . . .

Dani: What did we say about "hidden"? How did you do it? Could you tell about it or draw it?

Michal: I remember in general . . . all kinds of little sections, views from above to down below, views that disappear and then reappear. . . .

Dani: We see that your section [Figure 3] is as if it is continuing the hill.

Michal: I wanted people to approach the site without seeing that there is a building there. Only when they are actually there should they realize they are there. That was the idea. . . . My concept was that you come to a field school for the experience of nature. So you should not see a building, that is what you see all the time. You should walk through the trees and suddenly you see that this is the field school. This is the field and you are inside. . . .

Dani: How is the concept "experience in nature" expressed?

Michal: I tried to keep all the vegetation and I had a problem with wide margins. You have to see how to get back to the trees from all this dug-out, built-up area. That bothered me very much and I thought about it a lot. . . .

Dani: I see there, in the second section from the right [Figure 4], someone is standing near the table, with one arm stretched outside. I can't get into your head, but I'd interpret that as part of the experience of nature. It is very varied. In some places, we see nature framed in a kind of window. In another place, you can touch it. In another place, you can go out into it.

Figure 4. Section of Room in Field School.

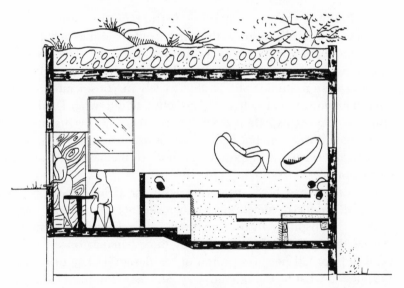

Michal: Also, different things can be seen from different heights. When you are on the lower level, you face the lower part. And if you are above, you see far into the distance. . . .

Later in the session Michal described how she had conceived of her *first* solution:

Michal: You can put it another way. I thought of what was wanted of me.

Participant: What do you mean by "wanted"?

Michal: It could have been satisfied, if I knew exactly what was wanted.

Participant: What did you feel was wanted from you?

Michal: A proper solution—it should be convenient, cheap. . . . I remember I had a problem of symmetry because of the WC that, in the front, was not so nice, etc. And I had this problem we were talking about, this elevation. . . .

Perhaps the most striking feature of this story is the vividness and enthusiasm with which student and coach tell it, even though they are eight years removed from the event. Now a practicing architect, Michal has saved the drawings from her first-semester design studio. She is able to tell in considerable detail what happened to her, what she thought and did, what Dani said, and how she reacted. Dani seems to remember the events in even greater detail than Michal does ("very unusual for me," he notes). Clearly, the event was important for both of them. What makes it so memorable?

Michal had been struggling with the field school project and had produced something neither she nor Dani liked. Dani calls it "uninspired, institutionalized, . . . a little like a motel" (earlier, he had described it as like "three bananas on a field"). Dani did not tell her his opinion of her design, but significantly, she guessed what he thought anyway. She herself decided the night before their session that "this is not what I want." The first critical moment seems to have been Dani's question, "What do you think? Do you like it? What do you feel about it?"

This seems to have come as a shock to Michal. It was true that she knew her design was not what she wanted and that she had already considered what she did want. But she had framed the situation as one in which *her* likes or dislikes were of little account. Rather, she had asked, "What was wanted of me?" She had tried to guess exactly what was wanted and felt she knew the answer: a "proper solution"—convenient, cheap, something much like what she had first drawn.

Dani at first "related to the project," talking with her about elevations, windows, symmetry. But then his question "Do you like it?" broke this frame. Surprised and relieved by his question (I think), Michal was able to tell him the truth, that it was not at all what she wanted, and she then described the three qualities she would have liked in her field school: nature should be dominant (the school should be "hidden in nature," as Dani later put it); the school should be a "social experience" for the groups of kids who visited it; and it should be a "place that will develop their senses."

Impressed by the clarity and conciseness of her description of the qualities she wanted to produce, Dani first of all told her "not to give up." Then he sat down with her, took a pen, and began to sketch. Later, Michal described what he did as "doodling":

> He made small sections and spoke and showed
> little schemes. That opened up all the physical
> possibilities for me.

Michal experienced what he did as a "kind of jump" to the stage at which she felt "it was really possible to actualize it." In his drawing, he "opened up possibilities," showing her *many ways* of producing the qualities she desired.

Energized by this opening up of possibilities and perhaps also by Dani's encouragement to actually go ahead and make what she liked, Michal went home, and that very evening ("very focused," as she says), she finished the building layout.

From the richness and enthusiasm with which Michal described the results of her work, it is clear that she still likes what she had done—even at a distance of eight years. Later, Dani stated explicitly what he liked about it:

> I began to see that all of the parts were answer-
> ing those possibilities that she defined. I was really
> pleased with those results, in that respect.

The story of the field school is a story of learning to design as experimentation in producing what one likes. In this process, the coach's functions are several:

- First, to ask what the student wants the project to be, thereby legitimating her own preferences and intentions—indeed, conveying the message that her personal preferences *ought* to be expressed and used to guide her design.
- Then, to encourage her to try to produce what she likes, demonstrating in quick sketches different ways she might do so, "opening up the possibilities." It is important here that Dani suggests many ways—not one best way—to achieve the effects Michal wants. He does not instruct her in the best way to do it; he works with her to open up a range of possible means for her experimentation.
- Finally, to judge the results of her work in terms of her effectiveness in "realizing those qualities she defined."

Dani presents Michal with an opportunity to learn how to practice, where "practice" is conceived as exploration and testing of alternative means of producing the qualities of product she finds appealing. She is invited to attend to her own appreciative judgments, surfacing preferences she might otherwise ignore or suppress.

Dani communicates, implicitly, that Michal should impose her own coherence on the design situation. So she makes the situation coherent by willing for her field school the three qualities of integration in nature, social experience, and development of the senses. She also unlearns, at least in this instance, her habit of dependence on a view of "proper solutions" that she has invested, heretofore, with the full authority of the school of architecture she attended.

In the same process by which Dani encourages Michal to produce what she likes, he guides her through a discipline in which appreciation regulates experimentation. Implicitly, he leads her to see the kind of objectivity achievable in a practice experiment—a kind that is dependent on her subjective preferences: she can judge for herself, independent of mere opinion, whether she has succeeded in realizing the qualities she says she wants.

Dani teaches "technique" here by demonstrating many alternative means of producing the desired qualities. Implicitly, again, he conveys the message that technique is to be learned through experiments that try out and evaluate alternative means of production. At the same time, Michal seems to learn here to observe in a finer-grained, more differentiated way. She seems, for example, to have learned the value of incorporating into the house a variety of ways of connecting with the natural surroundings, enabling the dweller to move from one such connection to another.

Taking all these functions together, it seems correct to say that Michal is being initiated into a process of self-education in designing, a process in which she is exposed both to an image of architectural practice and to an image of "practice" as a form of self-directed experimentation.

Dani seems here to have entered into a kind of contract with Michal, one that differs from Quist's request that the student "suspend disbelief." The elements of this contract seem to be as follows:

> You should step into the situation, advocating the qualities you want to produce; I will accept your preferences, without trying to impose my own on you.
> You must become an experimenter, testing out alternative ways of achieving your goal.
> I will become your coexperimenter, helping you figure out how to do what you want, demonstrating for you how you might achieve your goals.
> You must judge your work—and I will join you in judging it—on the basis of your success in producing what you intend.

This contract creates an interpersonal situation in which Michal and Dani sit, as it were, side by side, as coexperimenters, before the shared problem of producing the qualities Michal prefers:

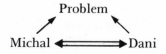

Sitting next to Michal in the presence of a shared problem that originates in her intentions, Dani escapes the dilemma of how to convey negative information to her without triggering her defenses. Information that might otherwise be seen as negative can now be seen, realistically, as helpful to her efforts to achieve her goals.

Dani has created with Michal a situation in which he does not have to struggle with her to get her to share his view of her designing, nor does he have to cope (privately or publicly) with the frustration he feels because his legitimate criticisms are interpreted by the student as personal attacks. He has framed his interaction with her in a different way. He has succeeded in getting her to declare her own preferences; he has joined her in the task of realizing those preferences; he has framed the shared problem as one of experimentation in producing what she likes; and he has defined his own role in that process as one of opening up new possibilities for action.

Conclusion

The possible outcomes of the studio experience are as varied as the possible evolutions of the learning predicament. The student must educate herself to design but can do so only through interactions with a studio master. Depending on the quality of their search for convergence of meaning—on the stance and theories-in-use that both parties bring to that process—the student's learning career is likely to unfold in one direction or another.

When student and studio master are in a learning bind, so that some of the essential elements of designing are frozen in miscommunication, and neither student nor studio master is able to initiate reflection on that process, then any of several unsatisfactory outcomes is likely. The student may become a *counterlearner*, like Judith, refusing to suspend disbelief or to enter into her teachers' views of designing—except to "give them what they want." Or the student may *overlearn* the studio master's message, construing it as a set of expert procedures to be followed mechanically in each situation. She may take as a general rule, for example, what the studio master conceives only as a limited illustration of a more complex idea. Such a student may develop a *closed-system vocabulary,** in which she can state the studio master's principles while performing in a manner incongruent with them and remaining unaware of that fact.

In contrast, a student like Johanna, with the kind of stance and competence she brings to her interactions with Quist and Northover, can succeed in listening actively and imitating reflectively, building up an extraordinary grasp of the essentials of their approaches to designing. Quist's and Northover's apparent disinclination to reflect on their interpersonal theories-in-use is no obstacle to Johanna, because of what she *brings* to the studio. But it is manifestly an insuperable obstacle to Judith. Between Judith and Johanna there are many shades and varieties of possible learning outcomes.

The story of Dani and Michal illustrates another kind of learning outcome and another approach to dilemmas rooted in the learning predicament. At Dani's instigation, he and Michal become coexperimenters in the task of producing qualities Michal has set as goals for herself. Student and coach reframe their interaction, thereby reducing the likelihood of falling into the kind of win/lose game that Judith and Northover play. But avoiding or dissolving a learning bind is itself a problem of experimentation. There are, as I have observed, many possibly effective approaches to it. In order to test any one of them, however, coach and student depend on reciprocal reflection-in-action and on the construction of a behavioral world conducive to it.

I have limited my discussions in this chapter to the interactions of student and studio master. I have not so far discussed the many ways in which the particular qualities of a studio milieu or the culture of the school in which it exists can

*I have borrowed this phrase from Jeanne Bamberger.

influence both the probability that learning binds will occur and the ways they are likely to be dealt with. In this respect, as in others, the institutional context of the school is critically important to the creation and conduct of a reflective practicum. Chapter Eleven will take up these questions.

❦ Chapter Seven ❦

Using a Reflective Practicum to Develop Professional Skills

In this chapter I draw from my observations of architectural design studios the general outline of a reflective practicum—an idea whose application to education for artistry in other fields of practice will be the subject of Parts Three and Four.

Designing, both in its narrower architectural sense and in the broader sense in which all professional practice is designlike, must be learned by doing. However much students may learn about designing from lectures or readings, there is a substantial component of design competence—indeed, the heart of it—that they cannot learn in this way. A designlike practice is learnable but is not teachable by classroom methods. And when students are helped to learn to design, the interventions most useful to them are more like coaching than teaching—as in a reflective practicum.

Why Designing Cannot Be Taught

Design professionals such as architects and urban designers, along with practitioners of such professions as law, management, teaching, and engineering, deal often with uncertainty, uniqueness, and conflict. The nonroutine situations of practice are at least partly indeterminate and must somehow be made coherent. Skillful practitioners learn to conduct frame experiments in which they impose a kind of coherence on messy situations and thereby discover consequences and implications of their chosen frames. From time to time, their efforts to give order to a situation provoke unexpected outcomes—"back talk" that gives the situation a new meaning. They listen and reframe the problem. It is this ensemble of problem framing, on-the-spot experiment, detection of consequences and implications, back talk and response to back talk, that constitutes a reflective conversation with the materials of a situation—the designlike artistry of professional practice.

Several features make this process learnable, coachable, but not teachable.

1. Skillful designing is a kind of knowing-in-action. It is possible to describe rules used in designing—for example, Quist's rules about the uses appropriate to slopes of various grades or Northover's rule that one must draw to scale. But some of the most important rules cannot be followed in a simple, mechanical way. Between a rule like "Draw to scale" and its concrete application in skillful designing, there is always a gap of meaning. In order to act on such a rule, a designer must learn a kind of experimentation— not "trial and error," which suggests an absence of reasoned connection between prior errors and subsequent trials, but a thoughtful invention of new trials based on appreciation of the results of earlier moves. The application of such a rule to a concrete case must be mediated by an art of reflection-in-action.

This helps to explain why students must practice in order to learn to design—suggests, moreover, that their practice must involve reflection-in-action—but does not explain why they cannot learn to design in the sequence of a normative professional curriculum: first classroom theory, then a practicum in its application. To explain this point, we must add that prescriptions like "Draw to scale" or "Impose a discipline, however arbitrary; you can always break it open later" make sense—sense useful for action—only when students are involved in an effort to design something. And for this, there is more than one reason.

2. Designing is a holistic skill. In an important sense, one must grasp it as a whole in order to grasp it at all. Therefore, one cannot learn it in a molecular way, by learning first to carry out smaller units of activity and then to string those units together in a whole design process; for the pieces tend to interact with one another and to derive their meanings and characters from the whole process in which they are embedded.

It is true, of course, that design processes may be broken into component parts by strategies of decomposition useful both to practice and to coaching. For example, Quist helps Petra learn how to go about a particular *phase* of designing: laying out the global geometry of buildings on a site. And with Dani's help, Michal divides the problem of the field school into three smaller problems, each of which consists in producing a desired effect. But in Petra's case, local experiments make sense only within the context of a larger-frame experiment. And Michal cannot make a total design by stringing together the solutions to her subproblems; moves that produce an effect like oneness with nature also have consequences for other effects. Although a larger design problem can be broken into parts, the total solution is not a sum of the smaller ones.

When a student has learned to carry out smaller units of design activity but has not yet learned how to integrate them into a larger design process, the nature of the larger whole is likely to seem confusing. Typically, coaches can describe the gestaltlike coherence of a web of design moves, consequences, and implications only in oblique, usually metaphorical terms (like Quist's "It would ruin the whole idea!" or "in a minor way, the major thing"). And students are likely to find such descriptions opaque until they have actually experienced the coherence of a whole design process in their own designing—at which point they may find an instructor's metaphor illuminating.

3. Skillful designing depends on a designer's ability to recognize and appreciate desirable or undesirable design qualities. If a designer knows how to recognize qualities like "enclosure," "privacy," "directionality," "softening of hard-edged forms," or "working slightly with the contours," he can regulate his move-experiments by reference to them. A student who knows how to recognize qualities like these can learn to experiment with different means of producing them, and an instructor can help her to do so. If a student does not already know how to recognize a particular design quality, however, she is unlikely to be much helped to do so by verbal descriptions alone (although, of course, some descriptions may be much more helpful than others). For one thing, an instructor may not be able to say what he means by such

phrases as "good form," "nice view," or "strong lines"; and even when he can do so, students may be unable to figure out just what *experienced* qualities those phrases are meant to denote.

A student may be helped to recognize and appreciate quality like "enclosure" or "directionality," however, without recourse to verbal description. A coach can show her examples, nonexamples, and variations of the quality in question, naming each of these as he goes along. He can demonstrate how a design configuration can be changed so as to give more or less enclosure or directionality. And he can then ask the student to discriminate among examples that have enclosure or directionality in greater or lesser degree. When he does these things, of course, his instruction is a form of coaching; he helps his student to learn to recognize design qualities by guiding her through a particular kind of learning by doing.

Even when a student learns, in this way or others, to recognize a design quality in someone else's production, she may still find it difficult to recognize it in her own. Typically, as we noted in Chapter Four, she learns to recognize a quality like "the softening of hard-edged forms" in the same process by which she learns to produce it.

4. What is true of the description and recognition of design qualities is more generally true of the description and recognition of skillful designing.

The description of one's own knowing-in-action is itself a skill, and designers may possess it in greater or lesser degree. Designers can learn to make better descriptions of designing— more complete, accurate, and useful for action—by continued reflection on their own skillful performances. How far they can go in this direction should remain an open question, however, testable in each new effort at description.

The limits of description may be set by a designer's inability to say what he knows or by the inherent inexpressibility of some aspect of design knowledge. It seems more reasonable to put these limits to the test in each new instance than to assert either that essential features of designing are inherently inexpressible in words or that design knowledge, if it exists at all, must be wholly describable in some formal symbol system.

Even when design instructors do succeed in making verbal or graphic descriptions of designing—descriptions that appear to *them* to be relatively full, accurate, and useful—beginning students are likely to find them strange, vague, ambiguous, or incomplete. Terms like *draw, use metaphors,* or *impose a discipline* may be especially confusing because their uses in the field of architectural design differ from their ordinary meanings or because they belong to the idiosyncratic vocabulary of a particular designer.

For any or all of these reasons, the meanings students initially construct for their instructors' descriptions of designing are very likely to be incongruent with the meanings their instructors intend.

The clarification of intended meanings and the discovery and resolution of incongruities between instructors' intentions and students' understandings are best achieved through *action*. It is when instructors act out their descriptions, as in Quist's demonstration, that students are more likely to see what they mean. And it is when students try to act on what they have seen or heard that they are likely to reveal, to themselves and their coaches, both the prior knowledge they bring to the studio and the understandings or misunderstandings they have constructed for their coaches' interventions.

5. Designing is a creative activity. A designer's reflective conversation with the materials of a situation can yield new discoveries, meanings, and inventions—as Quist, for example, came to see the gallery in a new way, as "the sort of artifice Aalto would invent." It is possible, of course, to talk about the creative side of designing. It is also possible—and far more useful—to illustrate it, as Quist did, by a demonstration. But no such description or demonstration can enable a student to make the *next* invention or discovery without engaging in her own version of reflection-in-action, for the process described or demonstrated is one of coming to see and do something in a new way. If it were fully describable in advance, it would not be new.

Again, there is necessarily a gap between description and action; and again, students can learn to fill it by engaging in the action of designing. Here, however, the gap results not from imperfect description or understanding but from the creativity inherent in designing.

For several reasons, then, a designlike practice cannot be conveyed to students wholly or mainly by classroom teaching:

- The gap between a description of designing and the knowing-in-action that corresponds to it must be filled by reflection-in-action.
- Designing must be grasped as a whole, by experiencing it in action.
- Designing depends on recognition of design qualities, which must be learned by doing.
- Descriptions of designing are likely to be perceived initially as confusing, vague, ambiguous, or incomplete; their clarification depends on a dialogue in which understandings and misunderstandings are revealed through action.
- Because designing is a creative process in which a designer comes to see and do things in new ways, no prior description of it can take the place of learning by doing.

From all this, of course, it does *not* follow that students cannot learn to become proficient at designing in all the senses listed above. They can do so, and they can be helped by exposure to explicit descriptions of designing. Some descriptions of knowledge useful for design—characteristics of site and program, for example, or directions of summer and winter sun—students may be able to understand before they begin to design. Moreover, students differ in their readiness to make use of an instructor's descriptions, just as instructors vary in the clarity with which they can say what they want their students to learn. The point is, rather, that under the best of circumstances—maximum readiness to understand, on the student's part, and maximum clarity, on the instructor's—some essential features of designing cannot be described ahead of time so that students can make useful sense of them. In order for such descriptions to become useful for action, students must be engaged in learning by doing and in dialogue with someone in the role of coach.

The Starting Conditions of a Reflective Practicum

As we have seen, a significant part of what a beginning student of designlike practice needs to learn, she cannot understand before she begins to design. She must begin designing in order to learn to design.

Not surprisingly, confusion and mystery reign in the early stages of a design studio or in any reflective practicum. Yet often, in a matter of a few years or even months, some students begin to produce in some significant measure what they and their coaches regard as competent designing; and student and coach achieve a convergence of meaning evident in the ease with which they appear to understand each other, finishing each other's sentences, speaking elliptically in ways that mystify the uninitiated.

Coach and student make this transition—those who do so— by joining in a particular communicative enterprise, a dialogue of words and actions.

Dialogue of Coach and Student. In their dialogue, coach and student convey messages to each other not only, or even primarily, in words but also in the medium of performance. The student tries to do what she seeks to learn and thereby reveals what she understands or misunderstands. The coach responds with advice, criticism, explanations, descriptions—but also with further performance of his own.

When the dialogue works well, it takes the form of reciprocal reflection-in-action. The student reflects on what she hears the coach say or sees him do and reflects also on the knowing-in-action in her own performance. And the coach, in turn, asks himself what this student reveals in the way of knowledge, ignorance, or difficulty and what sorts of responses might help her.

The coach's reflection-in-action revolves around two issues that are always alive in the dialogue (I shall presently add a third). He must deal, first of all, with the substantive problems of the designlike task. He must demonstrate designing, in various respects and at various levels of aggregation. He must also describe designing, in the modes available to him—advice, criticism, questioning, or explanation. But, second, he must *particularize* his demonstrations and descriptions. Demonstrations must be keyed to the tasks this student is trying at the moment to carry out. Description must be suited to this student's momentary confusions, questions, difficulties, or potentials. So the coach improvises, drawing variants of descriptions or demonstrations from his repertoire or inventing them on the spot. He also reflects from time to time on his own performance, asking, in effect, "Just what is it I spontaneously do in this situation?" so that he can more accurately describe the moves he may suggest to his student. His interventions are on-the-spot experiments. They test, at the same time, his understandings of his own knowing-in-action, his awareness of the student's difficulties, and the effectiveness of his interventions. In this process, the coach must be able to travel freely on the ladder of reflection, shifting, as the situation requires, from designing to description of designing or from description to reflection on description and back again to designing.

The student, for her part, tries to construct and test the meanings of what she sees and hears. She enacts the coach's descriptions ("Work back and forth between unit and total," for example) and reflects on the experience of enacting them. She may also reflect on her own spontaneous performances in order to discover what she already knows that helps or hinders her learning. She tries, through reflective imitation, to construct in her own actions the essential features of the coach's demonstrations. She, too, carries out improvisatory, on-the-spot experiments to discover and test what the coach may be trying to communicate to her. And in order to do these things, she adopts a particular kind of stance—taking responsibility for educating herself in what she needs to learn and at the same time remaining open to the coach's help.

The two dimensions of the coach's task become, in the student's case, like two vectors, each of which contributes to a learning circle. For her, as for the coach, two kinds of practice are involved in the practicum: the substantive designing she tries to learn and the reflection-in-action by which she tries to learn it. Each kind of learning feeds the other, and the resulting circle may be virtuous or vicious.

The student must be able to take part in the dialogue if she is to learn the substantive practice, and she must design to some degree in order to participate in the dialogue. To the extent that she has not mastered the skills of participation in the dialogue, her attempts to learn the practice are hindered. But as she learns the reflection-in-action of the dialogue, she increases her ability to draw from it lessons useful for designing. And the greater her design competence, the greater her capacity for the reflection-in-action of the dialogue.

Student and coach may begin to make the transition from an early stage of confusion, mystery, and incongruity to a later stage of convergence of meaning by the way they embark on the first round of the learning circle.

The coach may give some description of actions to be undertaken, to which the student may respond by doing something that falls roughly within the arena of the coach's expectations. However incompletely or mechanically she performs these initial operations, she can begin by doing so to learn what it feels like to do them and what changes they bring about. In Wittgenstein's potent phrase, she learns the meaning of the operations by performing them. Moreover, she puts herself into a state of mind in which she pays operative attention to the coach's showing and telling. She seeks to discover in her own doing what his messages mean. He, in turn, functions as an essential part of her experimental field—playing, in part, the role of "reality." Given her limited ability to tell for herself whether and in what respects her performance has succeeded or failed, it is on his perceptions that she must initially depend for detection and correction of error.

So the coach gives an instruction, observes the student's action, and instructs or demonstrates again to correct the error he has discerned. Or the student does something that feels wrong, as Petra felt her initial shapes to be wrong, but is unable to say why; and the coach gives her a way of understanding what is wrong and demonstrates an alternative, as Quist shows her how she might carve the geometry of the L-shaped classrooms into the slope. Or the coach may ask the student to do something and then help her reflect on the knowing-in-action implicit in her doing, as Dani helped Michal become aware of her belief that she must produce a "school solution."

In all such cases, the coach assumes that an initial instruction or demonstration will be sufficient to get the student to do *something*. This initiative, rooted in what the student already knows, begins the learning circle. Its function is to get the dialogue started. It provides a first occasion for feedback, which—given the qualities of a designlike practice, the student is very likely to find confusing or ambiguous. So the stage is set for a continuing dialogue of actions and words, of reciprocal reflection in and on action. Through this process, the student may increase her grasp of designing by participating in the dialogue and enhance her ability to learn from the dialogue through her increased capacity for designing.

But the communicative work of the dialogue, with its virtuous learning circle, depends not only on the ability of coach and student to play their parts but on their willingness to do so. Here, feelings as well as understandings are involved, each critically bound up with the other.

Affective Dimensions of the Practicum. The paradox of learning to design carries with it a predicament. For the student, having to plunge into doing—without knowing, in essential ways, what one needs to learn—provokes feelings of loss. Except in rare cases, students experience a loss of control, competence, and confidence; and with these losses come feelings of vulnerability and enforced dependency. It is easy, under these circumstances, to become defensive.

The coach's version of the learning predicament operates at two levels. He must accept the fact that he cannot tell his students about designing in any way they can at first understand, and then he must cope with their reactions to the predicament in which he has helped to place them.

Occasionally, a student like Johanna brings to the studio an ability to experience the predicament of learning to design without becoming defensive. She enters into Quist's view of designing, confident that she can always break it open later. More often, the student's vulnerability in the early stages of the practicum turns to defensiveness, and then the learning predicament can readily become a learning bind. Like Northover and Judith, coach and student may become locked in a cycle of miscommunication. Their dialogue may lead to learning or to a learning bind, depending on their stance toward each other, the behavioral world they create for themselves, and especially the coach's ability to foster a relationship open to inquiry. This is a third dimension of the coaching task, and like the first two—dealing with the substantive problems of performance, particularizing demonstration and description—it is alive in every interaction between coach and student.

Building a relationship conducive to learning begins with the explicit or implicit establishment of a contract that sets expectations for the dialogue: What will coach and student give to and get from each other? How will they hold each other accountable? These questions are not answered once and for all at the beginning (although early interactions may set the tone for later ones) but are continually being raised and resolved in new ways throughout the life of the practicum.

There is no single "right" contract or relationship. Different ones may be equally effective, depending on particular features of project, student, coach, and organizational context. For example, Quist's explicit demand for willing suspension of disbelief is suited to help a student learn a view of designing that she finds initially mysterious. Dani's way of involving Michal in a shared experiment seems particularly well suited to a student who can very clearly describe the effects she would like to produce but has been stifled by her belief that she must deliver school solutions. Quist's chosen model of coaching makes the most of his virtuosity and fluency but also makes it easy for him to avoid exploring what Petra makes of his interventions. Dani's approach liberates Michal from her confining assumption, encourages her to step into the situation with objectives of her own devising, and initiates a process of experimentation that she is able to continue by herself.

These and other approaches to coaching can be seen as policies toward the threefold coaching task. They set general frameworks within which a coach reflects-in-action—addressing the substantive problems of a designlike task, tailoring his moves to the student before him, and building a relationship conducive to learning. In his choice of such a model, the coach more or less consciously runs an educational experiment—one that may turn out to be well or ill suited to his own strengths and weaknesses, the particular student's difficulties and potentials, and the designlike task at hand.

When coach and student do become caught in a learning bind—and they may do so whatever a coach intends—their ability to escape from it depends on the coach's ability to reflect on, and encourage reflection on, the learning/coaching dialogue itself. Such familiar diagnoses as "lack of talent," "inability to grasp the covert things," "unvisualness," or "bad chemistry" may say less about a student's inadequacy than about a coach's failure to negotiate the ladder of reflection. But a coach's ability to encourage reflection on a dialogue that has gone awry requires a theory-in-use that minimizes unilateral protection and places a higher value on inquiry than on"winning"—a theory-in-use like the one Argyris and I call Model II.

Learning Outcomes

It is always difficult to say what a student has finally learned from the experience of a reflective practicum. It is especially difficult to say with reasonable certainty what she has *not* learned, for the experience of the practicum can take root in the subsoil of the mind, in Dewey's phrase, assuming ever-new meanings in the course of a person's further development. And background learning absorbed in a practicum may become evident only when a student enters a new context where she sees what she has learned as she detects how different she is from those around her.

More immediate judgments of what has been learned are bound to be partial and proximate. Nevertheless, it is possible to describe some of the dimensions of learning outcomes, as illustrated by the experience of students in architectural design studios. Each of the following oppositions identifies two poles of an axis along which a student's learning may fall:

- *Closed-system vocabulary/substantive understanding.* A student may be able to do no more than repeat the words she has learned, connecting them to one another but to no experience or action; or she may achieve a substantive understanding of the processes to which the words refer.

- *Unitary procedures/holistic grasp.* A student may learn to carry out discrete procedures, as Judith learns to "put in some metaphors," without being able to integrate them into a whole design process. Or she may learn to combine many different, partial procedures in a coherent web of moves, consequences, and implications.
- *Narrow and superficial/broad and deep.* A student may learn only to solve the problem of a specific project or may learn to see it, in various ways and to varying degrees, as an exemplar for future practice; at the extreme, as an instance of a way of designing applicable to any practice situation.
- *Overlearning/multiple representations.* A student may take the view of designing advocated by a coach as the one right way, committing to it as a true believer—"overlearning" it—or may see it as one view, a way of thinking and doing to be critically analyzed and juxtaposed and combined with other views.

Where a student's learning falls along these continua depends on how he makes sense of the practicum's messages in his own appreciations and performance—which depends, in turn, on the career of his dialogue with the coach. As that dialogue approaches the ideal of reciprocal reflection-in-action sketched earlier in this chapter, the student's learning tends to be broader and deeper and more substantive, holistic, and multiplicit. And the extent to which this happens varies with the abilities coach and student bring to their dialogue: the coach's ability to adapt demonstration and description to the student's changing needs; the student's initial capacity for the reflection-in-action of the dialogue.

In addition to these cognitive capacities, however, much depends on the fate of the student's learning predicament. If a student's initial defensiveness and a coach's reaction to it yield a learning bind that remains undissolved, then the student's learning is likely to take the form of a closed-system vocabulary. If the learning predicament leads to the student's protracted dependence on the coach, then overlearning is a likely outcome. The examples of Quist and Johanna and of Dani and Michal suggest very different forms of a dialogue of reciprocal reflection-in-action conducive to the student's deeper, broader, and more holistic and multiplicit learning.

These relationships are premised, however, on the assumption that a student's learning depends on the sense he constructs for a coach's demonstrations and descriptions. Other factors are also involved. Fellow students may, in various ways, play the coach's role. Other settings—other practicums or practice worlds—may help to shape the student's experience. And, most important, the student's self-education may transcend the practicum: what he gets from it may serve primarily to set the stage for later, more nearly independent learning.

Implications for Professional Education

These outlines of a reflective practicum, based on a study of the traditions of architectural studios, suggest issues and dilemmas central to the *creation* of a reflective practicum for any designlike practice.

A practicum is, as I have noted, a virtual world. It seeks to represent essential features of a practice to be learned while enabling students to experiment at low risk, vary the pace and focus of work, and go back to do things over when it seems useful to do so. A practicum may fail because its striving for realism overloads students with practical constraints or because (as architectural studios are often said to do) it leaves out too many important features of real-world practice.

In order to be credible and legitimate, a practicum must become a world with its own culture, including its own language, norms, and rituals. Otherwise, it may be overwhelmed by the academic and professional cultures that surround it. But if it succeeds too well in establishing its own culture, isolated from the larger worlds of university and practice, then it may become, in the pejorative sense, an artifice—in Hermann Hesse's words, a "glass bead game."

In architecture, some educators search for ways of introducing applied science and scholarship into a curriculum dominated by studio traditions. In other professions, prevailing models of professional knowledge and classroom teaching are bound to be hostile to the creation of a practicum in which overriding importance is attached to learning by doing and coaching. In both cases, the challenge is to invent a workable marriage of applied science and artistry, classroom teaching and reflective practicum.

Creation of a reflective practicum calls for kinds of research new to most professional schools: research on the reflection-in-action characteristic of competent practitioners, especially in the indeterminate zones of practice, and research on coaching and on learning by doing. Otherwise, the schools will find it difficult to determine how their earlier conceptions of professional knowledge and teaching stand in relation to competences central to practice and practicum; their efforts to create a reflective practicum may only produce a new version of a dual curriculum in which classroom teaching and practicum have no discernible relation to each other.

A reflective practicum is unlikely to flourish as a second-class activity. The professional school must give it high status and legitimacy or fall prey to the dilemma of Glazer's "minor professions" where students are forced to choose between low-status "relevance" or high-status "rigor." Coaches must be first-class faculty members, and criteria for recruiting, hiring, promotion, and tenure must reflect this priority. Moreover, the process of coaching and the learning experiences of the practicum must become central to the intellectual discourse of the school.

A reflective practicum is an experience of high interpersonal intensity. The learning predicament, the students' vulnerability, and the behavioral worlds created by coaches and students critically influence learning outcomes. Such issues are equally important in the classroom but tend to be masked there by conventional habits of lecturing and notetaking. Coaches in a reflective practicum are more obviously called on to examine the theories-in-use they bring to instruction; and professional schools, to create an intellectual environment receptive to such reflection.

These are among the issues we will address in Parts Three and Four as we explore the extension of the idea of a reflective practicum to other fields of professional practice.

🏵️ 🏵️ 🏵️ *Part Three* 🏵️ 🏵️ 🏵️

How the Reflective Practicum Works: Examples and Experiments

The three following chapters venture beyond the architectural design studio to examine other traditional or experimental forms of education for professional artistry: master classes in musical performance, psychoanalytic supervision, and a seminar Chris Argyris and I have developed to help students learn our "theory of action" approach to counseling and consulting.

These cases will be used to test the proposition that artistry in other fields of professional practice is designlike; and reflective practicums in other fields, similar in starting conditions, dialogue, and dynamics to design studios. Chapter Eight, on master classes in musical performance—another deviant tradition of education for practice—is closest to the studio. Musical performance is designlike, though radically different in its medium and content from architectural design; and the dialogues of coach and student in master class and studio are essentially similar, though different in ways that reflect differences in the two kinds of practice. Chapters Nine and Ten, on psychoanalytic supervision and "theory of action" seminars, extend the idea of a designlike practice and its reflective practicum to professions outside the arts or design in the narrow sense.

These three chapters develop the idea of a reflective practicum in different ways, not only because of their substantive contents but because they are based on different kinds of data. Like the studies described in Part Two, Chapter Eight uses a series of coaching vignettes to focus on models of dialogue and forms of coaching artistry. Chapter Nine compares vignettes and indirect descriptions of psychoanalytic supervision; it introduces the idea of a hall of mirrors where parallelisms between practice and practicum occupy a central place—for good or ill, depending on the coach's ability to exploit them. And in Chapter Ten, where we have access to the doing and thinking of coaches and students over long periods of time, we will examine students' learning cycles and coaches' reflections on coaching practice.

🌿 Chapter Eight 🌿

A Master Class in
Musical Performance

Musical performance is a kind of designing. It is true that the performer has access to a score that gives him the pitches and durations to be played, along with indications of fingerings, legato and staccato playing, dynamics, tempo, and such expressive descriptions as "furioso" or "andante cantabile." But the performer also has a great deal of discretion. He is free to decide on the groupings of the pitches and their accent patterns, tone quality and "color," and, within broad limits permitted by the score, dynamics, tempo, and rubato. All such decisions are realized by physical manipulation of the instrument: on the piano, fingering, tone production, and pedal; on stringed instruments, fingering and bowing; on wind instruments, fingering, tonguing, and breathing.

These are the physical means by which the performer makes and communicates the sense of a piece in performance. He must discover the meaning of the piece given to him as a score, frame it by the decisions he makes, and realize it by physical manipulation of his instrument. His enacted decisions are moves that he may hear as faithful realizations of his intentions, errors to be corrected, or back talk that reveals surprising meanings to be adopted, together with their implications, in further moves. So the performer makes his ephemeral, temporally unfolding artifact.

In a master class in musical performance, a master teacher works with an advanced student who has prepared a piece from the repertoire of his instrument. The teacher tries to communicate something about sense making and sense realizing in the piece at hand but may also communicate understandings applicable to the performance of other pieces—indeed, to performance in general.

Here, as in a design studio, the teacher confronts a threefold coaching task.

First, he must deal with the substantive problems of performance, drawing for the purpose on many domains of understanding—for example, technical properties of the instrument, acoustics of the physical setting, features of musical structure, style of composition, and details of a composer's life that may hold clues for interpretation. All such issues, together with their implications for the performer's decisions, a coach may communicate not by academic analysis but by a kind of analysis-in-action.

Second, the coach must tailor his understandings to the needs and potentials of a particular student at a particular stage of development. He must give priority to some things and not to others. He must decide what to talk about and when and how to talk about it, deploying for this purpose the full repertoire of media and language at his disposal. He may give verbal advice or criticism, tell stories, raise questions, conduct demonstrations, or mark up the student's score.

Third, he must do all these things within the framework of a role he chooses to play and a kind of relationship he wishes to establish with the student, taking account of the ever-present dangers of vulnerability and defensiveness.

Three Brief Examples

Consider the following description of a master class in cello. This is how Bernard Greenhouse, cellist of the Beaux Arts Trio, describes his early lessons with Pablo Casals:

> We spent at least three hours a lesson. The first hour was performance; the next hour entailed discussion of musical techniques; and the third hour he reminisced about his own career. During the first hour, he sat about a yard away. He would play a phrase and have me repeat it. And if the bowing and

the fingering weren't exactly the same as his, and the emphasis on the top of the phrase was not the same, he would stop me and say, "No, no. Do it this way." And this went on for quite a few lessons. I was studying the Bach D-Minor Suite and he demanded that I become an absolute copy. At one point, I did very gingerly suggest that I would only turn out to be a poor copy of Pablo Casals, and he said to me, "Don't worry about that. Because I'm seventy years old and I will be gone soon, and people won't remember my playing but they will hear yours." It turned out, of course, that he lived till the ripe old age of ninety-seven. But that was his way of teaching. . . . He was extremely meticulous about my following all the details of his performance. And after several weeks of working on that one suite of Bach's, finally, the two of us could sit down and perform and play all the same fingerings and bowings and all the phrasings alike. And I really had become a copy of the Master. It was as if that room had stereophonic sound—two cellos producing at once [Delbanco, 1985, p. 50].

Once this high degree of mimicry had been achieved, however, Casals did something surprising:

And at that point, when I had been able to accomplish this, he said to me, "Fine. Now just sit. Put your cello down and listen to the D-Minor Suite." And he played through the piece and changed *every* bowing and *every* fingering and *every* phrasing and all the emphasis within he phrase. I sat there, absolutely with my mouth open, listening to a performance which was heavenly, absolutely beautiful. And when he finished, he turned to me with a broad grin on his face, and he said, "Now you've learned how to improvise in Bach. From now on, you study Bach this way" [Delbanco, 1985, p. 51].

The task of letter-perfect imitation had been, then, in Casals's mind, a preparation for "improvisation in Bach."

Throughout the lessons, as far as Greenhouse describes them, Casals relied on demonstration. (Greenhouse does not tell us how Casals's reminiscences or discussions of musical technique may have related to the first hour's work on performance.) Sitting a yard from the master, the student was made to reproduce every detail of performance, achieving exact copies of the master's sounds by mimicking his every procedure and gesture. Then, once Greenhouse had learned in perfect detail how to construct *one* performance, with its bowings, fingerings, phrasings, and emphases, Casals presented him with a completely different but "absolutely beautiful" performance.

Here again, Casals gave a demonstration. This time, however, he did not expect Greenhouse to reproduce it. The second performance was to be taken, in juxtaposition with the first, as an object lesson in improvisation. And Casals's broad grin suggested that he had played a good joke on his student, as though to say, "You thought you were learning to play just like me, eh? But you have actually learned something quite different!"

Lest there be any doubt about the matter, Casals *tells* Greenhouse what he has learned—"Now you've learned how to improvise in Bach!"—and adds, indeed, that improvisation of this kind is a preferred way of practicing: "From now on," he commands, "you study Bach this way."

We may wonder, and neither Casals nor Greenhouse tells us, how the painstaking mimicry of one performance and the sudden demonstration of an entirely different one communicate the lesson of improvisation. We might imagine the following explanation.

The "lesson" has two parts. In the first, Greenhouse discovers by mimicry how Casals's performance is constructed in each phrase through the precise details of bowing, fingering, and emphasis. In the second part, Greenhouse sees and hears how an entirely different but equally precise configuration of bowing, fingering, phrasing, and emphasis within the phrase produces an equally beautiful alternative to the first performance. The lesson is not that there are *two* right ways to perform the piece but that there are as many as the performer can invent and produce—each to be realized, phrase by phrase, through a precise coordination of technical means and musical effects, each to be achieved through painstaking experimentation. Casals has opened up possibilities he intends Greenhouse to explore from now on through his own reflection-in-action.

In a deeper sense, the entire lesson consists of demonstration and imitation. In this sense, however, the imitation Casals expects from his student is of a different order, for Greenhouse can appropriately reproduce the larger demonstration only by creating new performances of his own. And, with some sense of paradox— this is perhaps the deeper meaning of the joke—Casals *commands* him to do so. All this reminds me of a story about a Hassidic rabbi whose followers reproached him because he had not followed the example of his illustrious father. "I am *exactly* like my father," he replied. "He did not imitate, and I do not imitate."

Let us turn now to a very different kind of coaching and learning. Several summers ago, I had the opportunity to watch a famous teacher of violin work with a group of gifted young performers. Each student performed the piece that he or she had prepared, while the teacher—whom I shall call Rosemary—sat impassively, listening. After each student had played, sometimes for as long as twenty minutes, Rosemary would begin by saying something like "That was wonderful, sugar." Thereafter, however, her responses were aimed at the particular student before her. Sometimes she talked about intonation (she kept an electronic tuning fork for such cases). Sometimes she focused on details of fingering or bowing. Once, in the case of a German student who listed precariously to one side, she talked about posture. The only time she talked about specifically musical issues was to a young Chilean woman who had chosen not a virtuoso exercise but the first movement of a Brahms sonata, which she had played with great musicality. Rosemary asked her to identify its prinicipal themes. The student obliged by playing first one, then another, then a third. The third one seemed to Rosemary to be a variation of the first. She asked the student whether there wasn't something "transitional." The student found it, played it, and agreed that it was, indeed, a third theme.

Rosemary asked her how she would describe the qualities of these themes. The student thought for a moment. Then she offered the opinion that the first was lively; the second, stormy; the third, reflective. Rosemary said,

> Suppose we wanted to accentuate the liveliness
> of the first. How would we do it?

Rosemary put her head in her hands, thinking about the problem. Then,

> There's an upbeat that goes to a resting place.
> Perhaps you could really *spring* off of it and land on
> the next—ta-*dum!*

The student tried it, produced the effect, liked it. Then,

> How about the third, how would you make it
> really reflective?

The student seemed puzzled. After a while she tried a fingering and bowing that gave a very gentle performance of the figure. Rosemary said, "Yes, you could do that. Or you could also *restrict* the bowing," and she mimed what she meant. The student tried it. Yes, that would work, too.

> Which do you think you'll use?

The student seemed puzzled again:

> I'm not sure, I'll have to think about it.

Rosemary sat back, obviously pleased.

Like the architectural studio master Dani, who asked his student Michal, "What do you want the field school to be like?" Rosemary asked her student, "How do you want these themes to sound?" In both cases, the coaches made it legitimate for the student to like or dislike something, and in both, they invited the student to reflect on the qualities liked or disliked. Then these descriptions were taken as the materials of a problem: how to produce what was liked? Coach and student stood side by side before the same problem. The coach suggested ways of producing the intended qualities, inviting the student to join in a process of experimentation, teaching by demonstration the idea of practice as experiment. And the relationship constructed was not of performer and critic but of partners in inquiry.

A composer and teacher of piano told me about an exercise he sometimes asks his students to do, a kind of experimentation similar to Rosemary's in some ways but different from it in others:

> It's a small, sensible thing. . . . I show them the score of a Chopin étude. Then I ask them to note the intensity of each of a set of high G's. I say, "Rank them from 1 to 5. Don't ask me whether intensity refers to loudness, texture, or the pivotal function of the pitch. Just do it!" They do it. Some assign different intensities to each G; others, the same for all. Then I ask them to play the piece and listen to the intensities they actually give to those pitches. Of course, the intensities they play are almost never the same as those they have written down. I want them to confront their notations with the descriptions actually built into their playing. I want them to hear "what they already know." Then I ask them, "How did you like what you did?" Of course, the exercise only works when two conditions are met—they actually do know a great deal, as revealed by their playing, and they can only partly, or incorrectly, describe what they already know. I want to help them make a description that enables them to get hold of what they already know and then to criticize it, to contrast it with other possible descriptions.

Like Rosemary, the composer invites his students to consider what they like. But here the judgment of "liking" is made in a different context. The students are asked to say how they liked what they *did* and compare it with the understandings implicit in their prior notations. They are asked to reflect on their descriptions as well as on their performance and to compare one with the other. In the "small, sensible" exercise, the students are helped—as in the examples of Casals and Rosemary—to become aware of new possibilities but, at the same time, to become aware of the choices implicit in what they already know how to do.

In each of these three examples, a coach helps a student become aware of differences in musical effects and methods of production that provide a framework for experimentation. There is *this* way of performing the Bach cello suite, with all of its coordinated fingerings, bowings, and emphases, and then there is this *other* way. There is this way of intensifying the quality you want this theme to have, and there is also this other way. There is this pattern of intensities built into your described ranking of the high G's in the Chopin étude, and then there is this other pattern of intensities produced in your performance, and there is, finally, the pattern you like once you have become aware of the possibilities. In each instance, the student learns to expand attention to include different musical effects achievable by different technical means and learns to consider, evaluate, and choose from alternative possibilities for action. He or she experiences practice in the mode of experimentation, where each run of an experiment reveals a new connection between technical means and musical outcome. The student is invited, sooner or later, to attend to his own preferences and to take these, rather than external authority, as criteria by which to regulate his actions. And in each of the three examples—though in very different ways—the coach opens up possible methods and materials for experimentation.

These examples represent variations on a way of dealing with the threefold coaching task: setting and solving the substantive problems of performance, tailoring demonstration or description to a student's particular needs, and creating a relationship conducive to learning.

A Master Class in Piano

In the case I shall now describe more fully, the master teacher is a world-famous pianist whom I shall call Franz; the student, an Israeli boy I shall call Amnon. Amnon, sixteen years old at the time of the lesson, was one of several students assembled at the Jerusalem Music Center for master classes with Franz.

I was not present at the lesson but observed a videotape of it in the course of a workshop on the musical master class in which I participated along with others—musicians, psychologists, and music theorists. Their comments and our discussions together have helped me to arrive at the following description of the lesson.

Franz and Amnon sit side by side, each at his own piano. In front of them, unseen by us as we watch the tape, there are television cameramen and, to the side, a small audience, which includes Amnon's mother and his teacher. In this setting, Franz has already given several master classes, each to a different student playing a different piece. Amnon is to play Schubert's *Wanderer Fantasy*, Opus 15, a piano piece whose second movement draws on a phrase from Schubert's song *The Wanderer*, a musical setting of a poem by Von Luhbeck (Schubert, 1822).

On Franz's piano there is a copy of the score; on Amnon's, there is none. Even without a score, however, Amnon seems able to begin at any point in the piece and play from memory.

The lesson begins with Amnon's performance of the first two movements. He plays fluently, with a triumphant air, beautifully but in a way that is also—at least in comparison with the way he will play it later in the lesson—rather flat, undifferentiated, not very moving or interesting. Franz observes and listens, his eyes fixed now on Amnon's hands, now on the score. Franz's face is middle-aged, worldly-wise.

When Amnon finishes, there is a round of enthusiastic applause. Franz quickly joins in and then makes a careful transition to the business at hand:

> Very nice. Beautiful, beautiful! I'd like to hear
> you go on. But one can't have everything. So if we're
> going to discuss it a little bit . . . it's very, very good.
> . . . My main criticism, it is, I think it's, I find it a
> little too gentle—

and then, perhaps in reaction to an expression of disappointment on Amnon's face,

> too gentle, believe it or not, for this piece. A little bit smooth, you are making it a little too unified. The same between loud and soft. It can be, you know, this piece, a sort of expression of despair.

He lands on "despair" with a rather theatrical emphasis. Then he begins to talk about the song:

> You know about *The Wanderer,* and the song. *The Wanderer,* this desperate, *desperate* searching for happiness that is somewhere *else,* you know. The last lines of *The Wanderer,* it says, "There where you're *not,* there is your happiness, where you're *not.*"

And quickly, gathering momentum as he goes,

> Of course, one doesn't have to play the whole piece like this, but some of it has that . . . tremendously unlimited despair! You make it a little bit too smooth. I know, you're probably afraid of making ugly sounds, and remember the last piece [performed in the master class] where we said, No matter how dramatic, keep it beautiful. It's a little bit different in this piece. If you sometimes go overboard a little bit with your sound, don't worry about it. It is that kind of a piece, especially in the last movement, which we haven't played, but you can really sort of let go . . . and already in the beginning.

And with this, he launches into the first few bars,

His playing of this passage does, indeed, convey a sense of desperation. The first two measures are very contained. The repeated rhythm holds the melody in one place, builds up energy that finally explodes into the sixteenth notes, and drives to the final chord.

This is the first theme of the fantasy. Franz will concentrate on it for a long time, considering now one aspect of it, now another. Then he will shift to a *subito piano,*

where Schubert interrupts the phrase—dropping back, as it were, to extend it and then rolling to a conclusion that ends the exposition of the first theme. Following this, there will be a development section,

which leads into a second theme:

Franz does not make explicit reference to what music analysts would call the "structure" of the piece. He does not use such terms as *first theme, development, second theme.* But in his selection of the places in the score to which he pays special attention, concentrating always on problems of performance, he highlights the structure through analysis-in-action.

When Franz has completed the first few bars, he pauses to comment on what he has done.

> It's not terribly beautiful, what I did, not terribly beautiful, but I don't think it *has* to be. You make it sort of triumphant [plays a little, "triumphantly"]. It *isn't* triumphant. It's desperate, you know.

Amnon now asks, "Should I try it?" and Franz replies, "Of course." Amnon plays the same few bars, Franz singing in accompaniment,

Yam-ba-ba-bum ba-ba-bum ba-ba-bum-<u>bum</u>!

Then,

> Yes, very good. Much better. But at the same time, *phrase* it!

And he plays the first two phrases again, singing,

Ya-ramp-pa-pa ya-ta-ta ramp-pa-pa ra-pa-pum-<u>pum</u>!

Amnon goes on to the second phrase now, Franz still singing with him. But midway through, he interrupts again:

> Wait! Wait! Don't come too soon!

Franz then plays again,

... pum-pum

His pause ("Three, four!") bridges the two answering phrases:

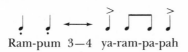

Ram-pum 3—4 ya-ram-pa-pah

His hands hover above the keys. At his "three, four!" he makes a sweeping gesture that articulates the pause, slowly moving down across the keys, "filling" the silence between the two answering phrases. In spite of the silence, the two phrases are connected. When Amnon repeats them, however, his pause somehow fails to establish their connection.

Franz does not dwell on this point but shifts his attention to another aspect of the first few bars:

> Now, don't overdo what I said. I said, it doesn't have to be beautiful. . . . By the way, [to the audience] I hope you all take this with a grain of salt. I don't mean it should be unbalanced. It should never, it should not be—

Ram-pum—three, four!—one . . .

. . . pum-pum

On the first playing, he demonstrates imbalance of emphasis on upper and lower pitches of the chords; on the second, balance. It need not be "beautiful," but it must be "balanced." And now he tells both what he means by balance and how, technically, to achieve it:

It should be still top, and less thumb.

That is, the little finger of the right hand, at the top of the chord, should strike its key with more force; and the thumb, at the bottom of the chord, should strike its key with less.

The same rules apply that we have been discussing all the time, of balance of sound. All I meant to say was, don't make it smooth. But same balance.

Franz plays the chords again and listens as Amnon plays them.

That's right!

Then he goes on to play the next few bars:

Ram-pa-pa-pah ta-ramp-pa-pa-pum.

Now see, we always say, no matter whether something is awfully loud, *pianissimo, mezzo forte, fortissimo,* the phrasing is the same, whether it's— [loudly]

Tim-ta-ta-tim da-da-ta-ta-tim

or [softly]

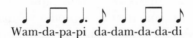
Wam-da-pa-pi da-dam-da-da-di

Franz is illustrating and trying to make clear what he means by phrasing. Whether the figures are played loud or soft, one must understand and communicate the underlying structure of the phrase—how the notes are grouped, how they have direction in their movement toward a goal, how they are shaped.

So, in his treatment of the first few bars of the piece, Franz has begun by criticizing Amnon's playing: it is too gentle, smooth, unified, too much the same between loud and soft; it should be "desperate." In his first, "not terribly beautiful" performance, he demonstrates "desperation." When Amnon imitates Franz's playing of these first few measures, however, Franz shifts his attention to another aspect of performance. He insists that Amnon also "phrase it." And he indicates by a variety of media and

methods what it means to do so. First, he plays the measures again.
He also sings over his playing, as in

Ya-ramp-pa-pa ya-ta-ta ramp-pa-pa ra-pa-pum-pum!

The syllables Franz sings are grouped in clusters, with a different
number of beats in each, exemplifying the groupings and levels of
groupings in the phrase, as shown above. Later, when Franz wants
to show what it means to hold phrasing constant while varying
dynamics ("whether something is awfully loud, *pianissimo, mezzo
forte, fortissimo . . .*"), he uses different syllables ("Tim-ta-ta-tim"
versus "Wam-da-pa-pi") to show how the character changes while
the phrasing remains the same. He also uses gesture in combination with playing and singing to indicate the direction of the
musical figure—the impulse toward the last *"pum,"* which also
goes *on,* as his gesture shows. With his combined playing, singing,
and gesture, Franz actually *designs* the phrase.

Then, as Amnon tries to reproduce what Franz has done,
Franz corrects him and shifts attention again—this time, because
Amnon ought to have "waited" between the first two phrases, as
Franz now demonstrates by counting, playing, and gesturing to
make the pause seem like a breath that both separates and connects
the two phrases. Finally, in a last shift of attention, Franz corrects
Amnon's "overdoing" of the not terribly beautiful sound. The
final chords of the phrase must still be "balanced." Franz plays the
chords, cites the rule of balance of sound, and gives a specific
instruction about the production of balanced sound: "still top and
less thumb."

Thus, in his treatment of these first two phrases of the
piece—some six measures in all—Franz has executed four shifts of
attention. He begins with the feelingful quality of desperation and
then turns to phrasing, metric order, the all-important pause, and
finally balance of sound. In each instance, his improvised response
to Amnon's playing goes beyond the manifest content of Schubert's score to its further meanings. Through qualitative descrip-

tion, technical instruction, and demonstration, he shows Amnon how to make *more* of what is there.

From the two phrases that announce the first theme, Franz proceeds to the next few measures, which build steadily toward a climax—interrupted, however, by a *piano tremolo,*

during which Franz exclaims,

> A tremendous . . . *[subito piano]!*

Franz plays the *subito piano* again and then again, emphasizing the sudden shift to the soft *piano tremolo.* He plays it again, singing, as though in accompaniment,

> I can't help it!

Now Amnon plays the passage, making the sudden contrast Franz has made and Franz exclaims,

> Yes!

As Amnon continues, however, Franz quickly interrupts,

> No, not faster, not faster.

There is no need to play faster, because at this point Schubert moves through a rolling sixteenth-note run to eighth notes that lead inexorably to a climax—a progression that must not be rushed. Franz plays the passage again, singing,

Ta-ta-ta-ta-ta-ta-ta-tum-tum!

Loud, the last one!

And as he does this, Franz actually stretches the last two chords. Amnon plays it now, while Franz says cuttingly,

No pity, no pity!

And then, as Amnon plays it yet again,

That's it!

Here, Amnon asks a question, the first that is audible on the tape,

> *Amnon:* Perhaps I want to hear *forte,* and then I want it immediately *piano*—
> *Franz:* Immediately *piano.*
> *Amnon:* So what can I do, because the pedal—?

And he plays the passage again, showing how the sound of his *forte* bleeds over into the *subito piano.* Franz says,

Depends on the acoustics. Of course, this [hall] is a pretty good place for this—so—

And he plays the *subito piano* again several times.

It's again, just like everything in life, something has to give, something you have to sacrifice. In a fairly live acoustic, where it's a little bit echo-y, if you want an immediate *piano* and don't want to wait, or rather, if you want it immediate *piano,* you have to choose between having the sound completely clean, in which case you have to wait, or not wait, and having the sound not completely clean. You can't have both. There's no trick of the pedal or anything where you can have both. It's either that

you have a little bit of overhang or that you wait.
And that's entirely up to you.

Unlike the earlier "Wait!" which marked a breath between the
first two phrases of the piece, this "wait" marks a clean break
between the *forte* and the *piano tremolo*.
Franz plays the *subito* twice again, singing,

                    Ra- pa-pi   Ra- pa-pi

He seems to be listening to himself, as though asking, Which of
these do I *really* do? Then,

            Of course, I know what *I* would like!

Amnon plays it now, waiting momentarily before the *piano
tremolo*.

        Franz: Yes, exactly.

Amnon goes on now to play the next few measures, but Franz
interrupts immediately,

            No accent, no accent!

He plays these measures, demonstrating their deliberate, accentless
progression, and Amnon repeats them:

                    Ra-pa-pa-pa-pa-pa-pa-pa-<u>pim</u>

        Franz: That's right!

Now he goes on the the next phrase,

and as he plays it, he says,

> Have the whole thing like an echo.

These measures, *pianissimo,* are to echo the first phrase, which Schubert had introduced *fortissimo.*

Amnon plays these measures while Franz intones in accompaniment,

> Have the courage, have the courage—nothing, nothing—oh, of course, of course!
> Now this—

He goes on, playing,

> That, we discussed that yesterday, that's technique, technique. To be able to play these seven notes *pianissimo* and exactly together.

And as Amnon plays them,

> Yah, yah. That is just as difficult and just as much to be practiced as— [He plays arpeggios.] You know, we always think that technique is only, is

mostly octaves and fast scales and jumps. It's everything!

Amnon plays the passage again, while Franz sings (using the same syllables he had used earlier to describe the first theme *pianissimo*):

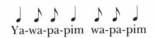
Ya-wa-pa-pim wa-pa-pim

Later, as Amnon goes on to "the next place," Franz again urges him to "phrase it!":

> *Cantabile, fortissimo* but *cantabile.*

Several measures further on, Franz returns yet again to the idea of constancy of phrasing:

> But don't forget what we said before, always the same phrasing, whether it's loud, whether it's soft, whether it's buried, whether it comes out on the bottom of a little burying place or on the top. . . . See, it's not enough to bring a melody, you have to bring it phrasedly.

With this, he turns to the second theme of the piece:

> Now we have a little bit of what we had in the A-major sonata, sort of two things happening. Sentimental song on top—

A-na-na-na-na-na-ti-di-di . . .

Again, he begins with the *character* of the theme ("sentimental song" here, just as the first theme had been "desperate") and proceeds to show how to intensify it. First, he plays the theme, inclining his head toward the left-hand rhythm offset against the right hand's sentimental song "on top." Then he shifts, after Amnon has tried it, to the technical means of production (just as he had done with "balance of sound"):

> Right hand more, close to the keys—more top, more top.

Finally, he turns to the intensification of "sentimentality":

> It's not quite sentimental enough, I mean sentimental in a good sense, full of sentiment—

Ya-ramp-pam-pi yum-pum-ra-da-di

And, going on,

Di-ra-di-di

He plays the full passage, adding, as though listening again to his own performance,

> Even if it involves a little *rubato,* don't worry about it.

Now, as with the first theme, Franz begins to analyze the musical—not by music-theoretic analysis but by an analysis-in-action that shows Amnon how to produce and intensify the theme's essential structure. As he plays the passage again, for example, he sings,

Come to the A...

indicating the direction and goal of the phrase. And he adds,

Yes, and left hand, a little more of this—

Yam-pa-di-di di-da-di-da-di-di

Again, he nods to the left to signal the left hand's answer to the right hand's sentimental song:

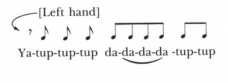

[Left hand]

Ya-tup-tup-tup da-da-da-da -tup-tup

[Right hand]

ta-ya-da-di ta-ya-da-di

And in a phrase, he sums up the character of the left-hand figure:

Sort of a different person playing.

As Amnon goes on, Franz shifts to the technical problem of producing the right hand's sentimental song.

> Keep it legato on top. Finger it, you must finger it. . . . Fingering it alone is not enough. You must finger it *and* play legato.

That is, you must play the octaves of the right hand so as to give a feeling of a smooth, legato sound and also use the fourth and fifth fingers of the right hand to help by connecting the notes to one another. The musical effect must be, as Franz says,

> Not dry, not dry at all.

And as if to illustrate these words, he plays the melody of another Schubert piece, the *Serenade,*

Da-da-da-dim da-da-da-da-dim da-dim da-da-da-da-dim

Then, without commenting on the subtle similarity of the two melodies, he offers a general remark on the performance of Schubert's music:

> The hardest thing in Schubert is to keep the balance, to keep it going, and yet get that leisurely—

Amnon goes on to the next, transitional place in the *Fantasy,*

and Franz urges,

> Now color, now color, color.

Here, Amnon stops to ask a question, unintelligible on the tape, and in response, Franz says,

> Well, what I like to think is, the rain begins. You know, in Schubert's rain, one gets wet. You know, it does. We see this again in the second movement, but here is already a preview. So do this without "ta-ka-ta-ka-ta" [playing].

When Amnon has played the same passage, Franz observes,

> It's a little stiff—I play it a little bit more, uh, unrhythmical. Get some of that swing into it!

And then, as Amnon plays again,

> That's it—sure, sure, absolutely—and don't forget, that's the new harmony. A new pedal because it's the new harmony. This was much too smooth, before, when you played it.

Now there is the beginning of something new, and as Amnon plays, Franz says,

> Only now, only now does it become—a tempest, yes, absolutely—

Later, Franz stops to ask Amnon a question:

> *Franz:*   Do you find that hard?
>
> *Amnon:*   It's not in my hand.
>
> *Franz:*   It's not in mine either. You have to—I used
> to find it hard, that place. It'll get easier with age.

Later still, as Amnon plays a new passage, Franz comments on its character:

> Now here I would suggest, because it's that
> kind of a key, make it full and make it victorious.
> Yes. To have a change.

Finally, as Amnon plays the last measures of the movement, Franz cautions him,

> Yes, still loud—the storm is still there—it
> hasn't subsided, it's still there.
>
> Can you do—?

He plays the passage, Amnon repeats it, and Franz says,

> No, *subito, subito.*

He plays, to show what he means,

and then he says,

A shudder among them—a touch of pedal—
end with the thumb and slide up—a little pedal on it.

What Happens in the Lesson

In Franz's coaching, the three parts of the coaching task are
evenly distributed. In the lesson as a whole and in each of its local
components, Franz intertwines design of performance, response to
the student's particular difficulties, and contribution to a relationship conducive to learning.

Design of Performance. Franz's approach to the substantive
task of performing the *Fantasy* first becomes evident in his global
critique of Amnon's playing. He contrasts Amnon's "too gentle
. . . smooth . . . unified" performance with his own image of the
wanderer's "desperate, *desperate* searching for happiness that is
somewhere *else.*" Thereafter, all of Franz's interventions serve to
elaborate his initial critique and implement his remedial program.
He begins by framing the problem of the performance in terms of
the image of the wanderer who moves from one place to another
through contrasting states of weather and mood, always onward to
the next place, drawn by what lies ahead—there where he is not.
Franz develops this image in terms of places on the piano and
places in the piece, as the performer moves through different and
contrasting keys and thematic ideas and through zones of contrasting musical character. Franz's interventions follow the wanderer's
journey, from its initial desperate figure to the tremendous *subito,*
the resumption of the rolling climax that has "no pity," the
sentimental song of the second theme punctuated by the ironic
left-hand commentary, the beginnings of the storm, the "big
surprise" of the tempest, its lingering, and its final, shuddering
demise. At each stage of the journey, Franz is concerned, first, to
appreciate the character of *that place,* in contrast to its surroundings, and then to produce an intensification of its distinctive
musical qualities. But his preoccupation with the wanderer/
performer's movement through places of contrasting musical
character is in tension with his emphasis on balance of sound and
constancy of phrasing. Across variations in tone quality and
dynamics, balance of sound must be maintained. And across

variations in tempo, dynamics, harmony, and character, the structure of phrases must be preserved.

Franz uses his references to story line, structure, musical qualities, technical operations, and associated contexts to describe and make operational a clearly defined and well-established image of Schubert's *Fantasy*. He knows, not only in general terms but in concrete detail, how he wants the piece to sound. The performance he has in mind is one he has already designed; in the context of this lesson, however, he reflects upon it and re-creates it for Amnon's benefit.

Particularizing Description and Demonstration. Franz helps Amnon to produce contrasting musical effects while preserving balance of sound and constancy of phrasing, by improvising on-the-spot responses to the particular defects he finds in Amnon's playing. He invents his global lesson plan to counteract the smoothness and gentleness of Amnon's first performance of the piece as a whole. Then, in each local context, he answers Amnon's attempts at imitation with descriptions and demonstrations tailored to Amnon's difficulties (as Franz perceives them). In his treatment of the first few measures, as we have seen, he shifts the focus of his attention four times, responding in each case to the problems of Amnon's just-completed imitation. He invents instructions to help Amnon achieve the legato effect of the second theme. And in one clear instance of joint experimentation, at the *subito piano,* he tells Amnon what choice he must make and then structures an experiment to help him make it. In all such instances, Franz reflects-in-action in relation to the particular weaknesses he finds in Amnon's performance, leaving its strengths untouched or merely appreciated. A different student with a different mix of strengths and weaknesses might have elicited very different responses.

As Franz leads Amnon through the *Fantasy,* he draws on an extraordinarily varied repertoire of media and language, using it in each new passage both to open up possibilities for performance and to match their description to the particular difficulties Amnon's playing has revealed.

Franz's *playing/talking* language of performance is very much like Quist's drawing/talking language of designing.

Sometimes, Franz talks over his own playing—"Have the courage, have the courage" as he plays a *pianissimo* passage in the development, or "I can't help it!" as he plays the *subito piano*. Sometimes he talks or sings over Amnon's playing, as in, "Yes, beautiful," "Come to the *A*," "Yes, and left hand, a little more of this." He moves so smoothly from talking over his own playing to talking over Amnon's and back to his own that it is difficult to tell from the audiotape alone just what is happening. One might say that his accompanying speech selectively describes aspects of his playing or, conversely, that his playing enacts his speech.

Much of Franz's speech, spoken or sung, consists of syllables whose sound, sequence, and accent structure communicate musical qualities. Thus, Franz renders the first few bars of the piece,

Ya-ramp-pa-pa ya-ta-ta ramp-pa-pa ra-pa-pum-<u>pum</u>!

Here, each new combination of syllables marks a grouping of notes that constitutes a phrase. The groupings of syllables override the metric boundaries, marking off the musical figures. And within the groupings, each syllable denotes a particular function, not always in one-to-one correspondence with the notes. The first "Ya" is a kind of send-off to "ramp," the first downbeat; in the second "ramp-pa-pa," "ramp" corresponds to the first two of six sixteenth notes that lead to the accented quarter note ("pa"). Accented syllables indicate the accent structure of groups of pitches, as in

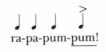

ra-pa-pum-<u>pum</u>!

And different kinds of syllables evoke qualitatively different renderings of the same musical figure. So the figure denoted above by "ya-ta-ta" later becomes

wa-pa-pim   wa-pa-pim

when it is played *pianissimo*, staccato, and exactly even. And the passage in the second theme, "two things happening," is

A-na-na-na-na-na-ti-di-di

It has the same rhythm as the first theme, but the different syllables convey its different, sentimental character.

Along with his playing/talking language, Franz also makes liberal use of gesture. In his treatment of the first few bars, for example, as he plays and sings,

Ya-ramp-pa-pa ya-ta-ta ramp-pa-pa ra-pa-pum-pum!

he sweeps his right hand far to the right at the *pum* to show the figure moving *onward* to what follows. Then he suspends both hands and allows them to fall slowly to the keys so as to measure the breath ("Three, four!") between the first and second phrases.

Franz's interventions are multimedia performances in which he coordinates playing, gesturing, talking, and singing (syllables or words) to communicate musical features of particular passages and concretize such abstract terms as *phrasing*. In these performances, he employs various levels and kinds of description, depending on the aspects of his overall design that happen to be salient for him at the moment.

Franz uses feelingful language to describe the character he wants in a particular passage—for example, "Not dry, not dry at all," "Much too smooth," "Have the whole thing like an echo," or *"Fortissimo* but *cantabile."* He calls the *subito piano* "tremendous" and exclaims, "I can't help it!" as he plays it. And as the piece starts up again, rolling to a climax, he proclaims, "No pity, no pity!" The first few measures must be "desperate, desperate," not "triumphant"; but at the end of the movement, there is a passage that should be "full and . . . victorious . . . to have a change." The second theme should be played in a way that is "sentimental in a good sense, full of sentiment."

Franz also conveys desired musical effects by references to quality of tone ("Now color, color"), tempo ("Not too fast!"), dynamics ("Still too loud . . . nothing, nothing"), and instrumentation (in a passage I did not quote where he talks of choosing to bring out the tone quality of either "violin" or "viola").

When he tells Amnon how to *produce* particular qualities of sound, however, he refers mainly to hands and their actions on the keyboard:

- "Still top and less thumb," to play the "balanced" chords (shorthand for "the higher notes, played by the little finger, louder; and the lower notes, played by the thumb, softer").
- The "wait" before the *subito piano,* to achieve a "completely clean" break.
- The seven-note *pianissimo* chords that must be played "exactly together."
- The octave passages where Amnon must "finger it *and* play legato."
- The second theme's sentimental song that must be played with "right hand more, close to the keys."

Franz does not make explicit reference to the structure of phrases or the larger musical structure of the piece, as a music theorist would do. But by his choices of moments on which to concentrate attention, his ways of linking technical means to

qualities of sound, mood, or character, he reveals the bones of
structure by an analysis-in-action that focuses exclusively on
questions of performance. So his vocalized syllables, playing, and
gestures indicate the groupings, directionality, and accent structure
of phrases. When it comes to marking off transitions in the larger
structure, Franz recommends a shift of pedal (because "there is a
new harmony") or a "full and victorious sound" (because there is
a change of key). His lengthy treatment of the *subito piano*
highlights Schubert's interruption and extension of the onward
movement of the passage. Franz never introduces the term *second
theme* but marks that theme, nevertheless, with evocative images
like "sentimental song" or "another person playing" and allusions
to contexts outside the piece like Schubert's A-major sonata or the
world of Schubert songs. And in the tempestlike development
section that follows the sentimental song, the melodies Franz urges
Amnon to "bring phrasedly" are variations on the first and second
themes. Although Franz never mentions "theme and variations"—
or "development," for that matter—he signals both by his selective
attention to features of performance.

Franz describes the structure of the piece in still another
way, by referring to its storyline. There is the onset of the rain—
"Schubert's rain," in which "one gets wet"—and then the tempest,
and the storm that lingers on, shuddering to a close. Above all,
there is the story of the piece as a whole: the Wanderer, with his
desperate searching for happiness that is "somewhere *else,* you
know . . . there where you're *not.*"

Franz manipulates these several levels and kinds of description in order to communicate to Amnon a particular way of
designing the performance of the piece. In the dominant pattern of
his discourse, he begins by asserting the musical character he
wants a passage to have—the "desperateness" of the first appearance of the first theme, the "echo" of its second appearance—and
then tells Amnon how to produce the desired quality, tailoring his
instructions and demonstrations to the particular defects he has
just discovered in Amnon's playing.

The end of the lesson is, in this respect, like its beginning.
Franz alludes to the "shudder" of the subsiding storm and then
tells Amnon how to produce it:

A touch of pedal—end with the thumb and
slide up—a little pedal on it.

Building a Relationship. The several participants in the
workshop expressed very different assessments of the impact of
Franz's coaching and the quality of his relationship to Amnon.

They agreed that the two performers began with vastly
different understandings of the piece. The participants also shared
an empathic feeling for Amnon's vulnerability as he played the
role of student in a public lesson that seemed to have as much to
do with show business as with education. Nevertheless, they
formed sharply contrasting views of and feelings about the process
they were observing.

Several observers saw the gap between Amnon and Franz as
unbridgeable. One of them, a student of artistic development, saw
in Amnon "a young boy, proud, looking like that—a young
warrior" and in Franz "a sage, worldly old man, with all the
accompanying *Weltschmerz.*" Franz, he thought, was "trying to
change the young warrior into himself," and he "felt sorry for the
young warrior being asked to give up his warrior's materials for
the detached, sensitive world of the old man. But how can the boy
do this?"

Others also saw Amnon as mystified by Franz and hopelessly distant from him. They disapproved of Franz's coaching
because it seemed to rest on the single principle, Follow me! To
these observers, Franz seemed to have no interest in understanding
Amnon's conception of the piece or in helping him to develop it;
rather, he seemed to be insisting that *he* held the one right
interpretation, which Amnon must "follow."

Others—some, but not all, of the musicians at the workshop
and I—saw Franz and Amnon as engaged in a dialogue of
increasing intimacy and effectiveness and were impressed with its
reciprocity. In our view, Franz continually responded to Amnon's
efforts, albeit in the light of his own preferred image of performance. We saw Franz as having framed the very problem of
performance in response to his appreciation and critique of
Amnon's playing, and we were struck by the plasticity of Amnon's
responses as he sought to reproduce in his playing what Franz had

just described or demonstrated. Most important, perhaps, we heard Amnon's playing change in the course of the lesson from an initial performance that, though fluent, accomplished, and triumphant, was rather flat to one far more differentiated, interesting, coherent, and alive.

We were not put off by Franz's "Follow me!" however much we recognized the underlying pattern of demonstration and imitation, because we understood the lesson to be about more than the performance of the piece at hand. We saw Franz as demonstrating and describing a particular way of designing a coherent performance of *this* piece in order to communicate to Amnon what it would be like to design a coherent performance of other pieces— trying, through this one well-crafted experience, to help Amnon build his capacity for further designing.

Conclusion

How do these vignettes of learning and coaching in musical master classes compare with our observations of the architectural design studio? What do they tell us more generally about the creation and conduct of a reflective practicum?

They confirm our argument from design—though with some important differences. They reveal the designlike character of musical performance and the strong family resemblance that master classes in musical performance bear to architectural studios. But master classes also differ from studios in ways that reflect differences in the media and contents of the two practices.

Designing Performance, Performing Design. When students are initiated into the artistry of musical performance, they learn a particular kind of designing. In the simplest case, they learn to adjust technical means to desired musical effects. In the case of the composer whose "small, sensible" exercise I described earlier in this chapter, students are helped to distinguish the effects they *say* they produce from those they actually produce in performance—as though to say, "Learn what you already do in order to be able to choose what you will do." In three of our vignettes—Casals, Rosemary, Franz—we found coaches trying to help a student learn to "improvise" on a musical score. By very different methods, they sought to communicate the idea that there is no one right way of performing a piece, but many possible right ways, each of which must be worked out both in its global structure and in the most concrete details of its production. In all cases, they tried to help the student envisage and produce local musical effects. Franz's case, especially, illustrated a process analogous to Quist's experimentation with reframing: global meaning imposed on the score of an entire piece and then elaborated in its implications for the musical qualities and technical means appropriate to each local passage.

As in the architectural design studio, students learn by doing, with the help of coaching. They prepare and play a piece or a part of one; the coach listens and then responds with criticisms, questions, advice, or demonstration; and coach and student engage in a dialogue of verbal discourse and musical performance. In these vignettes, because we have very little information about students' thoughts or feelings, we have no basis for deciding whether the paradox and predicament of learning to design are as pervasive in the musical practicum as in the architectural one.

Critically important differences in the practices of musical performance and architectural design show up in the dialogues of coach and student; but underlying similarities are also evident.

The entirely different contents and media of the two practices are reflected in the very different domains of discourse on which coaches draw and in the languages in which they conduct the dialogue—the drawing/talking language of designing, the playing/talking language of musical performance. In both cases, nevertheless, coaches employ a multimedia language of demonstration and description, and they analyze practice in terms of moves whose consequences and implications cut across different domains.

Musical performers work from a score; architects do no such thing. It is striking, nevertheless, how many degrees of freedom a musical performer has as she explores and tests alternative ways of designing a performance; indeed, much of the coaching in our master classes seems aimed at opening up possibilities for interpretation that students have not as yet imagined. And in architecture, the givens of site and program, as well as the precedents and prototypes on which designers draw, fulfill some of the functions of the musical score. In neither case is there unlimited freedom or a degree of constraint that demands "one right way."

Our examples of musical master classes differ from design studios in the immediacy with which the student and coach *perform* for each other. In the dialogues we have drawn from architectural studios, student and coach discuss a design the student has produced by herself. Only the coach designs on the spot, making a rough sketch to show how the actual designing might go. In the light of her reactions to the encounter, the student will go back again to work by herself. In the master classes, by contrast, Greenhouse, Amnon, and Rosemary's Chilean student respond to their coaches' interventions by performing in the action-present. The interplay of coach and student has directness and immediacy, so that Rosemary can tell right away what her student does with the second theme of the Brahms sonata, and Franz and Amnon can pass quickly through iterative cycles of demonstration and imitation.

This difference in "reciprocal immediacy" seems directly attributable to the different media involved: it usually takes longer to execute a phase of architectural design than to perform a musical passage. However, part of the difference may be due to the traditional habits of the practicum. Architectural students might be encouraged (and sometimes are) to execute some part of a design task in the coach's presence; and after a master class, student musicians often return to the privacy of their own practice rooms to continue to redesign their performance of a piece.

These observations on the distinctive features of education for musical performance raise a more general question about the idea of a reflective practicum: Is performance limited to what we normally call "the performing arts," or is it also central to some other kinds—perhaps to all kinds—of professional practice?

Our answer will obviously depend on the sense of "performance" we have in mind. Not all professional practice consists in *public* performance, before an audience, although much of it does. We need only consider a trial lawyer's appearances before a judge and jury, a teacher's performance in a classroom, a manager's public addresses to his employees or customers, a city planner's presentations, a physician's grand rounds. In such fields as these, more than a few practitioners specialize in the design and delivery of skillful public performances and even speak of themselves, in unguarded or lighthearted moments, as "performers." For many other members of these professions, however, and for most practices in fields like engineering, dentistry, nursing, or psychotherapy, public performance occupies a less important place in the map of practice.

If, however, we use *performance* to mean the execution of any skillful *process,* public or private, then it is clear that all professional practice consists in performance. For the most part, however, we do not dwell on performance in this sense nor distinguish it from the achievement of desirable professional outcomes. We tend to evaluate practitioners by their results—in some cases, their tangible products. We tend to call lawyers good, for example, when they win cases, protect clients from legal dangers, or write agreements that stand the test of time. We tend to call architects good when they make good buildings; physicians, when they produce accurate diagnoses and effective treatments. We focus on performance in this broader sense only when we take a detached, esthetic view of practice, admiring a physician's elegant clinical detective work, for example, or a manager's ability to get immediately to the heart of a complex organizational problem. But a physician who regularly makes accurate diagnoses or a lawyer who regularly wins cases has a characteristic way of going about the process of diagnosis or litigation. It is in the manner of these professionals' *performance* that their distinctive knowing-in-action resides.

Architectural design and musical performance can serve as models for two different ways of looking at practice. Whereas we tend to think of architecture in terms of its products (drawings, plans, buildings), we see practicing musicians mainly in terms of their processes (putting aside the fact that these are sometimes captured on disks or tapes). Nevertheless, as we have already observed, a musical performer like Franz *designs* his performance, and an architectural designer like Quist *performs* the process that results in his design.

As we have also seen, it is precisely in the context of learning the artistry of a practice that these relationships between design and performance become critically important. Quist performs for Petra because he wants her to see how to go about the particular kind of design process that yields a good global layout of buildings on a site. He wants her to learn not only to recognize a good design when she sees it but to recognize and deliver a good way of design*ing;* and his lesson with her is very much about the designing of design*ing.* Franz, in contrast, tries to help Amnon improve his performance of the Schubert *Fantasy* by helping him to understand how such a performance is put together; and by showing him what may be involved in a performance of the Schubert *Fantasy,* he also opens up issues and processes critical to the design of a performance of any Schubert piece or, in some fundamental respects, any piece at all.

It is useful to juxtapose practices we tend to see mainly as products and those we see mainly as processes, so that we can more easily see performance in the first and product in the second. For if, in a reflective practicum, it is critically important to see a practitioner as a maker of objects, it is equally important to see him as a performer whose knowing-in-action includes, as an essential element, the capacity to design his performance.

Models of Coaching. Some of the vignettes presented in this chapter are strikingly similar to some of the studio dialogues analyzed in Part Two. The dialogue of Rosemary and her Chilean student should be considered alongside the dialogue of Dani and Michal; and Franz's master class with Amnon, alongside Quist and Petra. The two comparisons suggest models of coaching that transcend the styles of particular instructors and cut across the usual divisions between fields of practice.

Each of the two models to be examined—"joint experimentation" and "Follow me!"—is a distinctive way of fulfilling the threefold coaching task. Each is appropriate to different contexts and demands different competences from coach and student.

Like Dani, Rosemary invites her student to choose the musical qualities she would like to hear in the themes of the first movement of the Brahms sonata. Rosemary leaves the choice of desirable musical effects to the student but joins her in an experiment aimed at intensifying those effects. Like Dani again, Rosemary is a relativist about effects, an objectivist about means.

As the Chilean student tries out different ways of producing the serenity of the second theme, for example, Rosemary helps her to see that she can judge her results by the evidence of her own senses; she need not depend on anyone's opinion or on the coach's authority.

It is crucial to Rosemary's way of coaching, as to Dani's, that the student imagine more than one way of producing the qualities she desires. Implicitly, Rosemary communicates the idea that technique is not a matter of following rules but of trying out and evaluating alternative methods of production. So when she coaches in this way (and it is important to remember that she also coached other students in other ways), she first helps the student to identify different themes whose qualities are important, then asks her what qualities she hears in them, mimes (just as Dani had sketched) different ways of intensifying those qualities, and finally asks the student to decide on the method she prefers.

In this process, Rosemary demonstrates a way of decomposing the larger performance into unitary problems, each of which can be solved by experiment. She treats the design of a performance as a series of experiments in the production of desired musical effects, just as Dani had done with Michal's qualities of oneness with nature, encouragement of social interaction, and stimulation of the senses.

Rosemary and Dani particularize their approach to the task of performance by focusing on *this* student's intentions and difficulties, then granting her the freedom to choose the option *she* prefers. And—from the point of view of relationship—they forge an alliance with the student, saying to her, in effect,

> Here is the problem *you* have chosen. Let us put it out there and see together how it might be solved.

They take up a position next to the student, sitting side by side with her before the shared problem.

For joint experimentation to be appropriate and feasible, several conditions must be met. There must be a way of breaking the larger task into manageable instrumental problems. The student must be able to say what effects she would like to produce—must know what she wants. And finally, the coach must be willing to keep instructional goals within the bounds of the model. Joint experimentation can be used to help a student see that she is free to set her own objectives. It can open up many possible ways of achieving a desired effect, introduce the idea of designing a performance through a series of local experiments, help to refine a student's perceptions of the qualities in her results. But joint experimentation is inappropriate when a coach wants to communicate a way of working, or a conception of performance, that goes beyond anything a student presently knows how to describe.

"Follow me!" lends itself to just this circumstance. Its dominant pattern is demonstration and imitation; its underlying message is "Do as I am doing," whether communicated explicitly, as by Casals, or implicitly, as by Franz and Quist. The invitation to imitate is also, in its way, an invitation to experiment; for in order to "follow," the student must construct in her own performance what she takes to be the essential features of the coach's demonstration.

In both the studio and the master class, we have seen variations on Follow me! Casals moves forthrightly to demonstrate his way of playing the Bach suite; he expects Greenhouse to follow him in the smallest detail. Quist first asks Petra what problems she has already encountered and only then demonstrates a way of going about the task in which her problems are reframed and solved. Franz starts with an overall critique of Amnon's playing; presents, in contrast, his own image of the performance; and proceeds to demonstrate in each passage how the new image may be realized.

There are also differences in the way each coach adapts his coaching to the particular student before him. Casals, as far as we can tell from Greenhouse's story (and there is independent evidence from other former students), taught *generically* by demonstration and imitation; he seems to have made no effort to take account of Greenhouse's individuality. Franz, however, responded continually to the specific strengths and weaknesses of Amnon's efforts at imitation, moving with reciprocal immediacy through cycles of demonstration, imitation, and criticism. Quist took Petra's specific problem as the starting point for his demonstration but, once launched on it, did very little to elicit or respond to Petra's particular difficulties.

In the matter of relationship building, Quist, Franz, and Casals basically assume that it is their business to show the way, and the student's, to follow them. Despite this shared basic assumption, however, their styles are different. In his forthright demand for letter-perfect imitation, Casals seems most peremptory and unyielding. Franz seems warmer and more intimate in his interaction with Amnon than Quist with Petra.

Franz and Quist seem to sense at times a danger of provoking their students' defenses, and they try to soften their impact. Franz edges ever so gently toward his first critique of Amnon's playing:

> Beautiful, beautiful! I'd like to hear you go on. But one can't have everything. So if we're going to discuss it a little bit . . . it's very, very good. . . . My main criticism, it is, I think it's, I find it a little too gentle—too gentle, believe it or not, for this piece.

And Quist ends the dialogue with Petra by saying,

> Go on, you are going to make it.

These softening and compensating tactics are understandable (however effective or ineffective they may be) given that Follow me! has a special potential for triggering a student's defenses. Follow me! calls on the coach to criticize the student's performance, rather than join him in a collaborative problem-solving task; and it necessarily evokes whatever special vulnerabilities and ambivalences the student may feel in the act of deliberate imitation.

Nevertheless, Follow me! is fundamental to a reflective practicum. The necessity for it is grounded in the paradox of learning to perform a designlike task. At times, especially in the early stages of the practicum, the student will have to follow her instructor even when she is unsure—indeed, just because she is unsure—what she will learn by doing so. Even joint experimentation is in one sense a version of Follow me! for Rosemary and Dani actually demonstrate, and expect their students to imitate, a new and critically important way of practicing and performing.

Chapter Nine

Learning the Artistry of Psychoanalytic Practice

Designing is, as we have seen, an essentially constructive activity. A designer gives coherence to a more or less indeterminate situation, testing his frame through a web of moves, consequences, and implications. Sometimes he apprehends the consequences of his moves as back talk that calls for a new round of frame experimentation. He conducts a reflective conversation with materials that recalls Edmund Carpenter's story of the Eskimo sculptor patiently carving a reindeer bone, eventually exclaiming, "Ah, seal!"

It is a rather small step from Quist's designing to Franz's design of a musical performance. Taking due account of the very significant differences between the two kinds of media and language, we can readily see Quist's design of the geometry of buildings on a site and Franz's design of a performance of the Schubert *Fantasy* as family-resembling examples of frame experimentation.

It is a much larger step—indeed, a leap—to see practitioners of professions outside the fine arts as designers. In order to see lawyering, managing, teaching, or clinical medicine as frame experimentation—sometimes as reflective conversation with the materials of the situation—we must adopt a constructionist point of view.

What makes this difficult, or odd, is that we tend to think that artists create things and practitioners of other professions deal with things as they are. According to the objectivist view of professional competence as technical expertise, skilled professionals have accurate models of their special objects and powerful techniques for manipulating them to achieve professionally sanctioned ends. But a constructionist view of a profession leads us to see its practitioners as worldmakers whose armamentarium gives them frames with which to envisage coherence and tools with which to impose their images on situations of their practice. A professional practitioner is, in this view, like the artist, a maker of things.

With the shift from an objectivist to a constructionist view of practice, such critically important terms as *truth* and *effectiveness* become problematic. We may still talk about true statements and effective actions, but only *within* a frame, just as we can talk operationally about the truth or effectiveness of the local experiments carried out by Quist and Franz. When we think of truth or effectiveness *across* frames, however, things become much more difficult.

When representatives of different professions take conflicting views of the same situation, as in our example of malnourishment (Chapter One), they are unlikely to resolve their dispute by reference to facts or judgments of the relative effectiveness of actions. With their different ways of framing the situation, they tend to pay attention to different sets of facts, see "the same facts" in different ways, and make judgments of effectiveness based on different kinds of criteria. If they wish, nevertheless, to come to agreement, they must try to get inside each other's points of view. They must try to discover what models and appreciative systems lead each of them to focus preferentially on one set of facts or criteria, make their tacit cognitive strategies explicit to themselves, and find out how each one understands the other's framing of the situation. Their ability to come to substantive agreement will depend on their capacity for *frame reflection*.

Conflicting views held by representatives of different schools of thought within a profession also tend to rest on frame conflicts, unresolvable except through frame reflection, as do disputes between professionals and laypersons.

In a reflective practicum, student and coach are initially in a state of frame conflict. Confusion and mystery reign, and the meanings held by coach and student tend to be incongruent. The coach's language refers to things and relations in a particular kind of world—familiar to the coach, strange as yet to the student. Since the student has not experienced that world from the inside and cannot experience it until he learns to construct it, the things and relations of that world are not yet *his*.

The frame conflict of student and coach differs from other kinds, however, in that these two parties come together with the manifest intention of resolving their conflict. It is expected that students will try to enter into a coach's view of the world and that he will try to help them. So their dialogue can be seen as frame reflection—unidirectional, at least, and reciprocal when coach and student try to make it so.

In this chapter, I shall make the leap from designing in architecture and the fine arts to designing in other kinds of professional practice. I shall describe as designlike a kind of practice we usually consider neither a design profession nor a fine art, and I shall treat its traditional form of education as a reflective practicum within which frame reflection plays a crucially important role.

Psychoanalysis is, from the point of view of these ideas, an exceptionally interesting profession.

First of all, it is a practice—a branch of medicine, a particular genre of psychotherapy. But it is also an overarching theory of human psychology, psychopathology, and development. When we study how a person learns to become a psychoanalyst, we study how he or she learns to practice in the light of such an overarching theory.

Second, it is generally agreed that the practice of psychoanalysis involves a core of artistry. As Erik Erikson has put it, each patient must be seen as a "universe of one." The analyst can learn to understand the patient's unique pattern of experience only by learning to listen in a special, "evenly suspended" way to the patient's freely verbalized thoughts and feelings (Erikson, 1959). He must learn to treat his evolving relationship with his patient as a field of experience and experiment in which the patient re-creates the underlying dynamics of his most important relationships to others and learns, with the analyst's help, to discover them.

The traditions of education for psychoanalysis reflect both its theoretical basis and its artistry. Students come late to psychoanalysis, usually in residency, after four years of medical school and one or more years of internship. They are expected to take instruction in psychoanalytic theory. Because their capacity to reflect on their own unconscious motivations is deemed essential to therapeutic effectiveness, they themselves are expected to undergo psychoanalysis. And they are expected to learn the artistry of psychoanalytic practice by practicing under the supervision of a senior analyst.

Further, the field of psychoanalysis has been for some time caught up in controversy over its epistemology of practice, a controversy between those who would frame psychoanalysis in objectivist terms, with its own form of technical rationality, and those who take an explicitly constructionist view of it. The controversy has important implications for psychoanalytic training.

The objectivists, who want to place psychoanalysis firmly within medicine, rely on theories of disease, etiologies, clinical histories, diagnosis, and cure. Their opponents deny that psychoanalysis is a branch of medicine and see it instead as a propadeutic or therapeutic art whose claims to validity and effectiveness are *sui generis*. A notable proponent of this view is Donald P. Spence, whose *Narrative Truth and Historical Truth* (1982) presents a constructionist, designlike account of psychoanalytic practice.

Finally, psychoanalysis is of special interest because it shares with certain other practices—teaching, management, and social work, for example—a powerful interpersonal component. Because an analyst's practice consists of interactions with other persons, a psychoanalytic practicum parallels its practice. It is unavoidably a hall of mirrors in which students read messages about psychoanalytic practice in a supervisor's behavior—whether or not he intends to convey them—and supervisors read in their students' behavior messages about the students' way of doing therapy. The effectiveness of psychoanalytic supervision depends significantly on the degree to which coach and student recognize and exploit such mirrorings so as to make their practicum a reflective one in this additional sense.

I shall begin this chapter by contrasting Spence's constructionist view of psychoanalysis with Erik Erikson's traditionally Freudian, medically oriented essay on psychoanalytic evidence and inference. Then I shall turn to examples of psychoanalytic supervision that progress along the ladder of reflection, culminating in an example that reveals how, in the special context of a hall of mirrors, a student and coach can move from frame conflict to frame reflection.

Objectivist and Constructionist Views of Psychoanalysis

Consider these two descriptions of the psychoanalytic process:

> [The clinician] can rely on the patient's capacity to produce during a series of therapeutic encounters a sequence of [freely associated] themes, thoughts, and affects which seek their own concordance . . . this basic synthesizing trend in the clinical material itself . . . permits the clinician to observe with free-floating attention . . . and to expect sooner or later a confluence of the patient's search for curative clarification and his own endeavor to recognize meaning and relevance [Erikson, 1959, p. 86].

Free-floating attention, then, could be better characterized as constructive listening in the service of understanding. This understanding is shared between analyst and patient; unwitting interpretations that facilitate the initial listening by the analyst lead directly to formal interpretations that supply continuity for the patient. . . . [Free-floating attention] is not the automatic decoder of free association. . . . An interpretation (seen as an artistic product) achieves its effect through something analogous to the well-known suspension of disbelief [Spence, 1982, pp. 279–280, 281, 289].

The two passages represent two very different views of the knowing implicit in an analyst's clinical work. In the first, the analyst is a clinical investigator who strives through disciplined subjectivity to achieve objective truth; in the second, an artist not only in manner or timing but in the very substance of interpretation and intervention.

It is no accident that the two passages were written some twenty-five years apart. Erik Erikson's "Nature of Clinical Evidence in Psychoanalysis" was published in 1959; Donald Spence's *Narrative Truth and Historical Truth,* in 1982. Their differing visions reflect a much larger movement of twentieth-century thought from objectivism to constructionism.

On the objectivist view, the truth of beliefs can be tested by their conformity to reality independent of anyone's way of seeing it; disagreements about empirical truth can be resolved, at least in principle, by reference to facts; and actions can be shown to be objectively effective or ineffective. On the constructionist view, perceptions and beliefs are rooted in worlds of our own making that we accept as reality. The knower is, as John Dewey put it, in transaction with the known, is quite literally a maker of the things he knows; and such familiar notions as true belief, effective action, and communicable and generalizable knowledge all become problematic (Dewey and Bentley, 1949). As a parable of the movement from objectivism to constructionism, I like Karl Weick's story (1979) of the three umpires: The first says, "I calls 'em like they *is!*"; the second, "I calls 'em like I *sees* 'em!"; and the third, "There ain't nothing *there* until I calls 'em!"

Technical rationality, an objectivist epistemology of practice, underlay the rise of the modern research university in the late nineteenth and early twentieth centuries. Practice was seen as instrumental problem solving, professional when based on systematic, preferably scientific knowledge. And, according to the professions' bargain with the universities, the schools of higher learning supplied research-based knowledge to the lower schools of the professions. Artistry was no more than style grafted onto the substance of professional knowledge.

On the constructionist view, a practitioner's feel for materials, on-the-spot judgments, and improvisations—the forms of his or her reflection-in-action—are essential to professional competence. The arts, crafts, and design professions are paradigmatic of professional artistry. Indeed, when objectivism fades, science, art, and practice all seem to be in similar, if not identical, epistemological boats.

Erikson, who wrote his essay when technical rationality was in the ascendant, treats psychoanalytic inquiry within the framework of clinical medicine and is at pains to show how subjectivity in psychoanalysis can be disciplined to achieve objective knowledge. Spence, who writes during the full flowering of the constructionist movement, presents a constructionist critique of Erikson's Freudian model.

Erikson's story begins with a dream report:

> A young man in his early twenties comes to his therapeutic hour and reports that he has had the most disturbing dream of his life . . . [one that] vividly recalls his state of panic at the time of "mental breakdown" which caused him to enter treatment half a year earlier. . . . He is afraid that this is the end of his sanity.
>
> The dream: "There was a big face sitting in a buggy of the horse-and-buggy days. The face was completely empty, and there was horrible, slimy, snaky hair all around it. I am not sure it wasn't my mother." The dream report itself, given with wordy plaintiveness, is as usual followed by a variety of incidental reports, protestations, and exclamations, which at one point gives way to a rather coherent account of the patient's relationship with his deceased grandfather, a country parson. Here the patient's mood changes to a deeply moved and moving admission of desperate nostalgia for cultural and personal values once observed and received [Erikson, 1959, p. 79].

Erikson listened to the report of the dream with free-floating attention that "turns inward to the observer's ruminations while remaining turned outward to the field of observations and which, far from focusing on any one item too intentionally, rather waits to be impressed by recurring themes" (1959, p. 80). Skillfully, he reconstructs the work of interpretation by which he placed the dream report within multiple contexts known to analyst and patient through their long and intimate association.

The first of these contexts is the analytic situation itself, within which the dream report represents a "crisis": is it the sign of "an impending collapse . . . or [is he], on the contrary, reaching out for me with an important message which I must try to understand and answer?" Erikson decides for the latter and subsequently explains why:

> [During the previous day's appointment] the patient had confessed to increased well-being in work and in love and had expressed trust in, and even something akin to affection for, me. This, paradoxically, his unconscious had not been able to tolerate. The paradox resolves itself if we consider that cure means the loss of the right to rely on therapy. . . . The dream report communicates, protesting somewhat too loudly, that the patient is still sick. We must come to the conclusion that his dream was sicker than he was, although his treatment was by no means near conclusion [1959, p. 89].

This will prove to be a decisive element in Erikson's reading of the dream report—a reading he compares to the scanning of an X-ray picture ("a dream often lays bare the stark inner facts")—but he adduces other interpretive contexts. For example, the motionless image of a faceless face suggests the analyst's own face ("My often unruly white hair surrounding a reddish face easily enters my patients' imaginative productions"). Erikson concludes that "the empty face had something to do with a certain tenuousness in our relation, and that one message of the dream might be something like this: 'If I never know whether and when you think of yourself rather than attending to me, or when you will absent yourself, maybe die, how can I have or gain what I need most—a coherent personality, an identity, a face?'" (p. 83). In passing, Erikson links this concern with his then-current studies of the "identity crisis" of a number of young people. Then he mentions the patient's failure, while attending a Protestant seminary (where, incidentally, his symptoms developed) to "break through" in prayer—to come face to face with God. He describes the patient's fondness and desperate nostalgia for a deceased grandfather who had "taken him by the hand to acquaint him with the technology of an old farm in Minnesota," an event described with "genuinely positive emotion" but also with a "strangely perverse tearfulness almost strangled by anger, as if he were saying: 'One must not promise a child such certainty, and then let him down.'" And finally, Erikson conjures up the "pretty, soft, and loving face" of the patient's mother "since earliest childhood . . . marred in the patient's memory and imagination by moments when she seemed absorbed and distorted by strong and painful emotions," which the patient attributed to his own willfulness and rebelliousness (pp. 87–88).

All this, Erikson builds into his formulation of a central theme:

> Whenever I begin to have faith in somebody's strength and love, some angry and sickly emotions pervade the relationship, and I end up mistrusting, empty, and a victim of anger and despair [p. 88].

Throughout his reconstruction of this interpretive work, Erikson recognizes that "some other clinician might have seen the dream report differently." Nevertheless, he defends his interpretation on the grounds that it meets the distinctive criteria of psychoanalytic inference. Its reconstruction of the patient's unconscious meanings is comprehensive; it accounts for all the relevant clinical material. It has evidential continuity, owing its clarity "to the fact that it responds to previous questions and complements previous half-answers." It lies at the strategic intersection of several "tangents" of interpretation that make up "the central core which comprises the 'evidence'" (p. 80). It is consonant with the overarching conceptions of psychoanalytic theory. And finally, it proves to be therapeutically effective.

When Erikson arrived at the inner signs of a right interpretation—it felt right; it promised, when appropriately verbalized, to feel right to the patient; and he felt himself compelled to speak— he

> reviewed with the patient in brief words most of what I have put before you; I was also able to tell him without anger, but not without some indignation, that my response to his account had included some feeling of anger. I explained that he had worried me, and had me feel pity, had touched me with his memories, and had burdened me with the proof, all at once, of the goodness of mothers, of the immortality of grandfathers, of my own perfection and of God's grace [p. 92].

Erikson tells us that the patient was delighted and that he left the hour with a broad smile and obvious encouragement. The analyst had "shown him that the [dream] image was in fact . . . a condensed and highly meaningful communication and challenge," had "talked back" without hesitation, accepting the patient's transferences as meaningful while refusing to become drawn into them, and had restored, in consequence, "a sense of mutuality and reality." This Erikson regards as "clinching the evidence" for his interpretation, untroubled by the problem of disentangling its truth from its effectiveness as an intervention.

Where in this elegant and parsimonious account is the analyst's artistry? It lies in his free-floating attention, his way of weaving together the strands of contextual meaning, the timing and delivery of his responses to the latent message of the patient's dream. But all such artistry belongs to the context of discovery (Reichenbach, 1951). In the context of justification, Erikson presents his interpretation as an inference objectively true to the patient's inner facts, testable by its completeness, its consonance with psychoanalytic theory, and its therapeutic utility.

Donald Spence would treat as problematic precisely what Erikson most readily accepts: the validity of the patient's dream reports, early memories, and free associations. Contrary to Freud's image of the free-associating patient as traveler sitting next to the window of a railway carriage, a passive observer of his own changing landscape of thought, Spence argues that a patient must continually translate "from the private language of experience [especially visual experience, as in the dream report of Erikson's patient] into the common language of speech" (1982, p. 83). "Free association is hardly free and the patient is hardly passive" (p. 83), nor can he be if he is to make himself understood in the analytic conversation.

Similarly, Spence sees the analyst's free-floating attention as active listening. Just insofar as a patient, following the basic rule, produces disconnected phrases free of the ordinary constraints of meaningful conversation, an analyst must construct their coherence. Convergence of meaning occurs only when both parties make an active effort to achieve a negotiated understanding.

Reconstructions of the past, like Erikson's patient's stories about his grandfather, Erikson uses as evidence for interpretation. But Spence regards them as negotiated constructions, inseparable from the unwitting interpretations and subtle modifications of meaning that pervade analytic conversation. He sees them as influenced by the analyst's private preoccupations, such as Erikson's "identity crises," and by the effects of transference and countertransference—"pernicious because they carry extreme conviction . . . and are often sensed as matters of fact" (p. 133).

The formal interpretations by which analysts eventually make sense of "facts," Spence sees as creative acts that work when they have *narrative truth:* tell a coherent story about other pieces of the patient's past and present life, conform to psychoanalytic theory, and lead to new therapeutic discoveries. But they are inherently unfalsifiable. "The search after meaning is especially insidious because it always succeeds," Spence says. It does so, first, because "the search space can be infinitely expanded until the answer is discovered" and, second, "because there is no possibility of . . . deciding that the search has failed" (p. 143). For example, an analyst preoccupied with the fact that she will be going on vacation in two weeks can almost surely find confirmation of the patient's presumed concern with this issue in some part of the patient's productions during the two-week period; she may even take the absence of evidence, or the patient's reluctance to admit any such concern, as negative confirmation.

Similarly, the claim that a "particular early experience is real is something like claiming you have lost a coin in your shag rug . . . if I search for the coin and fail to find it, you can always say that I have not looked far enough" (Spence, 1982, p. 142). As for Erikson's "strategic intersections of evidence," Spence points out that "two complex themes can almost always be found to share *something* in common" (p. 145). And the sense of inevitability that Erikson adduces as a sign of interpretive rightness, Spence sees as blinding the analyst to other ways of seeing clinical material.

An outside observer who possesses normative psychoanalytic competence and might see the clinical material differently cannot serve as a check on the treating analyst's judgments, because he lacks that individual's privileged competence. This competence "belongs to the analyst at a particular time and place in a particular analysis" (Spence, 1982, p. 216) but is also peculiarly vulnerable to misreading derived from the analyst's private associations. The evidential bind can be untangled, according to Spence, only by "naturalizing the text of an analytic session: the analyst would have to annotate every utterance in order to make his privileged competence accessible to a normatively competent reader" (p. 216). Failing that, clinical inferences are impossible to disconfirm. Different readings are never tried or confronted, because they are never seen; they are swallowed up in what has come to seem obvious to analyst and patient alike. But the criteria for a full naturalization of the text are extraordinarily strong; all or nearly all of the analytic literature falls short of them.

How, then, does Spence finally regard the knowledge claims of a psychoanalytic interpretation? He sees interpretation, first of all, as an "esthetic experience, claiming *artistic truth*" (p. 268). Interpretations are essentially creative; any number of different ones, equally coherent and complete, might be provided for any particular clinical event. But right interpretations must also have a power to persuade grounded in their esthetic appeal, by virtue of which they may also acquire *pragmatic utility* as "means to an end, uttered in the expectation that they will lead to additional, clarifying clinical material" (p. 271). In the words of the later Freud (1937/1976), we may produce in the patient "an assumed conviction of the truth of the construction which achieves the same therapeutic effect as a recaptured memory" (Spence, 1982, p. 274).

Such future-regarding "truths"—those that are "true" in light of their likely future effect on the patient—are always contingent on the unique circumstances of their generation. And their esthetic and pragmatic value is inseparable from the artistry of their formulation and delivery. In Goodman's words, "The distinction between convention and content—between what is said and how it is said—wilts" (1978, p. 125).

The debate between objectivists and constructionists quickly falls into a vicious circle that pivots on the "truth" of psychoanalytic interpretation, the "effectiveness" of intervention, and the generalizability and communicability of psychoanalytic experience. Such a debate could be resolved only by reference to particular clinical experiences. For example, analysts who side with Erikson must do so because they are convinced that in *their* clinical experience they have achieved objectively correct understanding of their patients' material. But how could these analysts ever convince their opponents unless they were able to transmit to them the essence of the clinical experience that forms the basis for their own beliefs? And it is just this transmissibility and communicability of psychoanalytic experience that their opponents refuse to accept.

However, a constructionist point of view need not lead to relativism and the abandonment of every claim to knowledge. A constructionist view of psychoanalysis allows for world-specific truths. When we treat psychoanalytic practice as designlike, we see the analyst as one who fabricates the facts of an analytic situation. Yet, within the world she helps to create, facts are resistant to mere opinion and cannot be wished away. Within a particular created world, it is possible for an analyst—as it is for an architect—to discover the consequences of her moves, make inferences she can falsify by experiment, and, indeed, establish by experiment whether her way of framing the situation is appropriate.

Nevertheless, two psychoanalytic worldmakers, debating with each other, could probably not settle their differences by reference to "the facts." These would be different in their respective worlds. And they could not resolve a debate about the effectiveness of intervention by an experiment, because each would frame and interpret its results differently. In order to come to agreement, they would each have to try to enter into the other's world to discover the things the other has named and constructed there and appreciate the kind of coherence the other had created. Each would have to try to understand the meanings of his own terms in the other's world and identify in his own world the (perhaps odd and unexpected) things and relations that corresponded to the other's terms. In such a process of frame reflection, each might discover how arguments compelling to him seemed utterly inconclusive to the other.

The constructionist point of view makes the communicability of "truths" into a puzzle, makes communication itself problematic in a way that corresponds to our actual experience. If each designer and psychoanalyst constructed in each new practice situation a unique world of his own, within which he formulated and tested his own world-specific truths, how on earth could he make his ideas understandable to anyone else? On this view, we would expect to find the very "babble of voices" which Leston Havens (1973) has described in his study of the schools of psychiatry and which many scholarly critics find in contemporary architecture. The wonder would be that two practitioners could ever move from such divergent starting points to a convergent understanding.

From an objectivist point of view, on the contrary, it is our experience of mutual *mis*understanding that requires explanation. And for this purpose objectivism needs a theory of error. The facts, the truth, the real state of affairs, are presumed to be out there; if we fail to agree about them, some illusion or blindness must be preventing us from doing so. Convergence of meaning, however, requires no special explanation; it is exactly what we would expect.

The advantage of the constructionist point of view is that it fits our experience of mutual misunderstanding, helps make sense of the fact that, often, the more we work at trying to understand one another, the more profoundly we experience the differences among our ways of seeing things. And the image of frame-reflective entry into one another's worlds suggests the experience we have (much less often) of passing from misunderstanding to mutual understanding.

Supervision in psychoanalysis is also usefully understandable as an exercise in communication across divergent worlds. When a resident in psychiatry embarks on the task of learning to become a psychoanalyst, he must try to enter a world that often seems initially strange, opaque, and incoherent. And in order to help him, the supervisor must find a way of bridging to the resident's world. When the process of learning and coaching succeeds—when a resident begins, in his and his supervisor's view, to think and act like an analyst—it has the quality of reciprocal frame reflection.

But in psychoanalysis, as distinct from architectural design, the process is complicated by the fact that the practice to be learned is also a process of entering into another person's world. So the learning/coaching process of psychoanalytic supervision bears a deep resemblance to psychoanalytic practice; and the artistry of supervision, to the artistry of analysis. Coach and student find themselves in a hall of mirrors which, on the one hand, presents them with special sources of confusion and, on the other, gives them special tools for frame reflection.

These are the phenomena we will explore in the two cases of psychoanalytic supervision that follow.

Resident and Supervisor

Let us turn to the protocol of a supervisory session.*

The therapist, a third-year resident in psychiatry, meets with his current supervisor, a psychoanalyst, for one of his weekly

_____

*The protocol discussed in this section was first recorded by two student researchers in the course of a seminar on professional education I

half-hour sessions. (He averages one such session for every seven or
eight sessions with his patient.) Because he has been troubled by
his relations with this supervisor, he has agreed to tape-record a
session with him for later discussion with the researchers.

He begins with the news that his patient, a young woman,
has returned to therapy after several months away.

> *Resident:* She had decided that she wasn't getting
> anywhere in therapy, and I agreed somewhat that the
> same issues were coming up again and again—and
> primarily the issue of her getting stuck in the
> relationship with the man she had been seeing for
> four or five years at that time, and advances on her
> part were matched by withdrawal, and vice versa.

The supervisor listens. Seeing the patient only through the
medium of the resident's stories, he does not listen in the analyst's
evenly suspended way, waiting for interpretations to emerge, but
asks immediately:

> In what way did she get stuck with you, I
> mean, in terms of the same way she got stuck in the
> relationship?

Focusing on the connection between "stuck in the relationship"
and "stuck with you," he frames a puzzle in terms of the patient's
transference: How does the transaction between patient and
therapist mirror her relationship with her boyfriend?

> *R:* Well, she tended to feel that any insights led to
> very little change, and we both noticed that even

---

conducted in 1978. The two students—Bari Stauber and Mike Corbett—
worked with the psychiatric resident to collect the protocol and the
interview material. Each of them wrote a term paper on the protocol.
Although my analysis departs from theirs in many respects, I am indebted
to them for the protocol and for their ideas.

though she saw the pattern of her relationship
outside the therapy, it didn't do much good in her
life—and it was difficult for her to really get emotionally involved in the therapy itself, that she was
[Pause] quite guarded about talking about her past
sadness and disappointments about them.

The supervisor asks whether that was also a problem in her
relationship with her boyfriend.

R: Yes, she tended to restrict the feelings that she
had in that relationship, especially the affectionate
ones—and the sad ones.

Summarizing, the supervisor observes,

So here she rather quickly brings into the
relationship that she's having difficulty and can't
express her feelings—she's stuck, that she feels
somewhat, maybe lowered self-esteem because she's
stuck.

Then he refers directly to the possible use of the transference:

Did you at any time tell her that it's not
surprising that what she experienced in her other
relationships is experienced with you, and that you
have the advantage of looking at how she gets stuck
and trying to work it out together . . . ?

The resident answers perfunctorily,

Yeah, that was part of the work. . . .

and goes on to describe the patient's reentry, the negotiation of fees
and times of appointments. He begins to reflect on these early
sessions:

> *R:*   She, during the first several sessions, repeated a lot of the pattern in the therapy that she had originally come in with in terms of feeling [Pause] very stuck—
>
> *S:*   [Interrupting] What does she mean when she says "stuck"? What's your experience?

This question stimulates the resident to produce a long example, which the supervisor probes with further questions:

> *R:*   Well—there's very much a pattern of her coming and telling me about a fight she has had, often around some kind of misunderstanding. For instance, about the third session, she was saying that they went up to their old haunt. . . . During the visit up there, he asked her whether or not a certain woman had called her. And this woman was a mutual friend, mostly a friend of his. . . . And the patient thought that this woman had been spending some time with her boyfriend. In fact, she knew that they had been together—
>
> *S:*   [Interrupting] What do you mean, "been together"?
>
> *R:*   That they had just visited together—she had some suspicions. [Pause] And she said they fought the rest of the time, mainly over the suspicions she had. Which has been one of their themes. That he goes out with other women and that she can't stand that. And he is not willing to stop. And she's not willing to lay down what she will and will not accept. And so she feels hurt and angry and suspicious when he's with any other woman. Meanwhile, he doesn't like it at all when she goes out with other men.
>
> *S:*   Does she go out with other men?

R: She doesn't, no—but that particular night, they fought the whole night. He took her to a restaurant and she said, "He knows I don't like lobster." He ordered her meal, which was lobster.

S: What d'you mean, he ordered her meal? You mean she was sitting there and doesn't say anything?

R: Yeah, I mean he takes control in many situations.

S: Did you ask her, I mean, how does that happen? If you don't like lobster, did you manage while sitting at the table to order something else yourself?

R: Well, in the past, she said that if she argues with him, there'll be a fight. And it is very painful. Either she has to go along with him and there isn't a fight. Or she argues and objects and there is a fight. And she feels she loses either way. If there's a fight, she invariably loses the fight.

S: How does she lose the fight?

R: Well, it seems that mostly it's because she feels terrible when the fight's over. That he attacks her in the fight with many ways he thinks she is inadequate. . . . She feels worse. And then the other part of it is, she's not willing to risk a total severing of the relationship. There have been a number of times now, she's told him she'll never call him again. And she doesn't want him to call her. And usually after a month, she'll relent.

The supervisor's questions seem designed to elicit stories that could illuminate the patient's stuckness. The incident of the boyfriend ordering her meal contributes to an emerging picture of her passivity and dependence. "How does that happen?" leads the resident to explain how she feels she loses whether she goes along with her boyfriend's demands or resists them. "How does she lose the fight?" induces the resident to describe her fear of feeling terrible after fights, her fear of being abandoned, her feelings of inadequacy.

The supervisor's questioning suggests a repertoire of psychodynamic patterns accessible to him (but apparently not to the resident). He uses these to flesh out the resident's stories until they seem ready for interpretation, at which point he shifts abruptly to a search for explanations:

> Well, what's your understanding of why it's this way. Do you have some sense of what the conflicts are?

With this, he indicates a direction of search: the patient's stalemated relationship with her boyfriend suggests a dilemma rooted in inner conflicts.

When the resident goes on to tell more stories, the supervisor pulls him back to the search for interpretation:

> You know, I don't get a sense of what you feel from seeing her. How would you characterize her problems in your own mind, psychodynamically?

The resident attempts an account of her difficulty in getting emotionally involved, "especially with men." This the supervisor brushes aside. He has an explanation of his own:

> S: You may be right—you know her better than I do, we'd have to wait and see. My own sense of it is that she's very disturbed at her own aggression. That she can't assert herself. . . . She can't even mail a letter for herself. You know, she becomes dependent, and when you say, "Well, why do you do it that way, end up eating lobster when you don't like it?" she says, "Well, what can I do?" And then she says, "If it leads to an argument, then I feel very guilty." And she's guilty, and part of her guilt is accepting as reality all of the criticisms that her boyfriend levels at her.

He urges the resident to use this hypothesis in the therapy:

> I would try to get her curious about it. Say, "Look, you seem able to assert yourself, and you get what you want [as the resident, trying to qualify the supervisor's hypothesis, had just argued the patient could do in school and work], but in this particular area you do seem to be stunted." But I think that her fear of being aggressive and asserting herself is at least in part based on her fear of separation, which is . . . that she's going to be left . . . and that she can't somehow take care of herself.

The resident plunges now into a new story about the patient's relationship with an alcoholic father, her anger at her mother for driving the father away, her recognition that she relates to her present boyfriend as she had related to her father, her early marriage, which was "subordinate, in a way, but unexciting."

> *R:* This is the other theme, that she feels a little dead. She feels lifeless, without conflict. Something has to be going on out there between her and someone else in a conflictual way.
>
> *S:* Yeah, I'm not—it may be that she feels dead. I don't know yet.

The supervisor refuses to join the resident's excursion into the patient's history and avoids committing himself to the resident's new hypothesis. He returns instead to the story of the patient's relationship with her boyfriend (illuminated, perhaps, by comparison with her "unexciting" marriage) and offers a new interpretation of his own:

> The man who's nice doesn't interest her. In order for the man to be exciting, [he has] to be a bit of a bastard.

This leads the resident to speculate that indeed the patient may have left therapy the first time because he was "too much of a nice guy." When she wanted to return, he became more "hard-nosed," demanding that she pay more money—perhaps, as the supervisor then says, "becoming the bastard [whom] she likes and expects you to be,"

> or that you might turn into him sometimes, or that you might be struggling and ineffective. And I would look for signs of one or the other developing in the relationship. But, you see, you have to ask yourself, "Is this all a way in which she can't be satisfied because she feels so guilty about it?"

As the supervisor develops this alternative, he demonstrates a particular way of drawing interpretations from the data of the stories:

> She can't even mail a letter for herself. You know, she becomes dependent, and when you say, "Well, why do you do it that way, end up eating lobster when you don't even like it?" she says, "Well, what can I do?" And then she says, "If it leads to an argument, then I feel guilty." And she's guilty, and part of her guilt is accepting as reality all the criticisms that her boyfriend levels at her.

From the fact that the patient allows her boyfriend to mail her letters and order her meals, it follows that she is unable to assert herself: she is dependent. Given her dependence, an argument with her boyfriend causes her to feel guilty (not merely "terrible," as the resident had put it earlier). The supervisor has now linked her dependency to feelings of inadequacy and guilt; and these, to her tendency to accept all of her boyfriend's criticism as reality. He has brought scattered bits of information together, grounding each partial interpretation in evidence drawn from the resident's stories. In contrast, the resident leaps to such interpretations as "the shaky boundaries of the self," "the feeling of deadness," and "the feeling of responsibility for the father's leaving." To each of these interpretive leaps, the supervisor responds, "I don't know yet—we have to wait and see."

The supervisor's chain of inference proceeds: "The man who's nice doesn't interest her"; "For the man to be exciting, he has to be a bit of a bastard"; and so "she constantly keeps herself frustrated." But constant self-frustration demands an explanation. He suggests two alternatives: being in love with frustration, or guilt. The two can go together, says the resident, and the supervisor agrees: "If she feels guilty, she wants punishment," which she then finds gratifying. But punishment for what? Again there are two possibilities: "angry aggressive thoughts" or "sexual wishes." In order to decide between these, he asks whether the punishing fights interfere with the patient's sex life. No, they sometimes stimulate it, says the resident. The supervisor concludes that punishment is a response to sexual wishes:

> If she is punished, then she can enjoy, or if she
> enjoys, then she needs to be punished, or something.
> I would see this as a woman who really feels quite
> guilty—about what, we have to decide—and really
> has, without knowing it, constantly thwarted her
> ability to be satisfied, and that's where she's stuck.

The repeated "really" suggests a coming to rest, as though the supervisor were now satisfied that he had answered his initial question.

Having built an interpretation to explain why the patient is stuck in the relationship with her boyfriend, he proceeds to show how it also explains why she is stuck in therapy. He invites the resident to reflect on the ways he finds himself becoming the person his patient wants and needs him to be. The resident should observe how he is being drawn into the patient's transference and, rather than collude with it, should suggest to her

> that what she experiences in her relationships
> is experienced with you and that here you have the

> advantage of looking at how she gets stuck with you
> and trying to work it out together.

He should get the patient interested in the puzzle of her self-frustration, provoke her curiosity about how, in this particular area, she is "stunted." This would test the utility of the interpretation whose plausibility the supervisor has just established; it would involve the patient in an inquiry like the one the supervisor and the resident have just undertaken, thereby helping her discover how she re-creates in therapy the pattern of her life outside it.

When the resident leaps to yet another explanation of the patient's guilt, the supervisor cautions, "Well, we don't know yet. It's too early to know all of these things." He returns instead to the general observation with which his earlier chain of inference began:

> I think if we can get some sense of this wom-
> an's frustration and of the way in which she con-
> tinues to frustrate herself. . . .

He means to keep his solution to the puzzle open-ended.

In the half-hour session recorded in this protocol, the supervisor has demonstrated a psychoanalytic frame experiment. First he has reframed the patient's problem as a puzzle located squarely in her transference. Then he has linked the resident's stories of her life in and out of therapy, accumulating, probing, and developing them until the precipitate of an interpretation seems ready to form. From observations close to the language of the stories themselves, he has gradually constructed an explanation that connects her recurrent dilemma to her inner conflicts: she can't be satisfied, because she feels guilty about it, and she seeks out the man who's a bit of a bastard because she wants punishment. Then, with his question about the effect of the fights with her boyfriend on their sex life, he conducts an experiment to decide what the punishment is for: "If she is punished, then she can enjoy. . . ." And finally, he proposes an intervention to test his interpretation and, at the same time, help the patient: get her interested in using the transference to explore the puzzle of her continual self-frustration.

What does the resident make of this demonstration? After listening to a tape of the session, he complains that the supervisor was not telling him what he wanted to hear; then, on reflection, he adds that *he* was not saying what he wanted to know. He doubts that the supervisor is an effective role model for him; he wants more help than he is getting but feels angry when he asks for it. He senses that the supervisor has formed but never expressed a negative judgment about him, and he explains it in terms of their different approaches to psychotherapy: "He is more psychoanalytic, while I deal more with the conscious phenomena." Yet, in the protocol he reveals an eagerness to join—indeed, compete with—the supervisor's psychoanalytic puzzle solving.

Clearly, the resident wants the supervisor's approval. He tries to get it by offering long stories peripheral to the supervisor's main line of inquiry, then proposes interpretive leaps of his own, and finally joins and embellishes the supervisor's train of thought. But the supervisor ignores his digressions and brushes his proposals aside with a faint "You know her better than I do" or "We'd have to wait and see." And although the resident finally tries to join the supervisor's reasoning, he never seems to grasp it fully. What eludes him is the system of understanding that lies behind it.

The supervisor, having fastened early in the dialogue on a question that informs his entire inquiry, never allows the resident to divert him from it. He interrupts frequently to get back to the main road whenever he feels the resident has departed from it. He asks for the resident's solution to the puzzle but rejects it perfunctorily in order to propose and develop his own. Yet he never explains why he drops the resident's proposal, never describes the story types and patterns that guide his search for interpretation, never reveals the thoughts and feelings that underlie his shifts from one phase of the inquiry to the next.

The resident does not know whether the supervisor is unwilling or unable to describe his own reasoning. The supervisor has not offered, and the resident has not asked. As he wistfully observes,

> I am not explicit about what I want from the
> supervisor and he is not explicit about what he gives,
> and so it just happens.

Nor has the supervisor tried to discover what the resident makes of his demonstration. His approach to instruction consists in demonstrating and advocating psychoanalytic inquiry while circumventing or fending off the resident's deviations from it. He exhibits his mastery of the material, and he keeps its sources mysterious.

The resident's approach to learning is also one of mystery and (passive) mastery. He does not express his dissatisfaction and frustration, question the hidden sources of the supervisor's demonstration, or state what he wants to learn.

The dialogue of resident and supervisor suggests the dialogue of Judith and Northover. Both pairs are locked in mutually incongruent understandings of the substantive material and their own interaction. Yet it is striking that these two therapists do not choose to climb the ladder of reflection to reflect on their own learning bind.

In one of his interviews with the researchers, the resident discovered this point. Excitedly he showed how his relationship with the supervisor resembled the patient's relationship to him. Like his patient, he felt stuck with the person who was supposed to help him, wanted more than he felt he was getting, and was angry at himself for wanting it. This analogy did not come up for discussion in the supervision, however. Had it done so, the boundaries of reflection might have been stretched to include the dialogue of student and coach; the supervisor might have reflected aloud on his own performance, and the resident might have glimpsed its mysterious sources.

A Case Conference Approach to Supervision

In two articles published in the mid 1970s, David Sachs and Stanley Shapiro present an approach to psychoanalytic supervision whose central principle they describe as "parallelism" between therapy and education.

Working with a mixed group of third-year residents in adult psychiatry and second-year residents in child psychiatry, the authors used case conferences to teach psychoanalytic therapy with adolescents. As one student presented a case, the others were encouraged to react to the material as though they were the therapist, interrupting the presentation whenever they wished. The supervisors explored participants' responses. They looked for shared, implicit assumptions, applying "the same method one uses in therapy in following the trend of a patient's associations" (Sachs and Shapiro, 1976, p. 395). They discovered that student therapists *reenacted* in the conference what had gone wrong in the treatment: they took their patients' roles and placed the group in a position analogous to their own. The supervisors then took as their chief task precisely the kind of reflection on the supervisory process that the resident in the preceding example had missed in his own supervision.

In their 1974 paper, Sachs and Shapiro describe a case strikingly similar to the resident's case. The patient, a sixteen-year-old girl, "reported to her therapist that she had asked her boyfriend if it was all right if she went out with someone else. She was not anxious to accept the date but felt that she could not turn the young man down lest she hurt his feelings. Her boyfriend was vague in his response but became upset and sulky for several days after the date. She was both upset and puzzled by his reaction, feeling that she had done the right thing by asking beforehand" (p. 53).

The residents were asked to analyze the situation and propose responses to it. Some of them saw the girl as "bitchy" and believed the therapist should tell her so, making her see that she had upset her boyfriend; they hoped to prevent her from doing the same thing again. Others saw her as trying to be "nice"; they thought she deserved support in her struggle to stand up to her unreasonable boyfriend. How could the matter be decided?

The supervisors noted that "both groups had evolved an intervention after first arriving at a value judgment about the patient's behavior" (Sachs and Shapiro, 1974, p. 54). Either position would put the therapist in an adversarial relation to the patient, they pointed out, thereby replicating her adversarial

relationship to her parents. They suggested she should be helped
to see that she had not fulfilled her intention to avoid hurting
anyone. She needed to see that she was in a no-win situation,
possibly the result of an internal conflict "where contrary wishes
or motives exist and . . . only one side of the conflict may be
conscious and accessible" (p. 55). No matter what course of action
she followed, she would hurt someone, just as she had once
become pregnant, hurting herself through a similar inability to say
no for fear of hurting someone else.

Once this pattern had been established, the student therapist
offered additional evidence for it. He reported that the patient had
begun to show some resistance, in the form of pauses and
"searching glances at the therapist for some response" (p. 58). She
also expressed annoyance at having to maintain the burden of the
conversation with her boyfriend and felt pressed by his demands
for sexual relations. She described a vacation trip on which "at
first she begged off sleeping with him because of a painful
sunburn and went to her own room, but she could not stand this
and came back some time later to spend the night" (p. 59). The
therapist reported to the conference that he felt the need to do
something in order to avert a crisis.

Although the group agreed that something had to be done,
they had no specific suggestions. It became apparent that they
wanted their supervisors to come up with the right thing to do.
Instead of obliging them, Sachs and Shapiro drew their attention
back to the case conference. They pointed out that the residents
expected them, as avowed experts, to know what to do and seemed
to feel justified, as novices, in expecting to be given the right
answer. They observed that patient and residents held the same
view of therapy. The patient believed she would be cured if only
she could find out some basic truth; the residents believed they
were supposed to know what was wrong, eliciting the right answer
from the patient by asking her the right questions. The therapist
in this case was very uncomfortable because he really did not know
what to say or do. In increasing frustration, he turned to the
conference for help. "Essentially, then, he was repeating with the
conference what the patient was doing with him" (p. 61). Both he
and his patient expected magical help from others in the form of

right answers. And the group became aware that, as they waited to be given the right answer, they were experiencing in the conference what the patient herself was experiencing in therapy.

The real task for both therapist and patient was to "examine the assumptions by which they find themselves . . . subordinated to a supposed expert to whom they have attributed such omniscience" (p. 64). Sachs and Shapiro proposed that the therapist help the patient learn to examine her own mental processes so as to "detect the operation of unconscious tendencies" (p. 67), becoming in this way a model for her. He could help her to identify, at least temporarily, with his way of looking at her actions as signs of transference that illuminated her inner conflicts. He could help her see, for example, how her complaints about her boyfriend's silence might also refer to unexpressed feelings toward the therapist's silence, thus helping to explain her underlying disappointment in therapy. She might be encouraged to "explore and articulate exactly what she wanted from the doctor" (p. 69). This would surface her inappropriate view of him as omniscient and give her an opportunity to examine the poor self-image that led her to overestimate other people—men, in particular.

In a later paper (Sachs and Shapiro, 1976), the authors describe another example of coaching based on exploitation of parallelisms between case conference and therapy. Here, the patient was a fourteen-year-old boy, suffering from enuresis and dyslexia, whose difficulties with sexual exploits, cheating in sports, and bullying gave his behavior a "delinquent quality" (p. 397). The student therapist had developed an easy and comfortable relationship with the boy, confining himself to listening and occasional questioning as the boy communicated a steady flow of material. In the case conference, the therapist's reports captured the flavor of the boy's street talk in an entertaining way. But the therapist regularly withheld from the boy his ideas about the possible meanings of the boy's material.

The supervisors noted that, in the hands-off attitude that prevailed in the conference discussions of this case and in the general enjoyment of the therapist's entertaining presentation of the patient's material, "the conference was stalemated in a way that paralleled that therapist's stalemate with his entertaining patient" (Sachs and Shapiro, 1976, p. 399). Like the therapist, the group was reluctant to disrupt the performance with challenging questions or suggestions. Instead of telling the conference about the therapy, the therapist was unwittingly reenacting it, putting himself in the patient's position as he put the group in the position of therapist. The supervisors argued that "what we did in the conference demonstrated what the therapist should have done with his patient" (p. 400): if he was unwilling to put his alliance with the patient to a test, the therapy would continue to be stalemated.

At a later conference session, the therapist reported that his patient had missed two consecutive appointments without canceling them in advance. Although he had just seen the patient that morning, he said there was very little to discuss with the group and proposed that they go on to another case. The group had no objection. But the supervisors wanted to know what had happened in the morning session. The resident then described what had happened:

> The patient explained that not only had he forgotten . . . his mother had forgotten also. It was just one of those things. He then went on to say that there was a lot going on at home. His sister had come home from the hospital and was found to have an infection under her cast. He commented on the poor care she was given by those doctors in the hospital. Then he complained about something his mother had not done for him. Next, the young man asked the therapist directly what could be done for facial pimples . . . why couldn't something be done about it? He then went on to relate how he had begun to exercise with barbells to build himself up [p. 401].

When the therapist was asked what he had been thinking when he heard these things, he acknowledged some frustration. He strongly suspected that a resistance was operating and hoped to learn more by asking questions. It was pointed out to him that the patient had already answered the resident's questions without knowing it: his reference to his sister might be a veiled comment about his own therapy; the therapist's facial acne might have led the patient to wonder how he could be helped by someone who had problems similar to his own; and the patient's disappointment with therapy, together with his self-prescribed barbell program, might be a way of saying, "If you aren't going to help me, I'll have to do it myself."

The supervisors observed that the patient might not be willing to unburden himself indefinitely without getting more than friendship in return. Disappointed in therapy, he was acting out his feelings rather than discussing them directly. Then they described what they thought was happening in the conference. The therapist had suggested going on to a new case, and no one in the group had challenged him. The group's passive compliance mirrored the therapist's stance toward his patient. And the therapist, like the patient, had lost interest in his treatment.

In response to these comments, the resident admitted frankly that he had wished to avoid presenting that day because of his disappointment with the conference; he had reached a dead end with his patient and was getting no help. The supervisors observed that the group had gone along with the therapist's avoidances, motivated by an exaggerated concern for the therapist's feelings— just as he had avoided upsetting his patient. "The stalemate in the conference was broken by our intervention, which did not permit dropping the case. . . . What the patient needed to be told was that he was disappointed with the treatment and was showing it by not coming" (Sachs and Shapiro, 1976, p. 405).

What produces such parallelisms between therapy and case conference? The authors suggest a complex answer. First, they introduce Freud's idea of the compulsion to repeat: the tendency of patients to act out what they have repressed. To this they add the idea of "identificatory reproduction": the therapist identifies with the patient, while the latter takes on the attitudes and behavior of his infantile object. So, the authors believe, their students acquire a compulsion to reenact the process, forgotten and repressed, by which they became identified with their patients. The basis for this identification is overlapping experiences of vulnerability: the patient's, in relation to his own problems; the novice therapist's, in relation to his patient. The therapist's "unexamined perfectionism"—his expectation that he ought to know what to do—signifies an unresolved need for omnipotence that resonates with the patient's similar need, "creating the identification . . . reenacted in the conference as a parallelism" (Sachs and Shapiro, 1976, p. 408).

The authors try to undo the therapist's identification with his patient. They refuse to meet his expectations for "right answers." These would only reinforce the need for and belief in omnipotence that underlies his identification with his patient and support the mistaken belief that he can be taught psychotherapy when actually he can only be "helped to learn how to do it." Moreover, belief in an expectation of right answers "places the students . . . in competition both with each other and with the instructor, to see who is 'right.' It takes the residents' attention away from the scrutiny of their own way of processing the clinical data by which they can begin to examine their own assumptions. As soon as 'the answer' is given by the 'expert,' there is a natural tendency on the part of the residents to turn off their own efforts. When this happens, learning stops" (Sachs and Shapiro, 1974, p. 73).

The authors' approach to supervision focuses instead on the "mirroring, reflecting, doubling" (Sachs and Shapiro, 1976, p. 401) by which residents unconsciously reenact their experience of the patient in therapy. Sachs and Shapiro seek to "point out the parallelism and trace it back to its source in the patient in an effort to undo the identification that has taken place. The aim is to provide the therapist with the means of unraveling the identification so that he can understand the patient's thoughts and feelings" (1976, p. 414). They try to become "teachers unlike any [the students] have known in the past, helping them to learn to examine their own mental processes and to detect the operation of unconscious tendencies" (1974, p. 67). By modeling this kind of teaching, the authors try to help their students practice it with their patients. Hence, they frequently admit their own uncertainties, make clear when they do not know what to do, and reveal the reasoning and feeling by which they sometimes grope their way to answers.

They anticipate, and encounter, resistance. Anxiety and vulnerability cause the students to withhold their thoughts and feelings. Students are reluctant to give up their belief in expertise, and they become anxious when invited to scrutinize their own responses. Early in the supervisory process, the authors try to deal with the sources of the students' resistance by expressing their view of the parallelism between treatment and supervision. They point out that identification is not only unavoidable but necessary to treatment (Sachs and Shapiro, 1976, p. 412) and that "the therapist's own empathic responses can be used as a source of information in understanding the patient" (1976, p. 412). When examples of the students' resistance arise, the authors treat them as "forms of communication indicating trouble in the students' ability to be candid" (1974, p. 72). They call attention to such examples and invite the students to reflect on them—just as they would like their students to respond to their patients' resistance.

Conclusion

We have now described several examples of designlike inquiry in psychoanalysis: Erikson's response to his patient's dream, the supervisor's reasoning out the puzzle of the young woman stuck in therapy as in her relation to her boyfriend, and Sachs and Shapiro's case conference discussions of adolescent patients. These several examples bear a strong family resemblance to one another. In all of them, inquiry proceeds from an overarching theory but does not, in any mechanical sense, apply it. The analysts conduct frame experiments according to broadly shared schemata of inquiry—reflection on manifestations of the patient's transference, for example—and develop variations on such themes as guilt, identification, repressed wishes, and inner conflicts. Analysts construct the meaning of material gathered through their special way of listening to their patient, reason their way to new understandings, and test their interpretations in many ways— ultimately, by the effectiveness of their interventions. In their use of psychoanalytic theory, they are more like artists than like technicians.

Students in psychoanalytic supervision experience versions
of the paradox and predicament inherent in learning to design.
They cannot be taught psychoanalysis, as Sachs and Shapiro point
out, but can only be helped to learn it for themselves. Their
feelings of uncertainty, confusion, and mystery recall the feelings
of architecture students like Judith and Lauda. The resident, for
example, finds his supervisor's world hopelessly impenetrable, and
his dialogue with the supervisor suggests a learning bind no less
impressive than Judith's and Northover's. Sachs and Shapiro
emphasize in their approach to supervision the central importance
of the novice therapist's vulnerability and anxiety.

Psychoanalytic supervision differs from the architecture
studio, however, in its characteristic dialogue. Because supervision
is a hall of mirrors, it contains potentials for frame reflection
beyond those available in the studio.

Both the supervisor and Sachs and Shapiro try to get their
students to reframe the patient's problem and the analyst's role.
But their different ways of doing so highlight the difference
between coaching that ignores the parallelisms between supervision and therapy and coaching that exploits them.

The supervisor demonstrates what it means to think like a
psychoanalyst. He reframes the patient's material in a puzzle that
centers on the patient's transference. He shows how to reason from
two streams of data—the resident's account of the therapy and his
stories of the patient's life—to a plausible interpretation consonant with psychoanalytic theory. And he shows how to test his
interpretation by involving the patient in shared reflection on her
self-frustration. But he does these things in such a way as to
illustrate a theory of action counter to the one he advocates.

In his stance toward the resident, the supervisor conveys a
secondary message:

- I know what you need to learn.
- I will show it to you.
- I will claim to be doing something other than this in order to
  spare your feelings.
- I will reflect on your interaction with the patient and will ask

you to do the same but will keep our own interactions undiscussable.

If the resident picked up this secondary message and used it to guide his behavior with his patient, he would be unable to follow the supervisor's explicit advice. On the contrary, he would show his patient what she needed to learn but keep the therapeutic interaction undiscussable whenever he feared its discussion might upset her.

Like the supervisor, Sachs and Shapiro frame the analyst's role as one of helping the patient see how she brings to therapy the attitudes, feelings, and assumptions that shape her relationships in the world outside. But they also help their students see how they bring to the *supervision* attitudes, feelings, and assumptions that shape their interactions with their patients. The secondary message of the supervisors' behavior is something like this:

- We will help you see how you are doing with us what your patient is doing with you.
- We will do with you what you might also do with your patient.
- And we will make both processes discussable.

In the interaction of supervisor and resident, the undiscussable incongruity between the supervisor's primary and secondary messages feeds the resident's confusion and sense of hopelessness. In the case conferences, Sachs and Shapiro reflect aloud on the therapy and on the case conference itself, moving deliberately back and forth between the two. They use their students' dissatisfaction and frustration in supervision to illuminate both supervision and therapy. They call attention to the relation between the behavior they recommend for therapy and the behavior they exhibit with their students, drawing on the latter's immediacy to illuminate therapeutic practice. And the various ways in which they do these things illustrate how the several mirrorings of a hall of mirrors can contribute to frame reflection.

In the transference, the patient does to the therapist what she has also done to others. In the parallelism, the therapist does to his supervisor (or case conference) what the patient has done to him. Both processes are forms of unconscious imitation in which one person reenacts with another a kind of worldmaking to which he has contributed elsewhere—makes the other into a part of the drama he has played out elsewhere—and thereby provides the other with directly inspectable evidence about his *way* of worldmaking.

The parallelism between therapy and supervision can be analyzed into two distinct components.

In the "parallelism of diagnosis," the therapist reenacts with his supervisor the world of his interaction with his patient. In the case of the sixteen-year-old girl, the therapist and other group members impose on the supervisors a magical expectation of right answers, like the girl's magical expectation of her therapist; and, like the girl, they treat the supervisors as experts. As the supervisors reflect on their experience of the position in which the therapist has placed them, they gain insight into the therapist's experience of the position in which the patient has placed him.

In the "parallelism of intervention," the parallelism of diagnosis is reversed. From his position as "therapist," the supervisor enacts with the resident the kind of intervention he would like the resident to pursue with his patient. Sachs and Shapiro do this by public reflection on the parallelism of diagnosis. They point out that the therapist's expectation of expertise mirrors the young girl's belief in some basic truth that will cure her. They invite the therapist to reflect on his reenactment of the therapeutic situation and ask him to notice the unconscious perfectionism and need for omnipotence that have induced him to accept the girl's demand that he tell her what to do. By example and explicit advice, they suggest to the therapist that he give up expertise in favor of a psychoanalytic way of thinking and doing, helping the patient reflect on inner conflicts revealed by the manifestations of her transference. Their advice is like the supervisor's, but in their case, it decribes an intervention like the one they have just carried out with the resident.

Not all forms of frame reflection depend on the parallelisms of a hall of mirrors. When the dialogue of student and coach takes the form of Follow me! a student can try to enter into a coach's

Figure 5. Some Forms of Frame Reflection Possible in a
Hall-of-Mirrors Practicum.

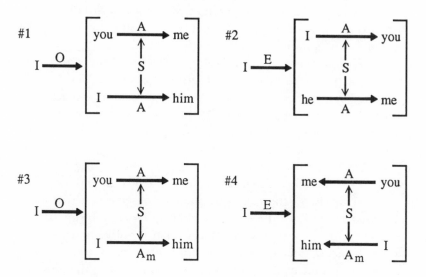

O   = observe
E   = experience
A   = act on
A_m = might act on
S   = similar to

way of seeing and doing. She can discover what it feels like to
follow a coach's instructions or do as the coach has done. And a
coach can reciprocate by reflecting on the student's attempts to
enter into his view. In a hall of mirrors, however, there are
additional possibilities for frame reflection.

     First, a coach can help a student discover how she has
framed a role or problem in practice by showing how she has re-
created it in the practicum. The student can now see in others,
from the outside, what she had earlier experienced from the inside.
So the student's framing of the situation can become *visible* to her
as an object for private and public reflection. Her awareness of the
way she has already framed a role or problem prepares her for the
task of entering into a new way of framing it.

Second, by doing to the student as the student might do with her patient or client, the coach can enable her not only to observe the kind of action she might carry out (as in Follow me!) but also to experience what it feels like to be on the receiving end of that sort of action.

These forms of frame reflection make use of inner and outer views of action—action as felt and action as observed. They exploit perceived similarities between interactions of a practicum and those of a practice world. They do these things retrospectively, in relation to events that have already happened, and prospectively, in relation to those that might happen.

Figure 5 displays possible combinations of these dimensions—inner and outer, practicum and practice, past and future.

In the first schema, I (the student) observe you (the other students) acting toward me as I have acted toward him (my patient or client). In the second, I experience what it is like to act toward you as he acted toward me. In the third, I observe you (the coach) acting toward me as I might act toward him. And in the fourth, I experience your (the coach's) action on me as he might experience my action on him.

So my earlier action becomes visible to me in your present action toward me; and my client's earlier experience becomes accessible to me in my present experience of interaction with you. I observe in your present action how I might act with my client, and I experience now what he might later experience with me. My efforts at frame reflection are enhanced as I ring the changes on parallelisms available in a hall of mirrors—integrating inner and outer views of my earlier practice and the new practice I seek to learn.

🌿 Chapter Ten 🌿

A Reflective Practicum in Counseling and Consulting Skills

For the past fifteen years, Chris Argyris and I have worked together, in our teaching and research, to develop both a theory of competent interpersonal practice and a practicum in the acquisition of its skills. Our work has focused on the practices of organizational consulting and personal counseling and on the interpersonal dimension of professions like business management, public administration, and teaching. Our students have come from schools of education, management, planning, and public policy, among others; participants in our research activities have included industrial managers, school administrators, lawyers, and academic researchers—indeed, at one time or another, representatives of most recognized professions.

We have proposed (Argyris and Schön, 1974, 1978) that human beings, in their interactions with one another, *design* their behavior and hold theories for doing so. These theories of action, as we have called them, include the values, strategies, and underlying assumptions that inform individuals' patterns of interpersonal behavior. We have distinguished two levels at which theories of action operate: There are espoused theories that we use to explain or justify our behavior. Managers, for example, often espouse openness and freedom of expression, especially about negative information—as in "My door is always open" or "I want no 'yes men' around here; managers in this company are expected to say what they think." But there are also theories-in-use implicit in our patterns of spontaneous behavior with others. Like other kinds of knowing-in-action, they are usually tacit. Often we are unable to describe them, and we are surprised to discover, when we do construct them by reflecting on the directly observable data of our actual interpersonal practice, that they are incongruent with the theories of action we espouse. For example, a manager who espouses openness may nevertheless systematically withhold or soften the expression of any information he or she thinks other people are likely to treat as negative.

Argyris and I have constructed a very general model of theories-in-use to describe interpersonal behavior, especially in situations of difficulty or stress. The values (or governing variables), strategies, and assumptions of this model, which we call "Model I," are listed in Table 2. Its values are "Achieve the objective as *I* see it," "Strive to win and avoid losing," "Avoid negative feelings," and "Be rational" (in the sense of using "cool reason" to persuade others). Its strategies include unilateral control of the task environment and unilateral protection of self and others.

Examples of Model I behavior have been described in previous chapters: Northover's and Judith's strategies of mystery and mastery, to mention one instance, and the supervisor's camouflaged dismissal of the resident's ideas, to mention another. Model I strategies rest on assumptions by virtue of which they seem to be plausible means of achieving Model I values—for example, "Interpersonal interactions are win/lose games" and "Other people will not detect my strategies of unilateral control." Model I theories-in-use contribute to the creation of behavioral worlds that are win/lose, closed, and defensive. It is difficult in Model I worlds to reveal one's private dilemmas or make a public test of one's most important assumptions. As a consequence, learning tends to be limited to the kind that Argyris and I have called "single loop": learning about strategies or tactics for achieving one's own objectives. In Model I worlds there is little or no "double loop" learning about the values and assumptions that drive one's own or the other person's behavior. A Model I consultant may learn, for example, how to keep a client focused on a predesigned agenda but is unlikely to examine the price paid for efforts to exercise unilateral control over the client.

Table 2. Characteristics of Model I.

Governing Variables for Action	Action Strategies for Actor	Consequences for Actor and His Associates	Consequences for Learning	Effectiveness
1. Achieve the purposes as I perceive them	Design and manage environment so that actor is in control over factors relevant to me	Actor seen as defensive	Self-sealing	
2. Maximize winning and minimize losing	Own and control task	Defensive interpersonal and group relationships	Single-loop learning	Decreased
3. Minimize eliciting negative feelings	Unilaterally protect self	Defensive norms	Little public testing of theories	
4. Be rational and minimize emotionality	Unilaterally protect others from being hurt	Low freedom of choice, internal commitment, and risktaking		

Source: Adapted from Argyris and Schön, 1974, pp. 68–69.

Table 3. Characteristics of Model II.

Governing Variables for Action	Action Strategies for Actor	Consequences for Actor and His Associates	Consequences for Learning	Effectiveness
1. Valid information	Design situations or encounters where participants can be origins and experience high personal causation	Actor seen as minimally defensive	Testable processes	Increased
2. Free and informed choice	Task is controlled jointly	Minimally defensive interpersonal relations and group dynamics	Double-loop learning	
3. Internal commitment to the choice and constant monitoring of the implementation	Protection of self is a joint enterprise, oriented toward growth	Learning-oriented norms	Frequent public testing of theories	
	4. Bilateral protection of others	High freedom of choice, internal commitment, and risktaking		

Argyris and I advocate a different model of theories-in-use, which we call "Model II" (see Table 3). Its governing variables are valid information, internal commitment, and free and informed choice. Model II aims at creating a behavioral world in which people can exchange valid information, even about difficult and sensitive matters, subject private dilemmas to shared inquiry, and make public tests of negative attributions that Model I keeps private and undiscussable. For example, a Model II consultant might publicly test a client's willingness to express disappointment with the consultant's performance. She might test how far she can go in making discussable issues of doubt and mistrust that frequently arise in relationships between clients and consultants.

In a Model II behavioral world, learning need not be limited to single-loop learning; it can also include learning about the governing variables that underlie behavioral strategies. For example, a manager and his subordinate might explore how they have colluded to keep from discussing issues that might bring them into open conflict.

From the early 1970s onward, Argyris and I have worked with people who are interested in examining their actual theories-in-use and exploring the transition from Model I to Model II behavior. We began with participants in a program for school superintendents (Argyris and Schön, 1974) and have continued, individually and together, with business managers (Argyris, 1976), research and development managers (Argyris and Schön, 1978), and consultants in business strategy (Argyris, 1982), among others.

From 1977 on, we began a series of seminars for graduate students in our respective programs at Harvard University and the Massachusetts Institute of Technology. After a first course conducted in the fall by Argyris, we would jointly teach a seminar for fifteen to twenty students who had completed the fall course and wished to continue developing Model II skills. Most of these students were enrolled in the Counseling and Consulting Program at the Harvard Graduate School of Education or in the Department of Urban Studies and Planning at M.I.T., although some participants came from other schools of management, social relations, public policy, or planning in the Boston area.

We held the first of these seminars in 1977, a second in 1978, and a third in 1983. I undertook a fourth alone, in 1984, while Argyris was on leave.

In the following sections, I shall describe in roughly chronological order some of the issues and experiments that have been most important to our students and ourselves. Their sequence will suggest an evolving picture of our students' learning and the ways we have tried to help them.

For Argyris and me, the seminars have been research settings in which we have pursued our inquiries into such topics as the nature of interpersonal theories-in-use, the conditions for and impediments to the transition from Model I to Model II, and the kinds of help most useful to those who wish to make this transition. In all this, we have tried, as will be seen, to involve our students not only as learners but as co-researchers.

From the perspective of this book, the theory-of-action seminars have a bearing on the more general idea of a reflective practicum. They provide examples of long-term cycles of learning and nonlearning and suggest how coaches can learn from reflection on their own cumulative experience. Perhaps most important, they suggest how the theories-in-use of coaches and students affect the potentials for frame reflection. The experiments described in this chapter illustrate one approach to creating conditions favorable to the success of any reflective practicum.

The Paradox and Predicament of Learning and Teaching
Model II Behavior

Typically, students come into our seminars after a course with Argyris in which they get acquainted with our two models, study examples of Model I behavior, and try to invent and produce interventions aimed at criticizing and correcting such behavior. Almost always, their interventions reproduce features of the theory-in-use they have criticized.

Argyris has developed a short case based on the transcript of an interaction between a supervisor, Y, and his subordinate, X. Y has been asked to "help X change his attitudes and behavior so that X could improve his performance." Y has also been told that, although the organization is genuinely interested in keeping X, X will probably have to be dismissed if his performance does not improve. These, then, are Y's comments to X:

1. X, your performance is not up to standard (and moreover . . .).
2. You seem to be carrying a chip on your shoulder.
3. It appears to me that this has affected your performance in a number of ways. I have heard words like *lethargy, uncommitted,* and *disinterested* used by others in describing your recent performance.
4. Our senior professionals cannot have those characteristics.
5. Let's discuss your feelings about your performance.
6. X, now you want to talk about the injustices that you believe have been perpetrated on you in the past. The problem is that I am not familiar with the specifics of those problems. I do not want to spend a lot of time discussing something that happened several years ago. Nothing constructive will come from it. It's behind us.
7. I want to talk about you today, and about your future in our system.

Each student in the course is then asked to answer three questions:

1. What is your reaction to or diagnosis of the way Y helped X?
2. What advice, if any, would you give Y to improve his performance when helping individuals like X?
3. Assume that Y met you in the hall and asked, "What did you think about the way I handled X?" How would you respond? Please write your response in the form of a scenario on the right-hand side of a page. On the left-hand side, write down any thoughts or feelings that you might have had during the conversation but which you would not, for whatever reason, communicate to Y.

Wherever the case is presented, there is near consensus that Y's interventions were not helpful to X. The reasoning processes used to construct the diagnosis involve inferences at varying degrees of distance from the relatively directly observable data (the sentences quoted above). Some comments require a short ladder of inference (a few steps from directly observable data to inferences about the data)—for example, "Y cut off X," "Y criticized X's attitude," and "Y quoted others to illustrate his points." These comments could be easily illustrated by reference to the transcript. Going up the ladder of inference, there are statements such as "Y was too blunt," "Y did not give X an opportunity to defend himself," "Y prejudged X." These inferences may be correct, but they are not self-evident. For example, Y might believe he was not too blunt, did give X an opportunity to defend himself, and did not prejudge him. Y might say that he was blunt in order to be honest, did not give X a chance to defend himself because he did not wish to open up the past, and expressed a top-management judgment of X's performance of which X was already aware.

In these sentences, the respondents make inferences about the meanings Y produced when "helping" X. A third and higher level of inference is illustrated by sentences that go beyond the meanings and motives attributed to Y, presumably to explain his actions—for example, "Y was not interested in getting at the truth," "Y was aggressive, cold, and detached," and "Y was not interested in understanding X."

Most of the respondents' diagnoses contain attributions and evaluations that require complex reasoning about Y's sentences. Very few of the respondents illustrate their inferences; most of them appear to leap from directly observable data to higher levels of inference. Embedded in their diagnoses, moreover, is a micro-causal theory of the interaction between X and Y. For example,

> If Y is blunt and negative, judgmental and offen-
> sive, threatening and lacking in sensitivity, not
> interested in understanding X, and dominating
> X,

> then X will feel rejected, prejudged, treated unfairly,
> and defensive.

> If the above is true, then: there will be little
> learning between Y and X, and X will not be
> helped.

If the respondents communicate their diagnoses to Y, they are likely to create for Y the same conditions for which they condemn Y for creating with X. If they tell Y that he is "blunt," "cold," and "insensitive," for example, Y is likely to experience *them* as blunt, cold, and insensitive. The respondents' causal analysis of Y's impact on X depends on reasoning which, if communicated to Y, would very likely create the very conditions the respondents deplore.

When students were given this analysis, most of them at first denied it and tried to prove the instructor's logic invalid. As the discussion progressed, however, many respondents began to agree with Argyris. An increasing number of them saw that, in their reactions to Arygris and one another, they displayed the same type of reasoning they had used with Y. They also noticed that, when Argyris made attributions and evaluations about the respondents' actions, he illustrated them and tested them publicly.

When Arygris asked the class to say what they were now thinking and feeling, most of them used such words as *shock, surprise,* and *disbelief.* However much they had studied and espoused Model II, most of them were shocked by the discrepancy between their initial expectations of their behavior and the Model I theory-in-use they had discovered in themselves.

Students react in various ways to this shocking discovery. Some drop the course. Others continue in a passive and defensive mode. But a substantial number—those who go on to participate in the theory-of-action seminars with which this chapter is concerned—are intrigued to explore and restructure their theories-in-use.

These students now share a predicament. They know what Model II looks like in the abstract and, for the most part, believe they understand and agree with it. Although they can sometimes recognize examples of Model II behavior, they know that they are usually unable to detect their hidden Model I reasoning or to invent and produce Model II responses to difficult interpersonal situations. Nevertheless, they readily detect Model I features in their colleagues' responses and, with others' help, in their own. Their dilemma is something like this:

- They know how they would like to change their behavior.
- They recognize the desired behavior in others when they see it.

- They recognize, with help, when they are not producing it.
- They do not know where to go from here.

As we work with these students, Argyris and I face a dilemma complementary to theirs. We are able to offer conceptual models, criticize their productions, and demonstrate the sort of behavior they would like to produce. But we cannot learn for them, and much of the help we have to offer them is inadequate or incomplete.

For example, we have devised Model II heuristics, such as:

- Couple advocacy of your position with inquiry into the other's beliefs.
- State the attribution you are making, tell how you got to it, and ask for the other's confirmation or disconfirmation.
- If you experience a dilemma, express it publicly.

But new situations continually suggest new heuristics equal in importance to those already available. Moreover, when Model II and its associated rules of thumb are taken together, they seem internally inconsistent. Making an attribution public, for example, may conflict with the effort to understand a person's thoughts and feelings. An attempt to surface a private dilemma may seem, in a particular context, like a bid for unilateral control.

Finally, although the propositions of Model II are generalizations, Model II interventions are always particular to a case at hand. A person skilled in Model II behavior exhibits in her interventions an intermediate artistry that is not part of Model II itself. Students who try to "apply the model" discover that they must acquire their own versions of this artistry—a very personal process that leads them to reappreciate themselves in the world around them.

A Failure Cycle

In the 1977 seminar, we first became aware of a cycle of failure whose structure we analyzed roughly as follows.

When students felt vulnerable to threat, they would produce "automatic intercepts." Negative feelings like anger, resentment, fear, or impatience would trigger such automatic Model I responses as "blowing up," withdrawal, withholding of information considered dangerous, or projection of anger onto the other person. Typically, a student would be at first unaware of the feeling that triggered his action, though aware of the action itself and its usually unproductive results. As he tried to design and produce Model II interventions, the student experienced psychological failure.

One student, whom I shall call Arthur, wrote in his term paper about such an experience. In the action described by his case and even in writing the case, he had been unaware of his anger toward a subordinate:

> Looking at the data from the case itself, the only negative feeling I was experiencing was fear ("It scares the hell out of me when you say you *think* the preparations for a meeting are all set"), and the only reference I made to anger was to Joe's anger ("Joe, I sense you are getting angry" and "He is really angry now"). . . . I was extremely concerned about appearing incompetent and out of control ("Experiencing that feeling of helplessness . . . is very scary to me"), yet I indicated no concern about dealing with anger, even though the case I reported was a difficult one in which anger played an important part. . . . It seems fair to conclude that, initially at least, if I experienced anger at all, I reported it as a different emotion, for example, helplessness, out of control, or fright; and I may well have projected my own feelings of anger to others—to Joe, for example, in my case.

Careful analysis after the fact, usually in combination with class discussion, led some students to formulate the reasoning associated with their automatic intercepts. In his term paper, Arthur described the class session in which he had first become aware of the crucial importance of his unexpressed anger:

> I began the session seemingly unaware that I was feeling angry. Midway through the session there

is evidence that I acknowledged my anger but doubted the wisdom of expressing it. Finally, I seem to have acknowledged that I should express the anger in order to become more effective. What happened during the class session which led to my recognition that I was feeling angry toward Joe and should express it? Three aspects of the class discussion seem important to me. First, the class, with [the author's] help, kept the focus on anger, a focus which I would not have maintained on my own. Second, the class made it legitimate for me to be angry. . . . Finally, the class analyzed my behavior, via the roleplay, to indicate that I had in fact expressed anger whether I experienced it or not . . . expressing fright in a way that conveyed anger. In essence, the class focused on data, made connections and analyses, and created meanings which I was unable to do for myself; yet these were the very data, connections, analyses, and meanings I needed in order to become more effective in the situation.

Later, Arthur recognized that his anger at Joe was also directed at himself. He had not been aware of this connection but recognized it when it was expressed, first by a student and later by Argyris.

As Arthur thought about putting these discoveries to use in an intervention, he became aware of an additional dilemma. If he failed to express his anger at Joe, he would become increasingly angry at himself and, consequently, ineffective. But how would anger ("blowing up") help him deal with Joe? Later, Argyris suggested the following intervention:

I've got two feelings. One, I'm scared as hell that when the teachers are here, the tables are not going to be set, and if I find myself in that position, I'm going to be angry at you and at me for not monitoring you.

Arthur's reaction was to say, "I think that's . . . what I really was feeling." But he noticed that *he* had been unable to produce a concise intervention that incorporated the several elements of his dilemma.

When students became aware of the automatic intercepts that triggered their cycles of failure, the feelings and reasoning hidden in their automatic responses, and the dilemmas inherent in designing Model II interventions, they realized that they could not handle the complexity of diagnosis and design without outside help. How, then, could they manage such processes on-line under conditions of stress and speed? Argyris and I asked ourselves, why at this stage of their learning should they expect to do so? Yet it was clear from their expressions of frustration and discouragement that they not only expected to make complete interventions that incorporated everything they had discovered through analysis but also expected to get them right on the first trial. Their unrealistically high aspirations reinforced their feelings of incompetence, increased their sense of vulnerability to failure, and produced a level of stress that made on-line reflection more difficult.

Things We Tried

Once Argyris and I had come to this diagnosis of the failure cycle, we presented it to the group for their reactions. Although most of them agreed with our analysis and claimed to find it enlightening, many still wanted a procedure that would always yield correct Model II interventions. Argyris and I knew we could not devise such a program. We thought that, at this point in the seminar, our students should know better than to crave procedural expertise. We wondered what feelings they might be trying to control or fend off in this way. Perhaps, we thought, we should invite them to describe their fears.

We asked them to write a brief paper about the difficulties, concerns, and fears they experienced when they tried to function as interveners, and we distributed a full set of the resulting papers to each of them.

The main themes of the twenty or so papers were the fear of being or appearing incompetent (the meaning of incompetence varying with the type of situation the writer found most threatening) and the associated fear of feeling helpless or impotent. For example,

- Situations I try to avoid: coming to a dead end, in my interaction with a client, without the sense of direction being clear. . . . The question "Have you ever done this type of project before?" used to paralyze me.
- [I fear that] clients will ask me questions . . . in a way indicating they expect me to have an answer, but for which I have no answer . . . clients will ask me in a hostile manner, or regard me as weak, uninteresting, ineffectual, an amateur. . . . I fear these situations, but added to this is that I often don't recognize these situations for what they are when they occur.
- I think I am most fearful, as a interventionist, of appearing to be incompetent—of not knowing what to do or say in response to a reasonable request.

The students' papers revealed a secondary theme of concern about exercising unilateral control, taking charge, or overadvocating—all aimed at fending off the sense of impotence. They wrote, for example, about their fear of being found out by a client when they've claimed to know what they really don't know, being controlled by a client's anger when they raise threatening issues, or missing a lot of what's going on because they put so much energy into "maintaining their consulting agenda."

As they read one another's papers, the students expressed relief at discovering how similar were the fears each had believed unique to himself. Further, they shared a sense that, as one student expressed it, "I don't consciously acknowledge these feelings as they occur." The very act of describing these feelings seemed to open up the possibility of reflecting on them so as to head off the automatic responses they usually triggered.

Toward the end of the course, when we asked the students to describe the trajectory of their semester's learning, several of them called the paper on fears a turning point.

At about the same time that we assigned the paper, we talked with the group about our sense of the need to change the seminar's direction. We acknowledged our uncertainty about how to proceed and owned up to the experimental character of our pedagogy—something we had pointed out at the very beginning but (by all available evidence) had not been seriously heard. At the same time, we proposed, at least for a while, to take a more active role in organizing the experiences of the seminar.

From the beginning, we had introduced our students to the "method of decomposition." We knew that the transition from Model I to Model II theories-in-use would require that students learn to *discover* the meaning of interpersonal situations in a new way, *invent* new strategies of action, and *produce* and *evaluate* the strategies they had invented. So, given a case description of a difficult intervention, we asked students to describe, first, the meaning of the situation, then the strategy they had invented to deal with it, and finally, what they would actually say or do.

As students attempted this task, it became clear, to them and to us, that their difficulties often began with the meanings they had constructed. For example, a student who defined his problem as one of getting a larger group to see what he had already intuitively seen might be loading the situation from the very outset in a way that made a Model II response unlikely. His very definition of the task would lead him to try to "win" by achieving the goal he had unilaterally set. But those who were able to construct a meaning consistent with Model II governing variables were not necessarily able to invent a strategy consistent with their meanings. And those who had invented such a strategy were often unable to produce it.

For example, one student proposed the following strategy for responding to critics of the teacher training program he had devised:

> Minimize reliance on abstractions and generalizations; maximize valid information through the use, or at least the acknowledgment, of directly observable data to support your conclusions.

But the intervention he actually delivered, in roleplay, was:

> John, what evidence to you have to support the belief that the teachers would have an impossible time of it?

Reflecting on this intervention after he had made it, the student agreed that it would be likely to promote defensiveness and create a win/lose situation; indeed, it sounded to him like a cross-examination. He was surprised at his implicit assumption that "John is not supporting his [criticism] with . . . data." For him, as for other students, the method of decomposition led to awareness of the reasoning that underlay his spontaneous responses.

After each such roleplay, we would pause to evaluate what had been done, reappreciate the meaning of the situation, design the next intervention, and produce it. We deliberately slowed the process down and invited the students to request a slowing-down whenever any of them wished to.

In one case, we dealt with the situation of a manager who had expressed dissatisfaction at the outcome of his meeting with a subordinate. Seeking help, the manager had prepared a transcript of the taped meeting and called in a consultant. One of the students (Tom) had played the role of the consultant and another (Larry) the manager. Tom had got into difficulty, building up rather quickly to the feeling that his client had got the best of him. His reformulation of the consulting task was as follows:

> Show Larry how he's been ineffective and ask
> for confrontation, and be strong!

But "strong," as he translated it into action, took the form of interventions that the class evaluated as aggressive and overbearing.

Argyris then reformulated the starting problem, as follows:

> How best to create a choice about how to
> proceed—his initiative or mine?—without sloughing
> off responsibility onto him.

This, Argyris turned into the following intervention:

> Some clients say they would like to start off,
> others prefer me to begin. Which do you prefer?
>
> *Larry:*   I thought you were supposed to know what
> to do.

Argyris accordingly reformulated the new problem,

> He challenges my competence, which requires
> advocacy of my competence, but without defending
> it, and without specifics.

Argyris then said,

> I do know what to do, which is to give you as much
> choice as you want to take.
>
> *Larry:* Well, I'd like to hear what you have to say.

Argyris's next formulation of problem and strategy:

> Take him at face value, move ahead. But hold
> open for his input. I don't want to face him with
> another choice; he's defensive enough.
>
> *Argyris:* I'd like to pick paragraph #1 [in your case]
> and explore other ways of handling it than you did
> there, and I'd like to invite you to question any
> suggestions I made as I go along.

In the discussions of this roleplay, issues arose that proved
to be important for the remainder of the seminar. It seemed, first of
all, that Argyris had no fixed program. Indeed, a *fixed* program—
as one student pointed out—would have put him in the position of
trying to maintain unilateral control. Rather, he seemed to have a
repertoire of ways of framing and responding to situations that
came up in answer to his initial interventions. Having access to a
repertoire, rather than a program, allowed him the freedom to
listen to the client's back talk and to construct new strategies in
response to the meanings he found in the client's utterances.

Moreover, no single intervention had to carry the burden of
all the meanings Argyris constructed for the situation. He could
act on one of these meanings (for example, the wish to give the
client a choice about how to proceed) while reserving for later
interventions such other meanings as the wish to be strong (in the
sense of advocating one's beliefs) and yet to avoid contributing to
the client's defensiveness.

To our surprise, it was a new idea for many of the students that, in this sense, most interventions *had* to be incomplete. After this roleplay, we formulated an "incompleteness theorem," which we described as follows:

- Do not try to be complete or perfect.
- Do not be afraid to be corrective on-line, correcting what you have to say after you've thought about it.
- Identify the major meanings that you infer from what the person is saying and is expressing through nonverbal language. If you believe your inferences validly represent the other's meanings, go ahead and respond.
- Advocate your position as clearly as you can and combine it with an invitation for challenge and correction.
- Do not hesitate to be incomplete, in the sense of expressing only one of several possible positions.
- If you are incomplete, you can say so and/or own up to it later.

Toward the end of the term, when we asked the students to write brief papers in which they described what seemed to them milestones in their learning process, most of them noted both our decision to slow things down and our incompleteness theorem. Arthur, in the term paper quoted earlier, pointed out how crucial it was for him to learn to take the time to work out his discoveries, strategies, and productions. He described his efforts to "work out the connections that explain why I'm angry and to work them out publicly," a process that was for him "tedious, time-consuming, and error-ridden" in comparison with Argyris's quick and efficient on-the-spot analyses. He also reflected on the power of the incompleteness theorem, referring to the class session in which the instructors had put it forward as "a class catharsis in which the class was saying, 'At last we have an explanation for the feelings of frustration, tension, and failure we have been experiencing for the last few weeks.'" But he went on to note that the heuristic did not have its "powerful, cathartic effect until after its meaning had been elaborated and applied in significant ways to the 'world' of the class members."

By the end of the term, Argyris and I, and most of the students, felt that the rate and quality of learning had changed for the better. We became aware of the frequency of "hybrid interventions." Students produced interventions with recognizable Model II qualities, except for some element, often stuck on at the end, that reverted to Model I. A student might say to someone she was trying to help, "Can you give me the data that led you to make that attribution?" but then add, "I felt you were out to get Steve" (without indicating what in the other's statement had led to that attribution). Or a student, roleplaying a dialogue with his boss, might state a need for help and an intention to seek it but then automatically chastise his boss for *his* defensiveness (getting the boss before the boss could get him). Moreover, we found that students would often succeed in producing a Model II intervention only to discover, when the other person came up with an unexpected or threatening response, that they could go no further.

As we tried to explain these observations, it seemed to us that our students were trying to act from Model II rules without having learned to create Model II meanings. As Model II rules led them to abandon some of their defensive strategies, they began to give data that disconfirmed their attributions, express feelings they would ordinarily have withheld, and surface dilemmas they would ordinarily have kept to themselves. But they continued, initially, to create Model I meanings (such as "get him before he gets you!") whose accompanying feelings triggered intercepts of a Model I kind.

The difficulty the students experienced in stringing together sequences of Model II interventions—each an improvised response to the other person's reactions—seemed to reflect their Model I meanings. For example, the "strength" they wanted to show continued to take the form of unilateral control over the other person, and "support" consisted in sympathetic reinforcement of the other person's perceived weakness. Given the complexity of an intervention situation, students seemed unable as yet to form a holistic appreciation of it in Model II terms.

Protectionism

Argyris and I taught our seminar again in the spring of 1978 and again in 1983. In these seminars, we recognized many of the same issues we had encountered in the earlier seminars and noted a general dynamic of the learning process similar to the one described above. In 1983, however, we became aware of a new phenomenon—or newly aware of an old one—and attempted a line of experimentation we had not previously tried.

About midway through the term, we noticed that, although the levels of frustration and discouragement did not seem very high, a group climate of risk aversion and passivity had established itself. With three or four notable exceptions, students selected and wrote cases in a way that minimized risk to themselves. They withheld their negative reactions to other members of the group or revealed them only when following up a faculty member's remark. And when they did venture a criticism, they tended to couch it in the form of a question ("I wonder whether you feel . . . ?"). They showed such concern to avoid hurting people that they ignored actions for which others might well be held responsible; and with one possible exception, they never confronted us or one another as we had confronted them.

Individuals did appear to be learning about themselves and others, progress varying with the individual. Competitive and win/lose dynamics had been moderate at the beginning of the seminar and had decreased since then. Yet, the predominant trend of learning had been to minimize risktaking.

All this seemed to us to make up a group climate whose prevailing norms were self-protection and protection of others— sometimes, indeed, a tacit bargain of reciprocal self-protection. In this situation, we thought, theory-in-use matched espoused theory. At the espoused level, students advocated the need to be concerned and caring about self and others. At the level of theory-in-use, they tended to avoid risktaking, exploration of issues in depth, and conflict with one another; and they were very willing, at the same time, to admit error, guilt, or helplessness. In such a climate, students might learn new skills, but their learning would be limited.

We had asked them to write brief papers in which they described the skills they particularly wished to learn. In these, as in their seminar participation, the twenty-three students fell into three rather clear patterns. The first, and by far most broadly shared, we called Pattern A. These students focused on fears, counterproductive features of theory-in-use, and the feeling of not being in control. They asked, "What is making it hard for me to do it? Why am I worried? What is it that makes me do what I do not like?" They were honest about owning up to weaknesses and short on what to do about them; hence, they appeared more pessimistic. The second group, Pattern B, consisting of no more than three or four persons, focused on their prior learning about Model I defenses. They tried to formulate learning programs in which they set questions to be answered, invented new strategies to be followed and end states to be achieved, and appeared more optimistic. Their attitude was something like "Let's see whether we can learn this!" A third group, Pattern C, composed of only two students, combined features of A and B: they noted some of their defenses, defined goals to begin to reduce them, and looked for ways of trying out those goals.

The Pattern A responses contributed to, and were reinforced by, the protectionist climate that had evolved in the group. The Pattern B people, with their greater willingness to conduct risktaking experiments, used more than their proportionate share of group time, but their example did not affect the overall climate. The group's protectionism seemed to be tacitly accepted—not discussed, perhaps because it was not publicly recognized.

We decided to devote a whole session to discussing the three student patterns and the protectionism of the group as a whole. That session provoked mixed reactions of agreement and disagreement. It also caused members of the group to recall early sessions in which, as they saw it, they had taken significant risks and had been "punished" for doing so. For example, a student who had made a strong bid to redirect discussion toward group process had been sharply confronted by another student because of his "controlling" style and had drawn back to a less visible and assertive role. Other students spoke of the feelings of "threat" they experienced in class, saying, for example, "I don't feel comfortable thinking out loud here."

Our intervention had the effect of opening up some of the group's protectionism. Several members who had been virtually silent made their first steps toward participation. Several students made tentative criticisms of the instructors. And there was a noticeable increase in the students' willingness to risk more daring, complex interventions.

Imitation

In this somewhat more receptive climate, Argyris and I discussed the possibility of trying a new experiment. We were aware that, as usual, students were able to spend a whole class session analyzing a particular point of intervention in a case. Such exercises were often productive, but they also had the effect of preventing students from attempting a longer sequence of steps at each of which they tried to produce Model II responses. A further difficulty was that, on the rare occasions when students did make such an attempt, they seemed to lack a sense of the shape, or schema, of such a process.

In early April, we proposed an experiment in mimicry. We would roleplay a whole dialogue and convert it to a script. A student would then read the script of the dialogue, with another in the role of partner. The students could put things into their own words but would stick to the broad outlines of the script. The participants, and the seminar as a whole, would reflect together on that experience, after which we would construct a schema of the dialogue to be fleshed out and adapted to other situations resembling the roleplay.

We were careful to present this program as an experiment. Although we were not sure what would come of it, and we proposed alternatives to it, we said why we thought it might be a good idea. Some students refrained from comment or assented without enthusiasm, as though to say, "We will go along if you think so," and a few confirmed that they had felt frustrated at being unable to experience a whole Model II interaction. But other students expressed abhorrence of the very idea of imitation, which seemed to them insulting or even degrading. One of the students, Karen, wrote her term paper on this episode.

She noted, to begin with, that I had posed two ways of helping students bring isolated Model II skills together: use of a general action map, "articulate enough to provide guidance for . . . a whole sequence of moves"; and an invitation to students to "quite literally mimic a sequence that seemed to us and you the kind of thing that in fact you'd like to do if you could make it your own." About the second, I had said, "We felt sheepish because— well, is it degrading? But this is how we propose it." Karen recorded the unspoken thoughts with which she had greeted this invitation: "Good. You should feel sheepish. What do they think we are, a herd of sheep or ducks imprinting on our parents?" And later in the class session, she said aloud,

> I feel a lot of caution about what we're doing. Perhaps it's because we're calling it mimicry. I find it offensive because it's monkeylike.

And to herself, she thought,

> Learning by mimicry is what I did as a child and is why I've been embedded in Model I.

Nevertheless, she had finally offered to "give it a try." And some other students had added their support for the idea:

> The people who learn the most quickly are the best mimickers, like in learning athletics.
> I'm intrigued that you can try this thing on and experience whatever feelings come with it.

Karen wrote that she was "amazed that the class was willing to conform so readily," although she herself had expressed her willingness to try it. She went on to write,

An individual who is learning through mimicking a successful Model II person is being
encouraged to stand inside that person's system and
to *try it on*. By standing within another's system, this
individual is unable to stand apart and seek out
information that might modify the system. In essence, s/he is imitating a double-loop example but is
doing so with a single-loop skill.

In our first attempt at this experiment, Argyris modeled a
consultation with one of the students, Ted, who had been
confronted by a young woman about a piece of work they had
done together. Another student had roleplayed a consultation with
Ted, and in the course of it, Ted had expressed his satisfaction
with the student's help. Now Argyris began by questioning the
basis for his satisfaction.

Argyris: Ted, as I listen to you and your consultant, it is difficult for me to understand what help
she's giving you . . .

The interaction went on for five or ten minutes. When it was over,
the students, Ted among them, felt Argyris's intervention had been
helpful and had been, indeed, an example of a Model II intervention. We then asked for volunteers to imitate in roleplay with Ted
the intervention they had just heard.

After a long silence, one student volunteered. He mimicked
Argyris's interventions in a manner that seemed to the rest of the
group—and to himself, as he later admitted—to make a mockery of
the exercise. Moreover, the students, who had done little notetaking during the intervention, had a great deal of trouble remember-
ing what had actually taken place.

For the next session, we asked students to prepare from their
tape recordings a script to be used in a second attempt at imitation.

A student, Ben, volunteered to produce his version of the
script, a copy of which he gave to Ted. When he had finished,
these were some of the comments:

Paul: At the beginning, I didn't think he was *thinking* as he said the words.

Karen: It sounded to me like canned phrases, techniques.

Susan: And yet, it's an artifice useful for learning.

Karen: What we need is "skeletal mimicry," which includes space for me to do it *my* way. I need this if I want to learn from mimicry.

Ben: I felt, "These aren't my words. I can't get it right."

Emily: What we need is to practice *being* the other person—neither Chris [Argyris] nor Ben but somebody else.

Paul and Jeanne then tried to roleplay, working from Paul's script. This led to Karen's saying:

It should be mimicry, not impersonating.

Another student gave an example of having learned to play tennis by mimicking his instructor but added that he had modified his performance by detecting and correcting errors as he noticed the *effects* of his actions.

Paul and Jeanne then tried the exercise again, this time without relying on the verbatim script. The students seemed to feel, this time, that the action had come alive; both participants had got into their roles. Paul said,

I felt some of the panic, but also some of the structure. I felt I could at least feel confident that I could explain my point of view.

Following this session, Karen interviewed Paul for his reactions to the experience:

> Well, I read my script, which was pretty much
> verbatim from Chris . . . it was kind of fun. I had a
> sense of security in that it was all there—knowing
> that I was going to do something right and that it
> was productive, although I was clearly pretending.

She also interviewed another student, who said:

> Mimicry was supposed to give me a sense of
> what a successful intervention would be like. I did
> not feel this because it was not my intervention, I
> hadn't come to the conclusions, and I wasn't
> thinking.

In the second part of her paper, Karen reflected on her initial
abhorrence of the exercise:

- I began to realize that the demands placed on me by mimicry
  were my own creation . . . I started to see how I often see only
  fragments of the present because I view the present through a
  distorting lens of the past. The limitations of mimicry are the
  limitations I place on it.
- The process of inverting my perspective is both liberating and
  frightening. . . . My attack on mimicry is a defense which tries
  to keep fear, and my responsibility for it, out of my awareness. . . . I am happier predicting how damaging mimicry will
  be, and then being happy that it is, than I am taking a risk to
  go beyond where I now am in my learning.
- . . . So through mimicry one can lose freedoms, but can also
  generate new questions and find new voice . . . by trying on
  another person's view, I am not just visiting . . . I hesitate to
  enter another's world out of fear of being swallowed, but if I
  am swallowed, it is my illusion to see it in this way.

Karen's conclusion recalls Johanna's feeling that she could enter
into Quist's world, in order to see things as he saw them, without
fear of being overwhelmed. "I feel that even if someone is very
dominant now . . . I will always be able to undo it later."

Meanings and Feelings

In the spring of 1984, with Argyris on sabbatical leave, I conducted a seminar for fifteen students, all of whom had taken the fall course. Two members of the seminar had also participated in the 1983 seminar described above.

I began by inviting the students to design their own learning experiments, focusing on the particular Model II skills with which they were having difficulty. I hoped, in this way, to help them take on a greater share of the responsibility for their own learning and, at the same time, make the seminar a setting for reflection on the process of learning Model II skills.

The students found it hard at first to understand what, exactly, I meant by a "learning experiment." They had experienced the design and discussion of intervention scenarios, but they could not see what, beyond this, a learning experiment might entail. They agreed, however, to try the idea out. In their first brief papers, most of them described a problem they had identified in earlier discussions of their cases in the fall course or in one of the small groups they created for themselves each semester. But they had difficulty going from a problem to a course of experimental action. Their action plans tended to be vague and general—for example, "To pursue a line of inquiry, advocating my position and being open to the other person's," or "To examine our group processes and dynamics in relation to our own Model I to Model II behaviors."

From the outset, however, they converged on one particular problem. As we began to discuss their new cases and as they redesigned the learning experiments they wanted to carry out, they grappled, more directly than I recalled students having done in earlier seminars, with the puzzle of trying to change meanings and feelings. If this is the meaning I actually create, they asked, and this is the feeling I actually experience, how on earth can I bring myself authentically to mean and feel a different way?

A student who had become aware of the strategies she used to get others to express approval of her attempts at intervention and saw approval as a sign of "caring" asked, "What's wrong with seeking approval?" When I asked her whether she wanted approval for *anything* she did and when others helped her see the conflict between uncritical approval and Model II inquiry, she asked, "But what if you really do feel a need for approval? How do you change a deep feeling of that kind?" She went on to say, "I'm not sure that you can change just by asking yourself to be disciplined."

Another student had become aware of her fear of failure and tried to redefine "success" as the recognition and admission of error; but she then found she had given herself "little incentive to improve my performance." Struck by the negative power of her self-evaluation, she expressed a wish to "escape my feelings' power over me."

A third student, in his analysis of one of the early class sessions, delivered a self-mocking account of his view of the entire class situation as a competition with the other participants to "appear smart":

> I have a number of questions, ideas, about what Don [Schön] is doing. I feel competitive for his approval. I am also angry at him for arousing such feelings. He's confusing me, so I'll be as critical as possible. I'll be quiet; I'm not sure if examining his behavior is valid. So suppress these childish thoughts and be as mature as possible (it might even earn you some approval on the way . . . damn! There you go again!).

His competitiveness, which he saw as childish and wanted to change, led him to deliver his insights into others' interventions in a way that they (and he) perceived as aggressive. This, too, he would have liked to change, but he could not see how to do it.

As the seminar progressed, the focus on meanings and feelings held. This topic was the subject of general discussion as well as work on the students' scenarios. Of course, it was embedded in the dynamics of this seminar group, which, as it evolved, revealed both similarities to and differences from earlier groups. From the beginning, for example, a few students took leading roles. They received special attention because of their greater willingness to put themselves on the line and their greater competence.

The group dynamics were also different because I conducted this seminar alone. For about two thirds of the group, familiar with Argyris's style of teaching, I was at first an unknown quantity. In the first two sessions, as they heard my analysis of their experimental designs, many of them expressed frustration. My analysis pointed to new layers of complexity and difficulty. Could they carry out such analyses for themselves? Some expressed a feeling of being "back at square one." My style was seen as lower-keyed, less sharply challenging, less given to on-line demonstration than Argyris's.

About a third of the way through the term, Argyris paid a visit to the group. He made what some members saw as a much sharper challenge and elicited a much sharper counterchallenge than we had experienced before. Argyris decided, after that session, to forgo further participation. He felt that the pattern of the group had already been established and wanted neither to disturb it nor, at that time, to work through the emotionally demanding issues that he thought would accompany his further participation. In the next session, we discussed the sharply defined dialogue of the previous week. One student—the one who had earlier expressed a need for approval—contrasted that dialogue with the "mucking around" we had previously done. Students differed in their perceptions of the previous session and their expectations of the seminar leader. I proposed that we try to share, among ourselves, Argyris's more active, confronting style.

Gradually, a pattern of group work evolved in which students actively roleplayed their attempts to redesign their cases. Conflicts erupted from time to time. There were underlying currents of competition for group attention. Toward the end of the term, however, the level of competition and defensiveness had noticeably declined. Students displayed great willingness to slow down their interactions and work at the difficult process of testing their understandings and meanings with one another. Indeed, time seemed to move more slowly and calmly, as students became more empathic with one another—each one more ready to see in the other's difficulties a version of his own and, therefore, less jealous of the time and attention devoted to others. In the very last session, as we reflected on the semester's experiences, the question of my leadership was revisited. Some students voiced challenges they had long been withholding and wondered aloud why, since the early sessions, there had been so little challenge to me along the way.

Four distinguishable subprocesses seem to have been important to the students' efforts to grapple with the problem of meanings and feelings.

First, all of them discovered constellations of meanings, reasoning, and action strategies associated with the feelings they found most troublesome. Their discoveries did not progress in a straight line. It was as though they periodically returned to the same issues, at different levels of difficulty, by reflections on class discussions or their efforts to conduct experiments they could now more clearly identify.

They subjected their constellations of meanings, feelings, and reasoning to conscious critique in the light of Model II values. It might be more accurate to say that the abstract language of Model II took on new meaning for them as they applied it to their own newly discovered constellations. Some students seemed to be asking themselves, more realistically than they had done before, "Do I really want to change?" At the same time, they began to see Model II less as a method for effective interpersonal action in the confines of their professional work and more as a way of understanding themselves, shaping their relations with others, and living their lives.

Some students concentrated on the search for heuristics. As they monitored the feelings they had learned to recognize, they considered what questions they should ask themselves and what strategies of behavior they should adopt. In some cases, they expressed the belief that new patterns of behavior, if only they could describe and adopt them, would entrain the meanings and feelings they wished to create.

Some of them placed a new emphasis on acknowledging feelings and meanings they had come to see as negative. They tried, paradoxically, as one student put it, to accept their feelings in order to change them. Frequently, it was through new layers of analysis that they succeeded in acknowledging negative feelings as their own.

How these processes were variously combined, we can see in one student's retrospective analysis of the seminar.

Jane brought to the seminar a case, a conversation with a friend, that seemed to her to illustrate a cycle of self-protection. She had tried, in presenting her case, to make her self-protection discussable. But the class's analysis of another student's case suggested to her how she had actually "controlled the conversation to make it discussable only on my own terms":

> By predefining the goal of the discussion such that I could prove my point, it became impossible to achieve joint control. In order to prove my point, I had to control the conversation unilaterally and was foiled by [my friend's] lack of understanding/acceptance of the point I wanted to make.

She saw how, by using abstractions like "protective cycle" and by withholding her "left-hand column," the silent thoughts that accompanied her utterances, she had reinforced her unilateral control.

In her case, Jane's friend had accused her of being a "private person." In a later seminar session, as part of a more general discussion, I applied the image of a "black box" to Jane:

> We're all black boxes to each other, more or less. For example, Jane, you're a black box to me almost 90 percent of the time. I haven't the faintest idea of what's going on in your head or what you're thinking about almost all of the time . . . and I wonder whether I appear that way to you or whether others appear that way to you.

In her thoughts, unexpressed at the time, Jane felt puzzled. She was chagrined at being singled out and angry that another student responded before she had a chance. Nevertheless, she wrote,

I found the black box metaphor very powerful. In it I also found a parallel with the "private person." And I discovered that the in-class behavior really wasn't so different from the one-on-one situation.

She diagnosed her behavioral strategy as follows:

When I believe someone is critical of me and I feel threatened:
- Believe they might be right or ... wrong but anyway I can't change how they feel or what they think
- Don't inquire into the validity of what I'm hearing or advocate how I experience their position
- Be hurt, confused, feel misunderstood
- Cover up hurt feelings, confused, etc.
- Privately test whether they're right or wrong
- Keep quiet, or direct conversation to ground where I feel more in control

She proposed this alternative intervention:

- Be aware of my emotional reaction to criticism and surface it
- Respond to what I hear; question my understanding of what I hear, by restating to test if I understand it
- Be aware of my habit and try not to short-circuit the discussion by changing the subject
- Don't feel compelled to have an answer—be able to leave the subject open

A friend asked her, in the small group that went on in parallel to the seminar, what governing variables she thought her strategies served. Some two weeks later, she came to this formulation:

- Feeling unsure or confused makes me feel incompetent, which makes me angry at myself because I want to be competent all the time (that is, win).
- I assume that I can control situations to protect myself from appearing incompetent and thus avoid "losing" to others who see my incompetence.

She formulated the underlying value as "Don't play if you can't win," which she thought led her to keep quiet in class—hence to avoid practicing enough to build confidence in Model II skills.

She now saw herself as caught in the following dilemma:

> On the one hand, I wondered how I could've been unaware of the discrepancy between how I act and what I believe in. On the other hand, I didn't see a way to resolve the discrepancy without having to give something up completely, rejecting either a commitment to moving toward Model II skills or some long-held ideas and values, the loss of which appeared even more threatening.

Later, in her small group, she worked on this dilemma:

> *Laura:*   You say you're in conflict about change?
>
> *Jane:*   I'm not in conflict about wanting to change, but I don't know what that change would look like, so it's a little frightening . . .
>
> *Carol:*   The paradox I see is that maintaining silence gives you *less* control of what happens, not more. But you see it the other way around.
>
> *Jane:*   What you said last night about having to own the feelings before being able to relate them—I think I've tried not to own them, which precludes relating them. It's a difficult awareness to come to, how much I've denied of my feelings.

In a synthesis of these experiences, Jane wrote,

> I feel threatened by someone's getting too close
> to things I'm most unsure about myself: my feelings
> of incompetence, inadequacy, unkindness. My strate-
> gies serve to prevent my discovering a more objective
> reality, which is only discernible through other
> people. While there may be a protective cycle at work
> in my dealings with other people, its most destructive
> aspect for me is how it keeps me sealed off from
> learning about and dealing with my internal pro-
> cesses. Learning to acknowledge the feelings that
> start the cycle off is an important step in unsealing
> those processes. . . . As long as I hamstring myself by
> maintaining my "secrets," moving toward mutual
> control will be impossible. I perceive my work this
> semester as progress toward uncovering those secrets
> and making it possible for me, with the assistance of
> others, to become aware of protectionist gridlock and
> start dealing more openly with its effects.

In Jane's case, learning to own the "secrets" she has
heretofore denied proceeds in tandem with rethinking her underlying wish for control and self-protection. She records a kind of
work that includes monitoring negative feelings, discovering
underlying constellations, and inventing new behavioral strategies.
She emphasizes the process by which she has acknowledged and
reframed meanings, feelings, and reasoning.

Other student's papers revealed similar kinds of reflection.
One spoke of an "increasing tolerance for feelings in myself and in
others which do not mesh with my espoused values." Her case had
dealt with an anxious student of hers, whom she had tried to help.
After the class discussion of it, she saw that she did "feel
responsible for [the student's] anxiety" and had projected onto the
student her own "fear of failure," of which she was ashamed. This
negative self-evaluation had led to her uncritical acceptance of
responsibility for the student's anxiety and had kept her from
helping the student to examine her own possible responsibility for

it. "Ultimately," she observed, "the more I can come to recognize my negative feelings about others as expressions of my negative feelings about myself as well, the more I can empathize with them and accept the human weakness in them and myself."

Conclusion

This account of the seminars Argyris and I conducted over seven years contains several themes relevant to developing the general idea of a reflective practicum:

- Versions of the paradox and predicament inherent in learning a designlike practice appear in the theory-of-action seminars and give rise there to a failure cycle that may be characteristic of an important class of practicums.
- In our response to the failure cycle, Argyris and I treated our coaching as material for reflective experimentation and tried to involve our students as co-experimenters—creating a variant of the hall of mirrors that opens up possibilities for use in other coaching situations.
- At different stages of the several seminars, we became aware of a variety of blocks to learning and devised experiments to deal with them. Both the blocks and the experiments may be pertinent to other practicums.
- The three models of coaching discussed in earlier chapters of this book are all present in the theory-of-action seminars. Their suitability to different learning contexts can now be explored.
- Model II was the principal subject of the theory-of-action seminars, but its utility to the communicative work of any reflective practicum can now be examined.

The Failure Cycle and Its Generalizability. Students in the theory-of-action seminars experienced a failure cycle, in part because of features that Model II behavior shares with all designlike practice and in part because Model II behavior is a particular *kind* of designlike practice.

At the time of their entry into the spring seminar, our students have been shocked into awareness of the gap between their espoused theory of action and the theory-in-use they actually displayed in exercises like the X/Y case. They have seen that Argyris can carry out Model II principles on the spot, under pressure, but that they themselves cannot. They hope now to learn to do as they have seen him doing, and they are prepared to believe that he and I can help them.

But they soon discover that the principles we give them—the formal description of Model II and the heuristics associated with it—are not enough to enable them to behave in accordance with Model II. They learn that there is, in addition, a kind of artistry by which such principles are converted to concrete actions and that, no matter how many principles they absorb, the artistry essential to Model II behavior still eludes them.

They discover that they have not yet learned to recognize in their own action the qualities distinctive of Model II meanings, objectives, and outcomes.

These discoveries pertain, as we have seen in earlier chapters, to features of any designlike practice and would be sufficient by themselves to account for the students' initial experience of failure. In addition, however, the students discover the power of their tacit Model I theory-in-use. Even when they have become aware of a Model I error—for example, their tendency to make unillustrated negative attributions to other people—they find that, under pressure, they cannot avoid making a similar error again. They learn to identify sources of error in negative feelings like anger and shame that arise under conditions of threat, remain below the threshold of focal awareness, and trigger automatic Model I intercepts.

This additional layer of difficulty may not arise in learning *every* designlike practice, but it is not unique to learning Model II. It holds whenever learning a new competence requires *unlearning* deep-seated theories-in-use or whenever, in situations of uncertainty, feelings of vulnerability linked to Model I expectations of "being in control" and "knowing what to do" evoke automatic defenses—in medical internships, for example, when students are helped to recognize clinical problems for which there is no readily available expertise, or when teachers are encouraged to listen to their pupils in order to discover what hidden sense may underlie their "wrong" or "crazy" answers.

Under such conditions, it would not be surprising to find that students experience a version of the failure cycle, the development of which affects their views of themselves as learners, their attitudes toward their instructors, and the group dynamics that evolve from individually experienced failure.

For the most part, like the residents in Sachs and Shapiro's case conferences, students hold unrealistically high expectations for their performance. Once they become aware of their errors, they believe they should be able to produce complete and perfect interventions. They see error as failure, and when they repeat their errors, they experience a blow to self-esteem. They do not as yet have the idea of a learning process in which imperfect actions are continually modified through reflection-in-action. Hence, their growing awareness of complexity and dilemma leads them to discouragement or even despair.

They are ambivalent toward their instructors. They feel they perform under scrutiny, and they are anxious to compete with one another for the instructor's approval (reproducing in this way the familiar idea of "school"). They tend to hide their feelings of uncertainty; criticism often makes them defensive. At the same time, they may feel awe at an instructor's competence, which makes the instructor seem more distant from them and amplifies the apparent size of the learning task.

Such feelings may reawaken the students' ambivalence toward the practice they have set out to learn. Do they really want to learn it, if *this* is what it entails? Like Sachs and Shapiro's residents, students sometimes respond with demands for sure-fire technique. They may read an instructor's inability to give them what they crave as a sign of incompetence. Emphasis on artistry may increase their discouragement and provoke their anger.

Discouragement and frustration may spread contagiously. The students' competitiveness and struggle for "air time" may lead them to speed up the pace of discussion and circumvent confusions, thereby contributing to further error. When individuals respond to these experiences by pulling in their horns, taking fewer risks and avoiding confrontation with others in the hope of reducing confrontation of self, the group climate turns to protectionism.

Responses to the Failure Cycle. As Argyris and I became aware of the students' failure cycle and began to experiment with responses to it, we invented coaching strategies broadly relevant to any practicum in which a version of the failure cycle appears. Indeed, we may have reinvented some of what other coaches had already learned.

When we asked the students to write brief papers on their fears, the effect was cathartic. It was helpful to them to see that they shared the same fears of failure, perceived incompetence, and loss of control. It was a relief for them to become aware of their unrealistic expectations for their own performance. The incompleteness theorem helped them both to lower their expectations and to see incompleteness, corrected on-line, as a necessary concomitant of effective practice. And our decision to slow down the work of the seminar and decompose learning into reflection on discovery, invention, and production helped students to manage the complexities they were beginning to perceive. It also helped us to formulate and test more accurate accounts of the difficulties our students were experiencing.

We tried to walk a fine line between emphasis on individual learning and attention to the evolving group climate. To focus only on the first would cause us to ignore a critically important context of the teaching/learning process. But if we paid too much attention to the second, involvement in group dynamics might overwhelm the primary learning task. Our approach was to present this dilemma to the seminars, initiating reflection on group process only when the group climate seemed to us to have become a critical impediment to learning. Later, during the periods of sustained reflection that tended to occur in the last months of the seminar, students themselves more easily managed to distribute attention between group and individual learning.

Our experiments helped students to perceive risktaking intervention and resulting error as a source of psychological success and stimulated reflection on underlying patterns of reasoning. But they also helped to fragment the learning task. We noticed that students who could occasionally make an effective brief intervention were often unable to sustain a longer and more complex one, especially when their first moves led to reactions for which they were unprepared. This was linked to our growing awareness that the behavioral strategies sprang from whole constellations of meaning, reasoning, and feeling.

Our response to this awareness was of two kinds—and in both respects incomplete.

When we invited our students to mimic the entire script of a complex intervention, some of them used it to get a feeling for the schema underlying a whole sequence of actions. But others reacted negatively to the *idea* of deliberate imitation, although they were quite willing to do it as long as they could ignore what they were doing. Indeed, Follow me! tends often to evoke negative reactions in coach and student alike, whenever it becomes explicit. Yet imitation is essential to learning, just insofar as students are initially unaware of what they need to learn, and it can be a creative act of considerable complexity.

Paradoxically, it is blind imitation, rather than imitation as such, that most threatens a student's autonomy; and it is blind imitation that students and coaches encourage when they keep imitation tacit. In order to encourage reflective imitation, coaches may need to invite students to reflect on their negative attitudes toward imitation, as Karen did in her term paper.

Our concentration on constellations of meanings, feelings, and reasoning surfaced a dilemma of authenticity and control: If skillful practice proceeds from meanings and feelings that are not under my direct control, how can I learn to create them? In the 1984 seminar, some students struggled explicitly with this dilemma. They tried to acknowledge and articulate the meanings and feelings that kept them from authentic practice; reflected on the unfamiliar meanings they sometimes experienced as they experimented with new behavior; and, perhaps most important, acted as though they were trying to learn not only a new technique but a new appreciative system and way of living that each individual had to evolve in his own way.

Our Version of the Hall of Mirrors. When Argyris and I first became aware of our students' failure cycle, we also became aware of our own predicament as a version of theirs, and we tried to involve them with us in joint reflection on the learning/coaching enterprise. We knew that in certain crucial respects we knew more than they; but we also knew the limits of our ability to describe our practice and keenly felt our uncertainties about coaching.

Like Sachs and Shapiro, we acknowledged our uncertainties about particular interventions. But we also took an experimental stance toward the entire seminar. When we described the students' failure cycle, we acknowledged our uncertainty about how to deal with it and our need to experiment in order to find effective ways of doing so. If this increased some students' anxiety, it also defused many students' anger and discouragement. And by communicating that we and they were, in at least one important sense, in the same boat, we decreased the psychological distance between them and us.

Thereafter, we tried to be explicit about the reasoning that led us to propose experiments—in decomposing tasks, introducing the idea of incompleteness, slowing down the pace, confronting protectionism, promoting deliberate imitation—and tried to get the students interested in participating in these experiments, both as subjects and as designers.

The paradox of our aspiration was, of course, that it depended on meanings and skills the students had not yet acquired. Nevertheless, we noticed that some of our students were manifestly more successful than others in joining our reflective experimentation. These students seemed to be distinguished by three qualities. They were highly rational, not in the Model I sense of cool reason, but in their ability to recognize logical inconsistencies when these were pointed out, their abhorrence of inconsistency and incongruity, and their readiness to test their assumptions by appeal to directly observable data. They were highly reflective, as evidenced by their readiness to analyze their errors, try out thought experiments, and critically examine their own reasoning. And they were inclined toward cognitive risktaking: more challenged than dismayed by the prospect of learning something radically new, more ready to see their errors as puzzles to be solved than as sources of discouragement.

These capacities alone do not ensure progress in acquiring a designlike practice, but they do enable students to join with coaches in reflective experimentation. Indeed, a predisposition toward rationality, reflectivity, and cognitive risktaking seems essential for students and coaches alike when a practicum takes the form of action research in a learning/coaching process.

Many students continued, after our seminars had formally concluded, to pursue their efforts to learn Model II competences and understandings. And when they reported to us on their further learning experience, they emphasized the sort of *inquiry* with which the seminar had helped them to become familiar. They spoke, for example, about their successful efforts to connect seminar experiences with their personal and professional lives. They mentioned "lights going on" when, in interaction with others outside the seminar, they recognized patterns of behavior similar to ones they had already analyzed. They continued the acquired habit of on-line reflection, analysis, and redesign of their behavior.

In this way, our seminars seemed to have been halls of mirrors. The reflective inquiry on learning and coaching in which we have tried to engage our students has functioned, at least for some of them, as an exemplar of a kind of reflective inquiry they try to re-create in the context of their everyday lives.

Three Models of Coaching Compared. In the theory-of-action seminars, Argyris and I joined with our students, from time to time, in collaborative experiments aimed at helping the students realize Model II intentions. Frequently, we invited them, explicitly or implicitly, to imitate the patterns of intervention we demonstrated. And, as I have just observed, we tried systematically to create a hall of mirrors based on parallel processes of reflective inquiry.

So we drew on each of the approaches to coaching—joint experimentation, Follow me! and hall of mirrors—illustrated in previous chapters. In the dialogue of coach and student, each of these approaches calls for a different sort of improvisation, presents different orders of difficulty, and lends itself to different contextual conditions.

In joint experimentation, the coach's skill comes first to bear on the task of helping a student formulate the qualities she wants to achieve and then, by demonstration or description, explore different ways of producing them. Leading the student into a search for suitable means of achieving a desired objective, the coach can show her what is necessary according to the laws of the phenomena with which she is dealing.

From her side, the student's artistry consists in her ability and willingness to step into a situation. She risks declaring what effects she wants to produce and risks experimenting with an unfamiliar kind of experimentation.

The coach works at creating and sustaining a process of collaborative inquiry. Paradoxically, the more he knows about the problem, the harder it is for him to do this. He must resist the temptation to tell a student how to solve the problem or solve it for her, but he must not pretend to know less than he does, for by deceiving her, he risks undermining her commitment to their collaborative venture. One way of resolving this dilemma is for the coach to put his superior knowledge to work by generating a variety of solutions to the problem, leaving the student free to choose and produce new possibilities for action.

But the artistry of joint experimentation can succeed only when the student can say what she wants to produce. It is bound to be inappropriate when she is unable to do so or when the coach wants her to grasp a new way of seeing and doing things that transcends the boundaries of a particular local effect.

In Follow me! the coach's artistry consists in his capacity to improvise a whole designlike performance and, within it, to execute local units of reflection-in-action. So here the relations between a whole performance and its parts, between the whole and *aspects* of the whole, are crucial. Beginning with a holistic image of performance, a skillful coach disposes of many ways of breaking it into parts and unraveling its various aspects, each of which he treats in turn—as Franz subjected the first few measures of the *Fantasy,* several times over, to analysis-in-action, or as Argyris and I led our students through analysis of the multiple dimensions of a Model II intervention. Then the coach reconstructs his image of the whole, reassembling in performance the several chunks and layers he has separated in his analysis.

Here, in the coach's demonstrations and responses to the student's attempts to imitate him, there is great potential for ambiguity and confusion. So an important part of a coach's artistry consists in his ability to draw on an extensive repertoire of media, languages, and methods of description in order to represent his ideas in many different ways, searching for the images that will "click" with this particular student. And the student's artistry consists in her ability to keep many possible meanings alive in her mind, putting her own intentions and objectives into temporary abeyance as she observes the coach and tries to follow him. She does as she has seen him do, reproducing his operations in order to discover their meanings. She deciphers his responses, testing by further words and actions how the meanings she has constructed are like or unlike his.

In the hall of mirrors, student and coach continually shift perspective. They see their interaction at one moment as a reenactment of some aspect of the student's practice; at another, as a dialogue about it; and at still another, as a modeling of its redesign. In this process, they must continually take a two-tiered view of their interaction, seeing it in its own terms and as a possible mirror of the interaction the student has brought to the practicum for study. In this process, there is a premium on the coach's ability to surface his own confusions. To the extent that he can do so authentically, he models for his student a new way of seeing error and "failure" as opportunities for learning.

But a hall of mirrors can be created only on the basis of parallelisms between practice and practicum—when coaching resembles the interpersonal practice to be learned, when students re-create in interaction with coach or peers the patterns of their practice world, or when (as in the theory-of-action seminars) the kind of inquiry established in the practicum resembles the inquiry that students seek to exemplify in their practice.

It is important to remember that the three approaches to coaching are ideal types. A coach may shift from one to another, as Rosemary did in response to the several students in her master classes, adapting herself to the needs and difficulties of each student before her. Moreover, the several approaches may be combined. Franz included brief episodes of joint experimentation in a lesson structured mainly as Follow me! Argyris and I combined joint experimentation with the hall of mirrors in our management of the "slowing down" of our students' attempts to discover, invent, and produce Model II interventions. And, in a more fundamental sense, however a coach may otherwise vary or combine the three approaches, he always uses Follow me! to communicate the practice of his practicum—for he demonstrates, and expects his students to imitate, the particular kind of learning by doing on which the practicum depends.

Use of Model II Behavior in a Reflective Practicum. As a student moves through a practicum, he frequently asks himself what he is to learn, whether it is worth learning, how he can best learn it, and whether the practicum adequately represents the realities of practice. Typically, he does not resolve such questions once and for all in a burst of clarity but gradually comes to see things in new ways and make new sense of them. He shapes his further learning by his evolving answer to the question "What am I learning?"

Coaches also ask themselves what their students are learning, where they are stuck, and how they make sense of the "help" they receive, and they use the answers to evaluate and guide their further coaching.

At whatever level a student learns—to execute a particular performance, or kind of performance, or way of designing a performance, or way of learning—her evolving practice depends significantly on how she assesses her own learning. And the evolution of a coach's practice also depends on his ability to assess his own and his students' learning.

Hence, coach and student, when they do their jobs well, function not only as practitioners but also as on-line researchers, each inquiring more or less consciously into his own and the other's changing understandings. But they inquire under difficult conditions. The behavioral world of the practicum is complex, variable, and resistant to control. At any given time, concurrent processes are underway, any one of which might cause a change in understanding. And some of the most important kinds of learning are of the background variety, revealing themselves only when a student moves out of the practicum into another setting. Often, therefore, it is impossible to distinguish strong signals from ambient noise or to attribute a clearly discernible change in behavior to the interventions that caused it.

In their respective inquiries into learning, coach and student depend on the other party's awareness of his or her experience, ability to describe it, and willingness to make it discussable—conditions not easily met.

Students are often unaware of what they already know and what they need to know; coaches are equally unaware of the knowing-in-action that informs their own flawed or skillful performance. Both parties are susceptible to myths of learning that cloud their awareness of experience and confuse their attempts at self-description. So students in the theory-of-action seminars and case conferences held the groundless belief that they ought to be able to deliver complete and perfect interventions and became discouraged when they failed to do so. Some students expect to be told what to do at each stage of their journey and become panic-stricken or enraged when a coach fails to meet their expectations. Some students and coaches think of learners as autonomous beings who ought to be entirely free to choose what they want to learn and how to learn it—proceeding in a straight line from "learning needs," to which they have privileged access, through milestones of progress visible in advance. When such beliefs are strongly held, they distort reports of actual learning experience.

Retrospective reports are not necessarily more reliable than present ones. When coach or student looks back, he tends to become historical revisionist, restructuring the past to fit his present beliefs. In order to preserve a picture of smooth and orderly progress, for example, he may wipe out earlier experiences of anxiety and pain.

In an adversarial relationship, student and coach tend to keep thoughts and feelings private, protecting themselves from each other. Even when their relationship is not adversarial, they may have derived from earlier experiences in school or the world at large a disposition to doubt the utility of any such effort at communication, on the grounds that "He's not ready to listen to this!" or "This would only confuse him."

Nevertheless, coach and student must somehow respond to their questions about learning, and the various ways in which they do so help to shape their learning careers.

They may put a stop to inquiry by exchanging doubt for true belief. A coach may say, for example, "It's only years later, when they're out in the workplace, that they'll see the value of what they learn here," or "The important thing is to take a position about what you think they need to know and stick to it." Because such beliefs are hard to test—and it is a rare coach who tries to test them—they readily become ideologies. Similarly, students may react to their doubts about a practicum by overlearning its lessons. In the theory-of-action seminars, for example, one student introduced the term *sinner* to describe those who appeared to accept unquestioningly the merits of Model II and, because they were usually unable to produce it, habitually accused themselves of error. Or students may revolt against the lessons of a practicum, creating a mirror image of true belief.

In either of its polar forms, the exchange of belief for doubt makes beliefs self-sealing and protects coach and student from productive confusion.

Mystery and mastery is a different kind of response to doubt. In this case, coach and student privately interpret and test the meanings of each other's actions. Neither one reveals the results of his private inquiry except by the indirect evidence of his publicly observable behavior.

When inquiry into learning remains private, it is also likely to remain tacit. Free of the need to make our ideas explicit to someone else, we are less likely to make them explicit to ourselves. Indeed, the ideology of mystery and mastery usually includes a defense of the tacit, as when coaches say, "When they finally get it, you'll know," or "If you have to ask, you'll never find out!"

Yet, tacitness may be functional. Students do learn to navigate in the waters of mystery and mastery, and they acquire in normal practicums, at least on occasion, some of the artistry of a new practice. And some practitioners of mystery and mastery do learn to become skillful coaches. Whether they learn these things in spite of or because of the prevailing norms of tacitness, it is difficult to say. We know little about the possible functions of the tacit.

We have had occasion, however, to note the limits of mystery and mastery in areas where the meanings of publicly observable performance remain stubbornly ambiguous—when the content of a student's learning is in question, for example, or when learning binds occur. And we have also noted cases (Dani and Michal, the case conferences, the theory-of-action seminars) where a coach helped students by eliciting from them a description of their difficulties and confusions, acknowledging his own uncertainties, or describing his picture of the changing experience of the practicum.

In a climate of mystery and mastery, undiscussability and indescribability reinforce each other. We keep ourselves unaware of what we already know because we habitually stay away from situations where we are called on to describe it. We describe it poorly because we get so little practice, which reinforces our disposition to keep it undiscussable.

But the connections inherent in this vicious circle may be used to support a virtuous circle of reflection on private understanding. When a coach reflects aloud on his own knowing-in-action and encourages his students to reflect aloud on theirs, both parties are more likely to become aware of gaps in their descriptions and understandings. Such a coach is more likely to test the utility of further reflection. And, insofar as he discovers the value of opening himself to challenge, he is more likely to take such risks again. Finally (and in this respect all reflective practicums involve Follow me!), he demonstrates a mode of inquiry that students can mirror by joining him in reflective dialogue.

Of course, not all knowing-in-action can be given a verbal description, nor is it always useful to try to give one. But a student's learning is enhanced when she *can* voice her confusions, describe elements of what she already knows, or say what she makes of a coach's showing or telling. And a coach's artistry is enhanced when he builds his capacity to negotiate the ladder of reflection. The potentials of awareness and describability are kept hidden—untestable by either coach or student—when constrained by an unexamined mixture of defensiveness and lack of practiced competence.

For these reasons, the skills necessary to the creation of a Model II behavioral world are crucially important to a reflective practicum. When coach and student are able to risk publicly testing private attributions, surfacing negative judgments, and revealing confusions or dilemmas, they are more likely to expand their capacities for reflection in and on action and thus more likely to give and get evidence of the changing understandings on which reciprocal reflection depends.

 *Part Four*

Implications for Improving Professional Education

In this final section, I shall return to the crisis of professional education with which our discussions began.

In Chapter One, I described the dilemma of rigor or relevance as it affects the professional schools. Educators, I pointed out, are increasingly aware of the zones of indeterminacy in practice that call for artistry but are bound by institutional commitments, to a normative professional curriculum and a separation of research from practice, that leave no room for it. So I have argued for the need to take artistry seriously. I have proposed an epistemology of practice that does make room for it— one based on knowing- and reflection-in-action—and I have examined some of the deviant traditions of education, mostly drawn from the fine arts, from which we can learn about education for artistry. Out of this study comes the idea of a reflective practicum. Its main features are learning by doing, coaching rather than teaching, and a dialogue of reciprocal reflection-in-action between coach and student. I have illustrated this idea, first in architectural design, which I have taken as a prototype of a reflective practicum, and then in other fields increasingly distant from the architectural studio.

I have considered the following questions:

- What are the characteristic dynamics of a reflective practicum?
- How are they similar and different from one field of practice to another?

303

- What are the principal issues, processes, and competences involved in doing the job of a reflective practicum well?

In addressing these questions, I have described the paradox and predicament inherent in learning a designlike practice, the characteristic dialogue of coach and student, conditions under which that dialogue may become one of reciprocal reflection-in-action, the threefold coaching task, and models of coaching—Follow me! joint experimentation, and hall of mirrors—that can be used to structure the communicative work of the practicum.

Now I want to place these ideas in the context of the professional schools.

In Chapter Eleven I shall consider the introduction of a reflective practicum as one element in redesigning professional education and shall set the problem of redesign in terms of the institutional predicament of the schools.

Chapter Twelve will draw from one experiment in curriculum reform, in the master's in city planning program at the Massachusetts Institute of Technology, some perspectives on redesigning professional education.

🌿 Chapter Eleven 🌿

How a Reflective Practicum Can Bridge the Worlds of University and Practice

Redesigning Professional Education

When we consider introducing a reflective practicum into the complex intellectual, institutional, and political context of contemporary professional schools, we face a problem of design. The issues and questions to be considered may take very different forms in the various contexts of the schools, but some of them are generic and relatively straightforward:

- What form shall a reflective practicum take? What shall count as a "project"? How shall projects be used? What kinds and levels of reflection are to be encouraged?
- At what points in the curriculum—or, more generally, the life cycle of professional development—might a reflective practicum be introduced?
- What shall be the relation of a reflective practicum, in sequence and content, to the courses in which disciplines are taught?
- Who shall teach the practicum?
- What kinds of research, and researchers, are essential to its development?

Such questions raise a family of secondary questions that have to do with the possible interactions between a reflective practicum and the existing systems of the professional school. When a reflective practicum of a particular form is introduced at some point in a curriculum, how might the rest of the curriculum be called on to change in order to accommodate it? Given the privileged position of coaches in a reflective practicum, what changes will be called for in the school's existing criteria for hiring, promoting, and rewarding faculty members? How will the forms of research essential to a reflective practicum fit into the existing research system of the school?

The answers to these questions will vary among professional fields and among particular schools within a field. But there are also certain constants—institutional conditions, broadly shared by professional schools, that work for or against the introduction of a reflective practicum and must enter into our framing of the design problem.

Inherent in the problematic situation of the professional school is a twofold relationship to the worlds of the practice and the larger university—a relationship mirrored in the relationship of discipline- and practice-oriented components of the school, as diagramed in Figure 6.

Figure 6. Dual Orientation of the Professional School.

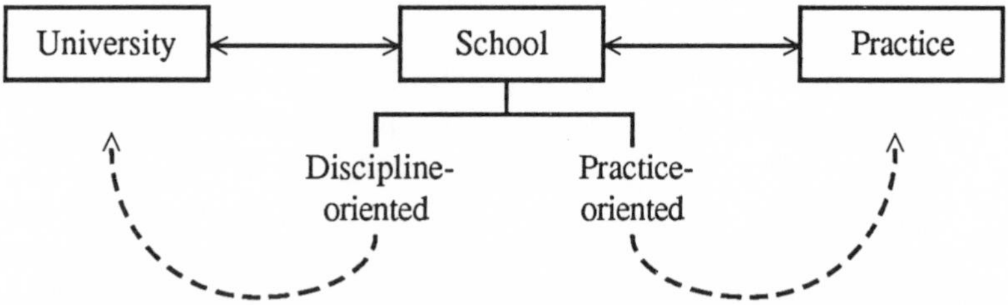

In its relation to the university, a professional school must cope with its Veblenian heritage: the disposition of faculties in mainline departments as well as in the professional schools themselves to see the professional school as a "lower school" wholly devoted to applying fundamental research derived from the "higher school" of the disciplines. In its relations to the world of practice, the professional school is concerned with what it means to prepare students adequately for a life in the professions, as such a life is currently understood by those who live it. Within a professional school, there are those sensitive mainly to the claims of the disciplines and those who hearken most to the demands of the practice world; and the two groups tend to be isolated from, or at war with, each other.

Herbert Simon introduced this way of describing the problematic situation of the schools in his well-known chapter "The Business School: A Problem in Organizational Design" (Simon, 1969). He wrote about business schools, being at the time dean of Carnegie-Mellon's school of business administration, but his argument might have applied to any professional school—and indeed, in *The Sciences of the Artificial* (Simon, 1976), he applied it to the entire field of professional education. It will be instructive, for the sake of its resemblance and contrast to my own view, to review his way of framing the problem of designing a professional school.

Simon's main worry, the "horror story" that he envisages, is the splitting of the professional school into two worlds inhabited, respectively, by discipline- and profession-oriented faculties, "the social system of practitioners, on the one hand, and the social systems of scientists in the relevant disciplines, on the other" (1969, p. 337). He believes that a professional school need not forswear fundamental research. On the contrary,

> The business school *can* be an exceedingly productive and challenging environment for fundamental researchers who understand and can exploit the advantages of having access to the "real world" as a generator of basic research problems and a source of data [1969, p. 341].

And he adds that a business school *must* become such an environment, for otherwise,

> The "practical" segment of the faculty becomes dependent on the world of business as its sole source of knowledge inputs. Instead of an innovator,

it becomes a slightly out-of-date purveyor of almost-
current business practice [1969, p. 350].

What all professional schools must fear, according to
Simon, is an "equilibrium state of death" in which practice- and
discipline-oriented faculty members separate from each other. To
avoid this fate, the schools must abhor departments and cultivate
communication between the two wings of their faculties. Most
important—and this proposal Simon develops at length in his
later book—they must build a science of professional practice on
which to ground their research and teaching:

> A full solution, therefore, of the organizational
> problem of the professional schools hinges on the
> prospect of developing an explicit, abstract, intellec-
> tual *theory* of the processes of synthesis and design, a
> theory that can be analyzed and taught in the same
> way that the laws of chemistry, physiology, and
> economics can be analyzed and taught [1969, p. 354].

In this way, he proposes to knit together the subworlds oriented to
university and practice.

But Simon's way of framing the design of professional
schools rests on assumptions that I have called into question. First,
he accepts—indeed, embraces—technical rationality. He accepts
Veblen's formulation of the ancient hierarchy of fundamental and
applied knowledge. He believes that the professional schools
should teach the application of a fundamental science and faults
them mainly because they lack one. He does not concern himself
with uncertainty, uniqueness, or conflict, presumably because he
regards his proposed science of design as applicable, at least in
principle, to the entire topography of professional practice.

My formulation of the design situation of the schools is in
some ways like Simon's. Like him, I give a central place to the
gaps between school and university, school and practice, and
discipline- and profession-oriented components of the school. But
unlike him, I am concerned about a different dichotomy: the split
between the technically rational world of the disciplines, on the

one hand, and, on the other, the reflection-in-action of competent practitioners and the reflection on reflection-in-action of those researchers who seek to develop a phenomenology of practice.

I am less worried by the split between discipline- and practice-oriented faculties than by the possible realization of Simon's vision—a proceduralized profession in which technical rationality wholly drives out artistry and a professional school organized around a science that wholly drives out education for artistry.

In contrast to Simon's image, my design for a coherent professional school places a reflective practicum at the center, as a bridge between the worlds of university and practice. The specifications for such a design depend on institutional forces, in the schools and their institutional environment, that I shall describe in two stages: first, the long-standing predicament that hinges on the dilemma of rigor or relevance; and second, a phenomenon of more recent origin that I shall call the "squeeze play."

The Institutionalized Dilemma of Rigor or Relevance. The normative curriculum of the schools rests, as we have seen, on an underlying view of professional knowledge as the application of science to instrumental problems. It begins with the relevant science and follows with a practicum in applications, separating the research that produces new knowledge from the practice that applies it. There is no room here for the research *in* practice, or, as I prefer to say, the reflection on reflection-in-action by which practitioners and practice-oriented researchers sometimes make new sense of indeterminate situations and devise new strategies of action. The tasks of the reflective practicum are out of place in the normative curriculum of the professional schools.

The schools' view of professional knowledge is a traditional view of knowledge as privileged information or expertise. They view teaching as transfer of information; learning, as receiving, storing, and digesting information. "Knowing that" tends to take priority over "knowing how"; and know-how, when it does make its appearance, takes the form of science-based technique.

The privileged knowledge held in the research university is broken up into territorial units. Each field of subject matter is the province of a department, and within each department, knowledge is further subdivided into courses, the provinces of individual professors.

Universities tend to see tasks or problems through the lens of their subjects and courses. When an issue cuts across the provinces of departments or professions, it requires "interdisciplinary" treatment. But because academic provinces are also political territories, interdisciplinary projects are quickly politicized—and the politics of the academy are legendary, fertile ground for satirists from Aristophanes to Alison Lurie.

Perhaps because the academy is familiar with its politics, it has evolved a behavioral world based on separation of spheres of influence and surface cordiality of relationships. Open conflict tends to be minimized by leaving to each professor the management of his own subject matter and courses; and in order to avoid confrontation among faculty members, public criticism tends to be suppressed.

Beyond this, there is in the behavioral world of the university—especially in the major research universities—a powerful norm of individualism and competitiveness. Faculty members tend to think of themselves as free-standing agents of intellectual entrepreneurship. Collaboration in groups larger than two is rare. Prestige tends to be associated with movement *out* beyond the boundaries of a department to other scholarly or practice settings around the world. Hence, it is extremely difficult in a university setting to achieve focused, long-term continuity of attention and commitment to work on the institutional and intellectual problems of a school.

In the light of these institutional characteristics of university-based professional schools, what changes would a reflective practicum produce? How might it disrupt the life of a school?

First of all, its introduction would reverse the usual figure/ground relationship between academic course work and practicum. In the normative curriculum, a practicum comes last, almost as an afterthought. Its espoused function is to provide an opportunity for practice in applying the theories and techniques taught in the courses that make up the core of the curriculum. But a reflective practicum would bring learning by doing into the core.

In order to accept a reflective practicum, a professional school would have to make room for it. The traditional program of the schools is divided into courses of a semester's duration, and students are usually expected to take four or five such courses each semester. But a reflective practicum demands intensity and duration far beyond the normal requirements of a course. An architectural studio, a psychoanalytic supervision, or a musical apprenticeship more nearly resembles what Erving Goffman called a total institution. Students do not so much attend these events as live in them. And the work of a reflective practicum takes a long time. Indeed, nothing is so indicative of progress in the acquisition of artistry as the student's discovery of the *time* it takes—time to live through the initial shocks of confusion and mystery, unlearn initial expectations, and begin to master the practice of the practicum; time to live through the learning cycles involved in any designlike task; and time to shift repeatedly back and forth between reflection on and in action. It is a mark of progress in a reflective practicum that students learn to see the learning process as, in John Dewey's terms, "the practical work . . . of modification, of changing, of reconstruction continued without end" (1974, p. 7).

In a reflective practicum, the role and status of a coach take precedence over those of a teacher as teaching is usually understood. The coach's legitimacy does not depend on his scholarly attainments or proficiency as a lecturer but on the artistry of his coaching practice. In order for a professional school to give a central place to coaching, it must tailor its incentives and career paths—its criteria for promotion, salary, and academic tenure—to provide institutional support for the coaching function.

A reflective practicum must establish its own traditions, not only those associated with project types, formats, media, tools, and materials but also those embodying expectations for the interactions of coach and student. Its traditions must include its characteristic language, its repertoire of precedents and exemplars, and its distinctive appreciative system. And the last, if the

argument of the previous section is correct, must include values
and norms conducive to reciprocal, public reflection on
understandings and feelings usually kept private and tacit.

Just to the extent that a reflective practicum succeeds in
creating a world of its own, it risks becoming a precious island cut
off both from the world of practice to which it refers and from the
world of academic courses in which it resides. If it is to avoid this
fate, it must cultivate activities that connect the knowing- and
reflection-in-action of competent practitioners to the theories and
techniques taught as professional knowledge in academic courses.
One such activity is a kind of research that studies processes by
which individuals acquire (or fail to acquire) practice artistry and
processes that make coaching more or less effective.

John Dewey has described one kind of research appropriate
to a reflective practicum in the following terms:

> A series of constantly multiplying careful
> reports on conditions which experience has shown in
> actual cases to be favorable and unfavorable to
> learning would revolutionize the whole subject of
> method. The problem is complex and difficult.
> Learning involves . . . at least three factors: knowl-
> edge, skill, and character. Each of these must be
> studied. It requires judgment and art to select from
> the total circumstances of a case just what elements
> are the causal conditions of learning, which are
> influential, and which secondary or irrelevant. It
> requires candor and sincerity to keep track of failures
> as well as successes and to estimate the relative degree
> of success obtained. It requires trained and acute
> observation to note the indications of progress in
> learning, and even more to detect their causes—a
> much more highly skilled kind of observation than is
> needed to note the results of mechanically applied
> tests. Yet the progress of a science of education
> depends upon the systematic accumulation of just
> this sort of material [1974, p. 181].

Although Dewey's description is intended to characterize research on teaching methods, it is generally applicable to several kinds of research appropriate to a reflective practicum. And to anyone familiar with the intellectual climate of most university-based professional schools, Dewey's list of features implies a corresponding list of resistances. The schools' prevailing assumptions about knowledge, the structural and political division of knowledge into departments and courses, the priority given to teaching over coaching, and the prevailing conception of normal science research—all militate against acceptance of the conditions essential to creation of a research base appropriate to a reflective practicum, as, indeed, they militate against creation of the reflective practicum itself.

We should add to these sources of resistance the current mood of vocationalism and consumerism among students in the professional schools—so easily translatable into a thirst for the "hard skills" embodied in sophisticated techniques. This mood is also likely to make students resistant to the demands of any reflection on practice that does not promise immediate practical utility.

But there are also forces favorable to the introduction of a reflective practicum. There is the ferment in the schools fueled by changing perceptions of the demands of practice and rising doubts about the effectiveness of traditional modes of education for it. There is, in the field of philosophy of science and in various social sciences, a palpable movement toward new ways of thinking about research and practice—ways that emphasize the merits of full, qualitative description of phenomena and the utility of well-worked-out cases of intervention, even when their translation into general rules is problematic. And there is evidence that a large and perhaps increasing number of students are attempting to create their own versions of the reflective practicum that the schools have so far failed to offer (Schön, 1973).

It is quite clear, as we consider these forces favorable or hostile to the introduction of a reflective practicum, that the design of its introduction engages the professional school as a whole—its curriculum, its intellectual and political life, and its relations with the worlds of university and practice.

The Squeeze Play. Superimposed on our basic picture of the institutionalized dilemma of rigor or relevance is a more recent complication: an uneven but nevertheless significant resurgence of technical rationality and an accelerating constriction of professional autonomy combine to squeeze out the very idea of education for professional wisdom or artistry. And this is happening just as some factions, in some schools, are becoming newly aware of the need for something like a reflective practicum. In its most dramatic form, this squeeze play threatens the very existence of the professions and professional education—at least as we have known them.

Technical rationality is by no means dead; on the contrary, it is on the rise—or, rather, seems in some ways and places on the rise and in others in decline. In more than one medical school, for example, the faculty is divided between those who embrace strictly biotechnical expertise and those who emphasize the psychosocial dimensions of illness and the clinical importance of uncertain situations where there is no biotechnical "right answer."

In the social sciences, there is a powerful counterreaction to the sorts of physical science modes of social research that flourished after World War II. In the past twenty years, there has been a perceptible movement toward such Continental approaches as critical theory, hermeneutics, and phenomenology. Nevertheless, some departments of sociology deny tenure to faculty members who do not take a mathematical approach to the discipline; and in cognitive psychology, the movement toward cognitive science, with its information-processing and artificial intelligence models of mind, is currently predominant.

Some schools fight over the choice of direction or divide into separate, more or less isolated camps. Some schools tilt in one direction or another. Some *fields* do the same. In urban design, architecture, and urban planning, for example, the heyday of analytic modeling seems to be over, at least for the time being. Schools of education, traditionally weak in quantitative, analytic modeling, sometimes put on a show of technical rationality, adopting techniques and frameworks that appear more precise than they are.

The second half of the squeeze play consists in a perceived erosion of professional autonomy: practitioners feel less free to think and act like professionals and educators, to teach what they believe in. In medicine, for example, the now-familiar crisis of malpractice insurance leads physicians, especially in fields like surgery and obstetrics, to practice "defensive medicine"; and freedoms to live up to professional standards of care are threatened, on one side, by the reimbursement criteria of Medicare and Medicaid and, on the other, by incentives and sanctions employed in the increasingly powerful for-profit sector. The reality of these threats to medical autonomy may be questioned, but the *perception* of the threat, on the part of physicians and educators, is undeniable.

How do the two halves of the squeeze play reinforce each other?

One interesting example, suggestive of the general case, is the plight of clinical research in medicine. This form of medical research, traditionally dependent on face-to-face interaction of physician and patient, is now subject to pressures from the increasingly strident claims of basic biomedical science, such as molecular genetics, and the increasing reluctance of administrators in hospitals and group practices to allow physicians to combine research with clinical practice. Reduced budgets due to stringent regulation of third-party payments, the rise of for-profit service delivery systems, and more complex and demanding regulation of medical care restrict physicians' freedom to conduct small-scale clinical research projects in conjunction with everyday practice. And at the same time, some voices from the community of fundamental medical science claim to be able to bypass clinical research altogether.

The more general form of the squeeze play is as follows: the growing power of technical rationality, where it *is* growing, reduces the professional school's disposition to educate students for artistry in practice and increases its disposition to train them as technicians. And the perceived constriction of professional autonomy makes practitioners feel less free to exercise their capacities for reflection-in-action.

Although the two trends have very different origins, they reinforce each other. Shrinking professional autonomy reduces practitioners' inclination to practice on-line research and reflection; and proponents of technical rationality claim to make reflection-in-action dispensable by replacing it with proceduralized, science-based technique. Under these circumstances, the dilemma of rigor or relevance takes on new and more desperate meanings.

In the three vignettes that follow—each a "collage" made up of features of schools I have observed at close range—I shall describe some variations of the squeeze play.

A School of Education in a Large Western University. This large school, with some 200 faculty members, educates teachers and school administrators for an entire state. The school is locked in combat with the state legislature, which has campaigned for the past several years to reduce costs of education, give relief to taxpayers, and return to "basic skills." The legislature's method has been one of increased control through "competency testing" of teachers, specification of curricula, and restriction of budgets.

In the background, politically conservative factions blame the permissiveness of the schools for a decline in standards of morality and religion. They consider university teachers hopelessly intellectual, liberal, soft, and ineffective and seek to whip the school of education into shape or dispense with it altogether.

The school of education is rather isolated from other parts of the university, with few connections to main-line disciplines, humanities, social sciences, or arts. Because it is large and linked to state functions, it has some power; but in comparison with high-status disciplines, it is considered second-class. It struggles for status within a university climate dominated by the usual epistemology of practice, with the usual political trappings.

Internally, the school is balkanized. Educational psychology, teacher training, continuing education, science education, educational administration, and counseling psychology function as separate territories. They maintain a cordial détente based on separation of spheres of influence, but when occasion arises (as in selecting a new dean or designing a cross-disciplinary program), they battle with one another for position, security, and control.

Most such battles end in political compromise that gives each unit a piece of the action.

The school places a premium on generalized, theoretical knowledge and formal methods of analysis. For example, a new teacher training program takes students through two years of general, theoretical instruction in subjects like pedagogy (with a heavy emphasis on classroom control), child development, and subject matter competence. Practicums are distributed through the program, in units of increasing length, with the explicit intention to provide opportunity for practice in applying theory and technique. Yet the faculty members who designed this program appear, in discussion, not to be strongly convinced of its rightness; they simply cannot imagine an alternative to it.

There are many, among faculty and students alike, who search for new ways of thinking about educational practice. For example, one group conducts research on "reflective teaching" aimed at helping students become aware of their existing knowledge and take greater responsibility for their own learning. Many faculty members espouse the idea that teachers should learn a kind of artistry that goes beyond classroom control and faithful adherence to a lesson plan. More than a few faculty members, in their own courses, try to help their students become excited about finding things out for themselves. And more than a few doctoral students study the practice of competent practitioners to learn how their demonstrated competence might bear on the education of teachers and administrators.

But it is very difficult to translate such interests into large-scale activities or institutional programs. Indeed, some faculty members consider their professional autonomy more immediately threatened by their own self-created institutional system than by the state legislature.

A Business School. This large school has a tradition of case teaching and practice-oriented research. For many years, it has described itself as a place where students learn problem-solving skills of general management through iterative analysis of hundreds of business cases. Its faculty members are dedicated case teachers, and it has invested heavily in case development.

In recent years, however, under some pressure from university leadership, the school has recruited bright young graduates in such disciplines as economics, history, applied mathematics, and social psychology. Now, as these recruits mature and come up for tenure, the dean and his senior faculty members wonder how they will be integrated into the school's traditions of case teaching and research. They fear that the young, discipline-oriented instructors will use cases only to illustrate theoretical principles rather than inculcate problem-solving skills.

As older faculty members approach retirement age, they see the shifting demography of the school reflected in a worrisome shift in course content. For example, the teacher of an introductory course in business policy, an outstanding professor and consultant to top management, has used the course to help students integrate specialized functional knowledge in marketing or finance into management decisions that require wisdom and artistry. Recently, however, the young professor who has taken over the course has used it to train students in a microeconomic model of business strategy. His model has gained a great deal of currency in the international business community, where there is a thirst for techniques of strategic analysis, but the senior faculty deplores the loss of the course's integrative function and its emphasis on managerial wisdom.

Concerns about the future directions of the school's research have recently led the dean to appoint a research committee. Among its chief findings is that younger faculty members up for tenure are subject to a double bind. For decades, the school's research has been bimodal. A relatively small number of faculty members have developed quantitative, analytic models of business phenomena (the committee calls this research "reductionist"), while a larger number of researchers have carried on the tradition of qualitative, empirical study of management and business phenomena (which the committee calls "field research"). The school is divided into broad functional departments—marketing, production, finance, general management—and in each of these, decisions on promotion and tenure tend to be based primarily on a faculty member's record of publication in peer-reviewed scholarly journals. But these journals are increasingly limited to papers of the reductionist variety. So a young faculty member who wants to associate himself with the school's tradition of field research must nevertheless prepare to be judged by reductionist criteria.

These and related experiences contribute to internal ferment. Faculty members are sharply aware of the need to integrate field and reductionist research, case- and discipline-oriented teaching, but are by no means clear as yet how to do so.

An Engineering School. This elite institution is dominated by the ethos of engineering science that swept over schools of engineering in the United States, in the wake of World War II and Sputnik, in the late fifties and early sixties. It supplies highly trained engineers, at undergraduate and graduate levels, for work in government and industry. In recent years, it has been dominated, like most engineering schools, by the dramatic rise in attractiveness of electrical engineering, in which over a third of its undergraduate majors enroll.

The dean of the school of engineering, along with several other university administrators, has two main concerns about the future of the school. First of all, engineering science has largely driven out courses in engineering design, and as a consequence, employers have tended to see graduates of the school as deficient in the ability to design. More recently, as concerns about international industrial competitiveness have heightened and engineering design has become a national policy issue, the dean of the school and some of his senior colleagues have begun to try to strengthen design education in such fields as mechanical engineering, computer programming, and electronic components.

A second area of concern, the dean calls "the humanization of engineers." This is by no means a new idea. For over twenty years, the university has expressed its allegiance to the idea of liberally educated, broad-visioned engineers, equipped with the capacity to think deeply about the social and ethical dimensions of technological change, and has experimented with courses in humanities and arts for engineers. But these have tended to become grafts on the main engineering curriculum and are generally regarded as having had a limited impact. Now, once again, the university administration has announced its intention to revitalize the teaching of arts and humanities and pursue their integration with the main building blocks of the engineering education.

But there are important constraints on the school's ability to pursue these initiatives. There is, for one thing, a growing tendency among industrial employers of engineering graduates to specify their requirements in ways that recall the "back to basics" movement in public education. Some larger employers tell the schools, for example, "You give them the basic courses in calculus, physics, and thermodynamics; once we get them, we'll give them the rest!" There is also the very considerable power of the special engineering departments that tend to conspire against radical curricular reform. Such departments as electrical engineering and materials sciences, increasingly overwhelmed by the amount of material to be taught in their fields, strive to protect and enlarge their intellectual territories and jealously guard their teaching prerogatives. The sum of their requirements easily fills up the free space available to students, forcing such ancillary subjects as design, arts, and humanities to the periphery of the curriculum. Moreover, the departments are powerful baronies, not readily coerced or cajoled into a change of direction they perceive as contrary to their interests.

Finally, there is the disposition of students themselves to think in vocational terms. Many of them have their eyes on jobs, are attentive to starting salaries, and plan their programs in order to maximize job and salary opportunities. It is only a minority among students—as among faculty members—who express any real concern with engineering design or the humanization of engineers.

Strait is the gate to curriculum reform, but there are some individuals at the upper levels of university administration who strongly wish to enter it.

Reformulating the Design Task

The squeeze play illustrated in these three cases gives us cause to rethink the task of redesigning professional schools. Its message intensifies the institutional dilemma of rigor or relevance, raising to a power the plight of artistry in practice and education for artistry in the schools. What constricting professional auton-omy makes unlikely, proponents of technical rationality claim to make dispensable. So Herbert Simon's vision of the schools threatens to become a reality.

More than this, the squeeze play suggests a need to recon-sider the institutional context of the schools, with their tenuous connections to the worlds of university and practice—the problem-atic situation within which the dilemma of rigor or relevance is embedded. It suggests the following criteria:

- The predicament of practitioners subject to constrictions on freedom of action in their organizational settings should be brought into the professional curriculum.
- It is more urgent than ever to develop new connections between applied science and reflection-in-action.
- There is a need to create or revitalize a phenomenology of practice that includes, as a central component, reflection on the reflection-in-action of practitioners in their organizational settings. And this phenomenology of practice must be substan-tively connected to traditional disciplines or risk (in a sense different from the one Simon had in mind) a bifurcation of the schools.

In my vision, these requirements can best be met by giving a central place to the reflective practicum as a setting for the creation of bridges between the school and the worlds of university and practice.

In order to build bridges between applied science and reflection-in-action, the practicum should become a place in which practitioners learn to reflect on their own tacit theories of the phenomena of practice, in the presence of representatives of those disciplines whose formal theories are comparable to the tacit theories of practitioners. The two kinds of theories should be made to engage each other, not only (as Simon proposes) to help academicians exploit practice as material for basic research but also to encourage researchers in academy and practice to learn from each other.

Traditional disciplines should be taught in such a way as to make their methods of inquiry visible. For it is true, paradoxically enough, that although normal science research cannot be conducted in practice, and its criteria are both more and less stringent than those of research in practice, experience in the methods of normal science research can be a superb preparation for reflection-in-action. A reflective practitioner must be attentive to patterns of phenomena, skilled at describing what he observes, inclined to put forward bold and sometimes radically simplified models of experience, and ingenious in devising tests of them compatible with the constraints of an action setting. Education in a traditional discipline can acquaint individuals with forms of inquiry, not literally applicable to practice in themselves, from which to improvise the kinds of inquiry that *can* work in practice.

The reflective practicum should include ways in which competent practitioners cope with the constraints of their organizational settings. The phenomenology of practice—reflection on the reflection-in-action of practice—should enter the practicum via the study of the organizational life of practitioners. And here a constructionist perspective is critically important; for the phenomena of practice in organizations are crucially determined by the kinds of reality individuals create for themselves, the ways they frame and shape their worlds—and what happens when people with similar and different ways of framing reality come into collision.

Now I shall sketch how such bridging functions might be carried out through a reflective practicum in schools like the three I have described in the previous section.

Consider a practicum for teachers in a school of education. Suppose that its students have had some working experience and are involved, during the period of the practicum, in some further teaching practice that gives them direct exposure to pupils in classrooms. Such a practicum might begin—like the Teacher Project conducted by Jeanne Bamberger and Eleanor Duckworth at M.I.T. (Bamberger and Duckworth, 1979)—by engaging teachers in tasks where they can explore their own learning. Teachers might work at math problems, study the movement of pendulums, construct tunes using Montessori bells (which look the same but have different pitches), or study the "habits of the moon" (to use Duckworth's phrase). As they did these things, they would reflect on their own processes of inquiry, examine their own shifting understandings—and compare their actual learning experiences with the formal theories of learning built into standard pedagogies. They might be helped in this process by exposure, later on, to experiments in and theories of cognitive development. Later still, they might shift their attention to the classrooms in which they interact with children. Here, they would be attentive to the ways in which children's learning is like or unlike the kinds of learning they have detected in themselves. They would be encouraged to think of their teaching as a process of reflective experimentation in which they try to make sense of the sometimes puzzling things children say and do, asking themselves, as it were, "How must the kids be thinking about this thing in order to ask the questions, or give the answers, they do?"

Life in the bureaucratic system of a school would be included, as the teachers begin to experience the difficulties of (for example) seriously listening to children in an actual classroom. The teachers would be encouraged to reflect on the ways in which they frame their own teaching practice in a setting that can often be hostile to reflection-in-action, to observe and explain how other teachers and administrators behave in the system of the school. They would be helped to imagine and experiment with interventions aimed at increasing their freedoms, within the school, to use new approaches to learning and teaching. They would be encouraged to think of adapting to or coping with the life of the school as a component of their practice equal in importance to their work with children.

In a school of business, a reflective practicum might center on the elaboration of case teaching. Skillful case teachers already know how to use cases in several ways. They put students into a mode of operative attention by asking them not only to analyze a situation or say what others should do but also to say (on the basis of admittedly inadequate information) what *they* would do in the case situation they have analyzed. They also know how to use cases as a way of helping students learn an art of applying known principles of management. A case might be used, for example, as a context in which students can discover how analysis of debt/ equity ratios can be used to determine whether it is wise for a company to "take a strike." This form of teaching can demonstrate, and help students try out for themselves, kinds of reasoning by which to determine what issues and principles are most usefully taken as central to the analysis of a given case.

Some case teachers are able to take a further step, helping students make sense of a problematic case situation where no known principles are involved. Here, the student is helped to perform a kind of frame experiment—to try out, in the "mess" of an action situation, a way of framing a problem that makes sense, a strategy of inquiry by which to test whether that problem can be solved within actual constraints, and an openness to unexpected back talk that suggests how the problem may need to be reframed.

All these things, some very good case teachers already know how to do, and such case teaching deserves to be called a reflective practicum. In addition, however, student-practitioners might also be encouraged to see the case situation as one in which they try to make explicit the underlying, tacit theories they bring to problem setting and problem solving. A case teacher might involve them in such a process, first, by asking them, as usual, "What would you do?" Then he might collect and compare a number of proposed courses of action and invite students to try to construct the values, strategies of action, and underlying models of phenomena that make such action proposals seem plausible to their proponents. When practicing managers are involved in this sort of task, their exposure to *multiple* theories of action often makes them aware of the extent to which their own practice is theory-laden; it suggests the surprising possibility of theories of action alternative to their own; and it creates interest in the problem of testing, synthesizing, or choosing among equally plausible theoretical options.

When cases used in this way are linked to disciplines like organization theory, social psychology, psychology of motivation, or theories of internal and external market behavior, students gain a different way of looking at the offerings of the disciplines. They tend to think differently about the theories offered by researchers when they realize that they hold comparable tacit theories of their own.

Again, when students develop a more lively awareness of their own capacity to think productively in situations of organizational action, they are more likely to become interested in interventions by which to make their reflection-in-action effective in an organizational setting. Case teaching can expand to include reflection on organizational practice. The question to the student is not only "What would you do in this situation?" but "By what particular interventions would you try to make your recommended actions effective in this organization?"

In a school of engineering, a reflective practicum might focus, in a rather broad sense, on engineering design. Students would undertake simulated design projects (as they do in some existing design courses). But the use of such projects might be extended in several ways. For one thing, students might be asked to reflect on and describe their ways of approaching a design task. They might be helped in this respect by exposure to other forms of designing—exercises in architectural design, for example—to which engineers usually have little or no access. Some design projects might be undertaken in groups where individuals play specialized technical roles; and reflection might then focus on group processes, divisions of labor, and forms of decision making by which the group does its work. Theories of designing and group functioning might be introduced for discussion just as students begin to become aware of their own tacit theories of design and group performance.

Special attention might be paid to the framing of design situations. If a given design problem is both rich in detail and vague in definition (a not uncommon occurrence in actual organizations), students will have to impose on the situation their own boundaries and images of coherence. And they can be encouraged to reflect, as they do so, on conflicting professional, organizational, and societal values at stake in framing a design problem. Here, exposure to the humanities, in the form of examples drawn from literature and literary criticism or from history and philosophy, may be brought into fruitful conjunction with the design task. For as students become aware of conflicting frames and appreciative systems, they acquire a new basis for interest in studies that reveal how human beings experience and cope with the sorts of dilemmas that arise when frames come into conflict.

Merely sketching these variations on the idea of a reflective practicum suggests how difficult it will be to bring them to reality.

Practitioners, coaches, and teachers of the disciplines will be called on to carry out layers of reflection that transcend normal educational practice. Practitioners will have to learn to reflect on their own tacit theories; teachers of the disciplines, on the methods of inquiry implicit in their own research practice; coaches, on the theories and processes they bring to their own reflection-in-action.

This order of reflection will require research of the sort I have earlier claimed necessary to the support of a reflective practicum, for in order to play the roles I have described, practitioners, coaches, and researchers will have to study their own practice.

Several further questions now present themselves:

What sorts of people will be willing, individually and collectively, to engage in this sort of reflection? What forms will their collaboration take? What rewards can they possibly get from their exertions to compensate for the loss of some of the comforts of normal academic life?

And what of the students who might participate in such a practicum: can they possibly do so unless they have already had a great deal of experience in practice?

By what sorts of processes, compatible with the world of an actual professional school, might such a practicum come into being?

These questions will be considered in the following chapter, which tells the story of an experiment in curriculum reform in a professional school—reform by no means as ambitious as that suggested above but not wholly dissimilar to it. The process by which the experiment came into being, its results, and the dilemmas to which it gave rise will suggest what it might be like to implement the kind of redesign of professional education that this chapter has proposed.

❧ Chapter Twelve ❧

An Experiment in Curriculum Reform

In Nathan Glazer's "schools of the minor professions" (which, as I have pointed out, his "major" schools of business, medicine, and law increasingly resemble) there is a high degree of ambiguity and instability in what counts as professional knowledge. Disciplines are often imported to enhance the prestige of the school, each professor tends to advocate his own discipline as a basis for professional knowledge, and curriculum tends to shift with shifting ideas in good currency in the larger professional field. Faculty members on opposite sides of the dilemma of rigor or relevance—high-ground and swamp-dwellers—tend to disagree about the proper course of professional education. And in this context, conflicts inherent in university culture sometimes reach a state of perceived crisis favorable to educational reform.

This description applies to university-based schools of city planning like the Department of Urban Studies and Planning at M.I.T., where I have taught for the past fourteen years.

Our department has endured frequent changes in curriculum, roughly coincident with changes in the national climate of city-planning practice, and it has initiated some changes in practice and curriculum that have spread to other university-based schools. Since 1972, I have been a part of these changes. My interests in professional practice and education have led me to study what the department was doing and, increasingly, take an active role in shaping its curriculum.

The story I want to tell here is about an effort, undertaken by a small group of faculty members between 1981 and 1984, to

327

restructure the first-semester core curriculum required of all students in the Master of City Planning (MCP) program.

The question of a core curriculum for the professional planning degree had been with the department from its origins. Until the early sixties, required courses reflected the clearly defined subject matter—plan making for the physical city—around which the department had won its independence from the School of Architecture. But with the emergence in the Kennedy and Johnson administrations of an "urban crisis" and the ferment of the civil rights, youth, and peace movements, the field of planning exploded. The earlier core curriculum was discarded by a new generation of faculty disenchanted with the obsolescence of earlier required courses and daunted by the challenge of making a core out of the new subjects—economics, sociology, psychology, anthropology, law—that had begun to proliferate in the department. The students were glad to see the old core go, resenting—in those heady times—any restrictions on their freedom of choice.

By the early seventies, however, freedom of choice had begun to be perceived as anarchy. There was a drive, as the new chairman of the department said, to "put some order back in the place." Under the general rubric of knowledge useful for planning practice, four main subjects were identified—economics, statistical methods, the planning process, and institutional analysis—each of which became a focus of debate. Eventually, the first three courses in this list were agreed upon. They were set out, as one faculty member put it, to represent "the department's view of useful planning knowledge." The courses were required, and students took them, always with some resentment and dissatisfaction.

In 1978, when a new department chairman came in, the makeup of MCP students and faculty had become fairly well established. A significant number of the students—among about forty entering each year—were preoccupied with questions that had become salient in the sixties: social justice, especially for racial minorities, women, and the poor. About half the students were women. Many students had come from careers in community development and advocacy. The department made valiant, if increasingly unsuccessful, efforts to recruit members of ethnic minorities. And many students preoccupied with issues of social justice were also concerned about their prospects for employment, which they tended to translate into an interest in learning "hard skills" like financial analysis, statistics, and computer programming.

The faculty consisted of about thirty full-time members, many of whom had graduated from the department. Some had links to traditions of architecture and environmental design; some had backgrounds as practicing planners; some were social scientists who had joined the department in the explosion of the sixties and early seventies. Like other faculty members in a research university, they tended to prize their freedom to conduct research and practice in the areas of their choice. Many identified with their original disciplines, or practice specialties, rather than with "planning." Research and practice were highly valued; teaching was taken very seriously but ranked second to research and practice; and administration tended to be regarded as an unavoidable and onerous duty.

When the new department chairman took over in 1978, he assumed the burden of coordinating the courses that made up the core. Nevertheless, students continued to resist required courses and, by 1980, had begun to express their dissatisfaction more overtly. Most of them accepted the idea that there should be a body of required knowledge but objected to the core as it then existed. They found it fragmented, divorced from an understandable context. They resented their isolation from faculty members, missed an emphasis on issues of fairness in public policy (expressed in shorthand as issues of "race, class, and sex"), and felt that they were treated in core courses as though they had no prior knowledge or experience.

The student protest led the MCP committee to form a Core Review Committee, which consisted of three faculty members— myself among them, as chairman—and seven first-year MCP students.

The atmosphere of the review was contentious and, as one student put it, "a little scary." But it also generated a great deal of energy.

In the spring of 1981, the committee carried out its work in a very public way, continually submitting products for the inspection of the larger student and faculty group—like "the planning process of old times," as one committee member put it:

> You had everybody in there. There was an extraordinary number of people. It was amazingly drawn out, a democratic process, which made a real effort to canvass . . . students and faculty.

The committee worked by sketching broad scenarios of possible future directions for the core. Debates centered on conflicting conceptions of the planning profession, the contents and levels of subject matter useful for practitioners, and the relationships of academic course work to practice. An important division of opinion arose between those who favored a "conceptual core"—a way of "teaching you to think," as one student participant said—and those who wanted to give priority to technical skills. An environmental designer on the committee proposed that the new core should be organized around a practicum:

> Somewhere along the line, the idea of a studio, or a case, emerged as . . . a shared context. It came partly out of some of my experience working with very diverse groups. . . . We all decided that we were talking different languages and that one thing we should do is have some common pieces to look at. And the conversation became more interesting. We decided, "That's what we need!"
>
> We would imbue in people the idea of playing, sketching, thinking things out loud through extremes . . . sort of, "What if we did this?" And it teaches you a lot about a thinking process, a way of attacking problems.

The committee's final report proposed an "ideal" scenario that included a "conceptual" approach to course content, supplemented by skill-building sequences, some compromise on issues of "coherence versus flexibility," contexts in which students had greater access to faculty members, "time for reflection" in smaller groups, pass/fail grades, and a recommendation that the "controversial issues" be included as a top priority.

By this time, several things had happened that can be seen, in retrospect, as having set the stage for the year and a half of planning that was to follow. Two students, young women, had emerged as committed participants—in the words of one faculty member, "very special people who had a lot of energy and a lot of imagination and staying power." I had urged one of these to continue to devote time to the process, arguing that she should consider it a prototype of the kind of leadership role she hoped to take in the future.

One of the faculty members most admired by the students, the environmental designer who had proposed the "studio" idea, agreed to take over the leadership of the committee—having determined, as he said, that the other members of the group were prepared to "hold up their end."

In the summer of 1981, we set up a study group that included the three faculty members previously involved, the two students, and two new faculty members who were expected to teach in the new core. Our group included the environmental designer, an institutional economist, an advocate planner, and two of the instructors in the existing quantitative methods course.

We created three basic courses surrounding a central, studiolike project. The three courses were new versions of the earlier set. "Economics" became "Political Economy for Planners," combining institutional economic history with units in micro, urban, and welfare economics. "Quantitative Methods" became "Quantitative Reasoning," organized around data analysis, estimation, modeling, and experiment design. The earlier "Planning Process" and "Institutional Analysis" courses were combined in one, "Planning and Institutional Processes," which examined some of the main traditions of city-planning theory and practice, placing programs and methods in the institutional contexts of their application. The studio project eventually settled on the problems of a region in Boston, a corridor beginning with Copley Square, where a massive new development project was going on, and proceeding up Blue Hill Avenue, a blighted neighborhood inhabited mostly by blacks and Hispanics.

As we continued to meet during the next academic year, we developed our own planning "traditions." We worked at listening to one another. At my instigation, we slowed the process down whenever necessary, to make listening possible. We tried to make our disagreements as clear and sharp as we could. We paid attention to the process by which we tried to surface and resolve our conflicting ideas, and increasingly, over time, we thought of ourselves as engaged in an experiment in collective inquiry.

The process was, as one participant described it, "burdensome and stressful" but also exciting. The professor of political economy later described it as follows:

> I knew something was going on at the point at which we weren't just using it as a forum for our own positions but started listening to each other. . . . The sense of being a part of something larger—that was very exciting. Early on, certainly Don and I knew, because we talked about it, that this activity was going to make the professional program the center of the department, and that was a good thing to do. . . . We joked sometimes about Don experimenting in terms of group process, trying different things out. We were all doing that, trying things out on one another, trying to teach one another about what we did. That fact in itself was very exciting.

A teacher of writing, who had been working for some years in the department, joined the planning group. She observed

> how thrilling it was to sit around the table to see people actually question how they could teach something best.

And one of the students felt we had made "incredible progress":

> To have started a process basically as a student issue and to have it become legitimate and have it become ongoing, having it become something that

> there was a commitment to on the part of the school.
> And to have it, in a sense, be a model process for
> them to do other things.

Not everyone shared her enthusiasm, however. One senior professor, a veteran of some twenty-five years in the department, expressed his skepticism about the very idea of required courses. In his view, no matter how enthusiastically they were begun, they tended to end up dry and uninspiring, unsuited to changing student interests. And the department chairman, who had managed the earlier core, though impressed with the energy and commitment devoted to the new venture, doubted that "one giant experience . . . made any sense at all." But he decided, as he said,

> Look, you want to do it a different way? You
> should do it.

Lessons from the Experiment

The date of the first delivery of the new core was fall 1982, and in spring of 1983, we evaluated it through interviews with faculty members and students who had participated.

Some of our intentions for the core were very clear. We had tried to achieve some, but by no means all, features of the ideally coherent curriculum described in the previous chapter.

We had tried to design our three courses so as to make their conceptual underpinnings clearer than they had been before and more clearly connectable both to one another and to the Copley Place/Blue Hill Avenue project. As part of this effort at integration, we had agreed to attend one another's classes.

We had tried, in the "Political Economy" and "Quantitative Reasoning" courses, to make a workable synthesis of broad, conceptual material and technical content. We wanted to stimulate intellectually interesting and personally meaningful reflection on values important to planning practice, especially values related to the "controversial questions" of race, class, and sex.

We wanted to help students develop "generic competences," some of which we described as follows:

- To take dir'y data and make something sensible out of them.
- To write clearly about complicated issues.
- To deal with people who see the world very differently and get something productive to happen.
- To be able to live through hard interpersonal and political issues and hang onto important ideas.
- To be able to deal with people who disagree with you in a productive way.

We wanted our studiolike practicum to serve several functions. We wanted to use it as a prism through which to see the utility of ideas and methods presented in the courses. We wanted it to be, in addition, a vehicle for student and faculty reflection on the process of framing problems in messy, conflictual situations drawn from actual planning practice—a setting where students would reflect on the tacit theories they brought to their project solutions and try out their newly acquired methods of quantitative description and analysis. However, we had not tried to use the practicum as a setting for coaches' demonstration and public reflection on their own planning practice. We had not, in any significant degree, tried to bring into the practicum the organizational experiences of planning practitioners. Nor had we tried to teach our disciplines so as to reveal methods of research that students could use as prototypes of reflection-in-action.

Some of our intentions were fully realized; others, marginally or not at all.

We discovered exciting conceptual connections among disciplines previously treated as intellectual islands. For example, the professor of quantitative reasoning, who had been initially skeptical about the benefits of faculty members' attending one another's lectures, later expressed "genuine disappointment at certain times at the end of the semester when certain faculty members were not there on certain days." He gave an example of the kind of insight into conceptual connections that became possible when other faculty members joined his class.

Thinking back about QR, one of the most
extraordinary classes . . . actually happened early on

when I was trying to explain the difference between a case and a variable, and I had about thirteen pages worth of lecture notes and I got through a page and a half. And that was . . . at the time very frustrating for me. Because it was a lecture which led to a lot of comments by Don, a lot of comments by [other faculty members], and a lot of comments by a lot of students about different ways to approach the question of research about that particular problem, and leaving that, I felt very frustrated and had a long conversation with Don about that. And Don persuaded me that that was a very important conversation to have had, and in fact, in our discussions, that has sort of become a model for [what] is possible with several faculty members present at the same time. Rather than the sort of thing that is costly. . . . But it is interesting how your immediate impression is different from your long-run impression.

In the session to which he referred here, he had asked the class what "cases" and "variables" they would choose for quantitative study if they had to describe deteriorating housing in a center city slum. One faculty member proposed to study entire *blocks* of housing, because of their significance for environmental design and the "contagion" of disrepair. The political economist claimed that it would be essential to study patterns of *ownership*. A practicing planner argued that the choice of cases and variables must reflect the kinds of *actions* that might be taken as a result of the analysis. It became clear to what extent the choice of things to count—the very starting point of quantitative reasoning—depends on disciplinary and political-economic perspectives.

It was clear, to faculty and students alike, that discussion of race, class, and sex had been "too stylized," too much dominated by the views of white, male instructors; inadequate in its treatment of women in planning; insufficiently attentive to the vexed question of race in the history of planning in Boston. Many of the students felt that these questions, which they saw as central to the planning profession, had not become integral to the core.

The professors of "Political Economy" and "Quantitative Reasoning" felt constrained by the limited time available to them for the technically challenging components of their courses.

As to the practicum, the Copley/Blue Hill Avenue project raised issues linked to the core courses and drew on course-related methods of analysis, data gathering, and design. But faculty members had found it difficult to define a level of realism and difficulty that matched the time allocated for project work. Some of them described the small groups as "a tremendous drain of energy" that "may not have been worth it." They felt that the small groups gave them an opportunity to get to know a few students well, but they also felt overwhelmed by the multiple, inadequately defined objects of the exercise—as practicum, time for reflection, and forum for discussion of the "controversial issues." As the environmental designer put it, "You can't do a studio out of three hours a week." And he added,

> The irony is that we put as much time into it as into any other piece of the core and I think in many ways it was the least successful.

Some students spoke positively about the experience of working with other students to achieve a shared understanding of a complex and vaguely defined situation. They liked the idea of working with other students of different backgrounds to produce a product in a limited amount of time. As one of them said,

> It got you to personally figure out some difficult things: working in groups, struggling with how you define something. These are things you can't really teach someone. There is a lot of anxiety. How can we think we are capable of deciding how to approach this problem? It was not easy; it was good. There are dilemmas you must experience.

But others reacted negatively to these very features of the experience. They found it frustrating to try to get a shared view of a problem about which they all had different ideas. They objected to the vagueness of the task. Some felt they had come to the work with inadequate experience, understandings, and tools of the trade. They didn't know how to tell, as one of them put it, whether "we were in the ball park, hitting a home run, or . . . in the bleachers."

Quite apart from the question of our success in realizing our intentions, we became aware of several unintended consequences. These seemed, if anything, *more* important than some of our intentions.

A practicum more nearly like the experiences described in earlier chapters of this book, and much more successful than the small groups, was the design of the core itself. The small group of faculty members and students who criticized the old core, planned for the new one, and taught it for the first time were self-consciously engaged in a design process. Over a three-year period, as they familiarized themselves with one another's research and practice, they learned, by doing, to construct a new curriculum. They created an environment for intellectual debate about teaching and, in the process, also created an intellectual community—thereby discovering how much they had missed belonging to one. There was a serious side to their occasional, humorous acknowledgment that the core meant more to them than to the students for whom it was intended!

Moreover, as their comments reveal, members of the core committee were aware of some features of the process by which they had built their reflective practicum. The long-term, "old-time planning process in which everyone participated" and the pressures generated by student dissatisfactions and expectations helped to create an environment of high energy and involvement. Gradually, members of the group had been able to test out one another's commitment to the stringent demands of the design task. Competition and bickering characteristic of normal curriculum planning gradually dissipated as individuals learned to listen to one another with greater attention and critical appreciation. Norms for discussion and ways of resolving conflicts were established, with surprising rapidity, as "traditions."

Those who taught the core courses found it intensely burdensome to sit in on one another's courses and participate in directing the small groups. They doubted whether such intense involvement could be sustained. But they also found extraordinary rewards in the experience of teaching together. One of the younger faculty members remarked,

> I thought it was really good to have other professors in the room. There were certainly occasions when I was nervous or would think twice about what I was going to do, but then I realized it was really good . . . students should see us criticizing one another.

Another faculty member talked about the benefits of mutual accountability:

> If something goes wrong, everybody knows about it quickly. It has to be dealt with; it can't be pushed away. Just the fact of having to be accountable to one another provided a really good discipline.
> [You see yourself] in a situation where your own personal success depends on the success of the group. That is the point at which you transcend your own individual competitiveness and move on to something else. And that happened for us a long time ago, even before the first class. It really did, and we had fun!

Nevertheless, the very success of the Core Committee's reflective practicum—its cohesiveness and excitement—gave rise to problems.

Some of these had been predicted by faculty members opposed to the new core. The Core Committee "in-group" helped to create an "out-group" of other faculty members who regarded the new core with disinterest or suspicion. After the first three years, as the usual patterns of faculty discontinuity reasserted themselves, it became difficult to sustain the climate of intense, collective involvement. Still, it proved feasible to attract new faculty members to teach in the core, especially in the small groups. For the most part, new faculty members found the climate of the core refreshing and contributed new skills and points of view. With each passing year, more student "alumni" of the core participated in the new year's core, bringing to it a feeling for the traditions of previous years. And a few members of the original group sustained their commitment to the enterprise. Hence, faculty discontinuities were damaging but not fatal.

There was a more significant, unexpected, and intractable dilemma inherent in the very idea of the core: the curriculum design created through the faculty's reflective practicum showed a very strong tendency to drive out the students' reflection.

It was not as though our students did not have a significant *capacity* for a reflection on their experience. Indeed, a study I had done in the early seventies (Schön, 1973) suggested that students in city planning at M.I.T. had a considerable ability to reflect-in-action on their own professional education. At some point in their careers, many of them learned how to stage a dialogue between their field and classroom experiences and used this discovery to direct and control their own learning. Seeing their courses as pieces of a larger educational puzzle, they used their movement between classroom and field to build up a sense of the practice competences they wanted to acquire. They sized up what they needed to learn and weighed the value for professional practice of the knowledge they were getting at school. Similarly, they used the movement between field and classroom to test their career goals and their visions of the practice they planned to enter. In their discovery of the possibilities inherent in the dialogue of field and academic careers—limited, to be sure, by their understandings of both—they created a reflective practicum of their own. And according to my informal observations of students over a decade, there were always some who continued to make this discovery.

But in spite of the students' capacities for reflection and the fact that the core was a reflective practicum for those who designed it, the experience of *taking* the core led many students to feel like passive recipients of other people's knowledge. One student complained of having

no time to think . . . just time to prepare
projects, keep up with the reading and get to class

and keep from falling asleep. The pace almost killed
me.

Another pictured

> little slides of my life: so many hours spent in
> the reading room, staying up all night to type . . . a
> lot of physical pain from not sleeping or eating . . . I
> can't believe all the time people spent doing all that
> work.

And one faculty member described the student experience as a
"marathon," adding,

> There ought to be spaces in it, where people
> can just go off somewhere and try to think.

For some students, the core seemed to take over their lives,
becoming their whole world. They found themselves preoccupied
with absorbing information, getting problem sets right, passing
examinations. Some of them felt they were being drawn into
beliefs in spite of themselves. The experience of being continually
lectured at made them "feel like an audience."

Other students denied that the totality of the core experience
drove out reflective thought. They spoke of their excitement about

> getting practical . . . sitting with a group of
> people to come up with a definition of a problem . . .
> and showing that it works.

Some found, as they went on to courses in the following semester,
that "we did synthesize some things and are using them now."
They were to "see the effects of what we have learned." Others
spoke of their discovery that

> no matter how many models you build, you
> really have to deal with every day differently, because
> so many unexpected things come up.

Nearly all the students and several of the faculty members mentioned the strong sense of intimacy and cohesiveness the students seemed to feel with one another. One faculty member commented on

> how remarkable it was that a group of forty people sort of thrown together at random had developed [early in the semester] that kind of cohesiveness and respect for one another and affection for one another. How it was created, how it could be created again, is completely mysterious to me.

But solidarity also had its negative aspects. The sense of membership in a community could be seen as a trap. As one of the students put it,

> We were in an environment that was almost like a bubble within the university.

Coda

When evidence of students' capacity to manage their own education is juxtaposed with their experience in the core, where many of them felt overwhelmed by the very completeness of the curriculum design, it raises an important question: Is it possible to combine a coherent professional curriculum with the conditions essential to a reflective practicum? For the more we integrate in a curriculum the knowledge and skills that students, in our judgment, need to learn, the more we make it difficult for them to function as reflective designers of their own education.

In part, this dilemma has to do with time, or the perception of time. The densely packed core left insufficient time for the practicum we tried to build into it—a practicum that might have given students the opportunity to explore questions of competence, satisfaction, learning, trust, and identity that underlay the self-managed movement of earlier students across field and academic careers. But the problem was not only one of time.

During the period since 1982, as we continued to teach the core and learn from our earlier mistakes, we tried, in various ways, to reduce pressures on the students. We redefined group work and reduced our expectations for student projects. We allowed each group to address a different task. In a number of areas, we cut back on readings, assignments, and requirements. But our results were paradoxical. Cutting back on requirements does not seem to have reduced the students' feelings of pressure—which suggests that the sense of overload may be, at least in part, of their own making.

Those who felt overloaded to the point of "having no time for reflection" may have adopted, with our unintentional help, a passive stance. They may have suffered from a paucity of prior, practice-related experience on which to reflect. And this, if true, suggests that a reflective practicum of the sort we tried to create may most appropriately occur, not at the beginning of a student's professional career, but in the midst of it, as a form of continuing education.

However, it remains to be seen whether, through a curriculum design based on a better understanding of conflicting demands, we can achieve, at least at threshold level, conditions essential both to a coherent professional curriculum and to a reflective practicum. We may be led to a positive view if we focus— as we have been trying in recent years to do—on timing, pace, and direction. If the entire experience is long enough to allow free time for reflection on course work, if simulated practice occurs when students are equipped to use it to try out ideas and methods they have learned in the classroom, and if we create opportunities for students to connect classroom knowledge to their prior experience, then we may be able to combine faculty-generated ideas about what students need to learn with students' active management of their own learning.

From the perspective of faculty participation, the results of our experiment in curriculum redesign are highly suggestive. They suggest that it is possible, at least over a period of several years, for a small group of faculty members to become committed to collective inquiry into teaching and learning. It is possible to create surprisingly durable "traditions" that channel faculty and student interactions in new ways. Faculty members can find it exciting, even liberating, to make their own teaching into a subject for mutual exploration. And when they do so, their substantive research interests are engaged.

Most important, many faculty members thirst for an intellectual community. When such a community presents itself as a real possibility, it taps a powerful source of energy for reflection-in-action in curriculum redesign.

The core experiment also suggests how a reflective practicum can become a first step toward remaking the larger curriculum. The base of faculty participation can be broadened. The thrust of the experiment can be sustained even in the face of the discontinuities inherent in academic life. The development of a reflective practicum can join with new forms of research on practice, and education for it, to take on a momentum—even a contagion—of its own.

References

Ackoff, R. "The Future of Operational Research Is Past." *Journal of Operational Research Society*, 1979, *30* (2), 93–104.

Alexander, C. *Notes Toward a Synthesis of Form.* Cambridge, Mass.: Harvard University Press, 1968.

Arendt, H. *The Life of the Mind.* Vol. 1: *Thinking.* San Diego, Calif.: Harcourt Brace Jovanovich, 1971.

Argyris, C. *Increasing Leadership Effectiveness.* New York: Wiley, 1976.

Argyris, C. *Reasoning, Learning, and Action: Individual and Organizational.* San Francisco: Jossey-Bass, 1982.

Argyris, C., and Schön, D. A. *Theory in Practice: Increasing Professional Effectiveness.* San Francisco: Jossey-Bass, 1974.

Argyris, C., and Schön, D. A. *Organizational Learning.* Reading, Mass.: Addison-Wesley, 1978.

Bamberger, J., and Duckworth, E. "The Teacher Project: Final Report to the National Institutes of Education." Massachusetts Institute of Technology, 1979. (Mimeographed.)

Barnard, C. *The Functions. of the Executive.* Cambridge, Mass.: Harvard University Press, 1968. (Originally published 1938.)

Brooks, H. "Dilemmas of Engineering Education." *IEEE Spectrum*, Feb. 1967, pp. 89–91.

Coleridge, S. T. *Biographia Literaria.* (J. Engell and W. J. Bates, eds.) Princeton, N.J.: Princeton University Press, 1983. (Originally published 1817.)

Delbanco, N. *The Beaux Arts Trio.* New York: William Morrow, 1985.

Dewey, J. *Logic: The Theory of Inquiry.* New York: Holt, Rinehart and Winston, 1938.

Dewey, J. *John Dewey on Education: Selected Writings.* (R. D. Archambault, ed.) Chicago: University of Chicago Press, 1974.

Dewey, J., and Bentley, A. F. *Knowing and the Known.* Boston: Beacon Press, 1949.

Erikson, E. H. "The Nature of Clinical Evidence in Psychoanalysis." In D. Lerner (ed.), *Evidence and Inference.* New York: Free Press, 1959.

Freud, S. "Constructions in Analysis." In J. Strachey (ed. and trans.), *The Complete Psychoanalytical Works of Sigmund Freud.* Vol. 23. New York: Norton, 1976. (Originally published 1937.)

Glazer, N. "The Schools of the Minor Professions." *Minerva*, 1974, *12* (3), 346–363.

Goodman, N. *Ways of World Making.* Indianapolis: Hackett, 1978.

Gusfield, J. " 'Buddy, Can You Paradigm?' The Crisis of Theory in the Welfare State." *Pacific Sociological Review*, 1979, *22* (1), 3–22.

Havens, L. *Approaches to the Mind: Movement of the Psychiatric Schools from Sects Toward Science.* Boston: Little, Brown, 1973.

Hughes, E. "The Study of Occupations." In R. K. Merton, L. Broom, and L. S. Cottrell, Jr. (eds.), *Sociology Today.* New York: Basic Books, 1959.

Illich, I. *A Celebration of Awareness: A Call for Institutional Revolution.* New York: Doubleday, 1970.

Kassirer, J., and Gorry, G. A. "Clinical Problem-Solving: A Behavioral Analysis." *Annals of Internal Medicine*, 1970, *89*, 245–255.

Kuhn, T. S. *The Essential Tension: Selected Studies in Scientific Tradition and Change.* Chicago: University of Chicago Press, 1977.

Lindblom, C. E., and Cohen, D. K. *Usable Knowledge: Social Science and Social Problem-Solving.* New Haven, Conn.: Yale University Press, 1979.

Lynton, E. "Universities in Crisis." Unpublished memorandum, Boston, 1984.

Lynton, E. *The Missing Connection Between Business and the Universities.* New York: McGraw-Hill, 1985.

Mill, J. S. *A System of Logic*. London: Longmans, Green, 1949. (Originally published 1843.)

Piaget, J. *Play, Dreams and Imitation*. New York: Norton, 1962.

Plato. *The Meno*. (W.K.C. Guthrie, trans.) London: Penguin Books, 1956.

Polanyi, M. *The Tacit Dimension*. New York: Doubleday, 1967.

Reddy, M. "The Conduit Metaphor: A Case of Frame-Conflict in Our Language About Language." In A. Ortony (ed.), *Metaphor and Thought*. Cambridge: Cambridge University Press, 1979.

Reichenbach, H. *The Rise of Scientific Philosophy*. Berkeley: University of California Press, 1951.

Rein, M., and White, S. "Knowledge for Practice: The Study of Knowledge in Context for the Practice of Social Work." Working paper, Division for Study and Research in Education, Massachusetts Institute of Technology, 1980.

Riesman, D., Gusfield, J., and Gamson, Z. *Academic Values and Mass Education*. New York: Doubleday, 1970.

Rogers, C. R. "Personal Thoughts on Teaching and Learning." In C. R. Rogers, *Freedom to Learn: A View of What Education Might Be*. Columbus, Ohio: Merrill, 1969.

Ryle, G. *The Concept of Mind*. London: Hutchinson, 1949.

Sachs, D., and Shapiro, S. "Comments on Teaching Psychoanalytic Psychotherapy in a Residency Training Program." *Psychoanalytic Quarterly*, 1974, *43* (1), 51–76.

Sachs, D., and Shapiro, S. "On Parallel Processes in Therapy and Teaching." *Psychoanalytic Quarterly*, 1976, *45* (3), 394–415.

Schein, E. *Professional Education*. New York: McGraw-Hill, 1973.

Schön, D. A. "A Study of Field Experience." Unpublished memorandum, Massachusetts Institute of Technology, 1973.

Schön, D. A. *The Reflective Practitioner*. New York: Basic Books, 1983.

Schubert, F. *Wanderer Fantasy*, Op. 15. In *Schubert's Piano Pieces*, Vol. 1, No. 29. New York: Lea Pocket Scores. (Written in 1822.)

Shils, E. "The Order of Learning in the United States from 1865 to 1920: The Ascendancy of the Universities." *Minerva*, 1978, *16* (2), 159–195.

Simon, H. *Administrative Behavior*. (2nd ed.) New York: Macmillan, 1969.

Simon, H. *The Sciences of the Artificial.* Cambridge, Mass.: M.I.T. Press, 1976.

Spence, D. P. *Narrative Truth and Historical Truth.* New York: Norton, 1982.

Sullivan, H. S. *The Interpersonal Theory of Psychiatry.* (H. S. Perry and M. L. Gawel, eds.) New York: Norton, 1953.

Tolstoy, L. N. "On Teaching the Rudiments." In L. Wiener (ed.), *Tolstoy on Education.* Chicago: University of Chicago Press, 1967. (Originally published about 1861.)

Veblen, T. *The Higher Learning in America.* New York: Hill and Wang, 1962. (Originally published 1918.)

Vickers, G. Unpublished memorandum, Massachusetts Institute of Technology, 1978.

Weick, K. *The Social Psychology of Organizing.* (2nd ed.) Reading, Mass.: Addison-Wesley, 1979.

Wittgenstein, L. *Philosophical Investigations.* (G.E.M. Anscombe, trans.) New York: Macmillan, 1953.

Index

ISBN 1-55542-220-9

90000